Addicted to
Life & Death

MEMOIRS OF AN EMT &
DEPUTY CORONER

Life is precious.
Handle with care.
Janice Ballenger

by
Janice Ballenger

Addicted to Life & Death
Memoirs of an EMT & Deputy Coroner

© 2008 by Janice Ballenger

Cover Photo Credit:
The Washington Post and Katherine Frey

Library of Congress Number: 2008909066
ISBN: 978-1-60126-143-4

Masthof Press
219 Mill Road
Morgantown, PA 19543-9516
www.masthof.com

Contents

Acknowledgements

So many people have impacted my life in supportive and positive ways that it would be impossible to name each of you. I am forever indebted to each person who helped cushion the bumps in the road during my travels. I have chosen to list several of you, alphabetically, as you are each so very important to me, and my life has been deeply blessed by having you in it.

Angie Sensenig. What would I do without you? You have helped me make it to, and through, so many of my trying calls. I am forever indebted to you for your friendship.

Elva Stauffer. For the many good times we've shared; your friendship and continued support of my ventures.

Ernie & Pam Givler. Your love, friendship and belief in me, when I doubted myself.

G. Gary Kirchner, M.D. For sharing your wisdom and insight; for providing me the opportunity to prove myself as a competent deputy coroner; for reminding me to never underestimate people.

John Cox. They say you can pick your friends but not your family. I'm blessed to have you as my brother and my friend. Your unwavering support means more to me than you'll ever know.

Katherine Frey. Thank you for letting me cry, and then listening to me. It took me a long time to understand what you saw, as I sat on the church altar steps. You understood my overwhelming grief and anguish.

Kevin Wolf. For setting positive examples and great leadership as our Ephrata Ambulance EMS Manager. Thank you for your friendship, tolerance and patience.

Larry & Cathy. You are truly a special couple. Through you, I see The Lord work.

Lisa Rosica. Another angel on Earth.

Lori Cowell. What can I say? You are my daughter as well as my best friend.

Maria Coole. For the many times you encouraged me to get back up after I fell down.

Paul & Jo Cox. For helping make my dreams come true and the comfort of knowing that you're always there for me.

Robert L. Good, M.D. Your kind, caring and gentle nature has been an inspiration to me.

Chapter 1

Nothing Is Worth More Than This Day

Life and death. I'll admit it. I'm addicted to both.

While most people can relate to being in love with life, death is a cold, harsh word that most people try to avoid. To enjoy dealing with dead people is not a common addiction. It is a sordid atrocity from which most any human being would turn away.

Most people assume that because it's 10:00 am, they will see 11:00 am. It doesn't always work that way.

My plans were to write my book of memoirs upon my retirement. October 2, 2006, found me counting bullet wounds in young, innocent, dead Amish girls. That was not in my plan.

I thought I'd return home from the Nickel Mines Amish schoolhouse tragedy, and neatly tuck the horrific images that consumed me into a room I've constructed in my mind. A room to store the indelibly etched images that I couldn't bear to see anymore. But the room was full.

I didn't know what to do with these images that were playing havoc with my mind and body. I wanted them to disappear, but they wouldn't.

I couldn't drive past a farm, or see a horse and buggy, without shaking uncontrollably. While I continued to function as a human being, I didn't feel like a human being. I felt like I had been lifted from the earth and replaced by a functioning robot.

My role at the Nickel Mines' murders thrust me into the national spotlight. News media stalked my every move. Being one of the few people to have entered the school, with the dead bodies still inside, every reporter wanted to be my best friend.

My phone rang constantly. I finally asked one reporter, "How did you get my number?" He answered, "It's in the phone book." I wanted to throw my phone through a window. I took it off of the hook.

I didn't want to talk to anyone. I closed my curtains. I locked my doors. I was scared to drive. I became paranoid, and I was convinced reporters were stalking every move I made.

They wanted me to share the horrific scene I had witnessed firsthand. The surreal images consuming my being. The shattering of a rural, gentle, Amish community. The shattering of a "seasoned deputy coroner." It was overwhelming. I wanted to disappear. I wanted to scream to the world, "Leave me alone!"

The day after the shootings, I drove back to Bart Township. I don't know why, but I had to go back to the scene. Along the way, I noticed the Georgetown United Methodist Church had a sign out front. Its words were plain and simple, "Open for prayer."

I drove around the block and read the sign again, this time also looking to see if there were many cars in the parking lot. I checked my rear view mirror to see if any cars were following me. There weren't. I decided to go inside and pray.

As I entered the sanctuary, I didn't see anyone there. Then I saw flowers, cards, and notes on the altar. I cautiously inched forward, and read one of the notes, "Our prayers are with all of the families." I looked at the flowers that had been left by other visitors.

What had I brought for them? Nothing. I felt selfish. How could I have not brought anything along to leave for the families? Other people had, what was wrong with me? I tried rationalizing that I had not intended to stop at this church, but it just didn't work. I was distraught.

The horrific images continued to consume me. All of the emotions that I had kept bottled up inside me during the past twenty-four hours exploded. I sat on the steps of the altar and cried. I couldn't stop crying.

Why had I been subjected to this horrific scene? What was I to do now? Was I once again to put on the happy face, and say, "I'm fine, how are you?" This time, I couldn't do that. I didn't know what to do, other than to cry, and pray for the families.

I had shattered the notion that coroners must be men. Being the first female deputy coroner in Lancaster County, I had proven my ability to perform the job, while maintaining the highest standards of professionalism. But now my life was shattered. I felt I had left my body inside the schoolhouse, and I'd never be the same person again.

My crying finally subsided. I gathered some sense of composure. As I fumbled through my purse for a piece of paper to write my expressions of sympathy on, a woman approached me. She said she had seen me crying. She mentioned that she had taken some pictures, and she asked if that was ok.

"If that was ok?" She could have told me she had taken my purse and I couldn't have cared less.

She asked if I was a friend or relative of the families involved in the shootings. I mumbled, "No, I was only the coroner at the scene."

The following day, a photograph of me, sitting and crying in the church, was on the front page of *The Washington Post*!

At first, I was angry and appalled. How could she do that? I tried to convince myself that she was just doing her job. But I couldn't understand why anyone would put that photograph in the newspaper, especially on the front page.

After purchasing one of the newspapers, I returned home to numerous messages on my answering machine. One friend said she saw the picture, and she felt it captured my despair. So now I was the poster child for "despair?" I didn't like that idea.

Another friend said, "The picture of you in the church conveys the agony that every average person is going through." So now I was the poster child for the "average person?" I liked that theory better, but I certainly didn't feel average or normal. I just wanted everyone to go away and leave me alone.

I retreated to the safe haven of my home office, with my phone off of the hook, and I began writing my book. I couldn't wait until my retirement, as I realized, I might never see my retirement, just as one may never see the next hour or day in their life.

Writing provided me a venue to stage everything I've been recording in journals for many years. Wearing the hat as an emergency medical technician (EMT), provides me the opportunity to save lives. My role as a deputy coroner provides me with a unique look at the dead.

I could release all of my thoughts and emotions in the solitude of my book. I could expose my guarded secrets. Secrets that have shaped every facet of my life. My journey through terrain where most will never venture.

I've been keeping a journal since I began "running" (being a member of an organization that responds to emergency calls), with pre-hospital emergency services.

Years ago, I read an advertisement, "Volunteers needed to help people in emergency situations. No experience necessary." It sounded perfect. I remembered my high school days, when I thought I would go to college and become a doctor. I could help people in "emergency situations."

But sometimes events occur in your life that lead you down a different road. I have never regretted the road I chose. I submitted my application to Ephrata Area Rescue Services that same week. I never once looked back and questioned why I had applied. Those initial years provided me with my first sights of horrific deaths.

One of my first calls with the rescue was for two occupants, trapped in a red Corvette that had rolled so many times, it looked like a crushed Coke can. As I held the tarp over the dead man, my body felt numb, and I felt disconnected. I couldn't stop staring at the dead man's head, whose nicely cut hair now framed what looked like a dish of eggplant parmesan.

I couldn't stop looking at his brain, spilling out of his head like gray pudding. I became nauseous. I searched for comfort in the midst of chaos. But I did my assigned job. I knew then that I could do this work.

My heart has been so deeply rewarded with comfort and satisfaction, while at the same time, it has been broken, torn and scarred. I've often wondered, "Will my heart ever heal? Will I ever feel normal again?" It seems to heal to a certain point, and then I am left with scars and pain that I know will always remain a part of me.

I started my journal as a way to vent and record my feelings, after returning home from a call. Some were quite eventful, others quite uneventful. But all were worthy in some means, especially to the person and family members experiencing the emergency.

My brother, John, gave me a blank, lined journal. I definitely needed the lines for my writing to be legible, after many of the calls. The cover of the journal reads, "Nothing is worth more than this day."

Some days I returned home from a call and was too exhausted, mentally or physically, to write in my journal. I would throw some meat and cheese between two slices of bread, plop my drained body into my recliner, and turn on a Lifetime movie. It didn't matter if it was a movie I'd already seen. I would enter someone else's world, and try to forget what I had just witnessed. I could live someone else's life for a few hours.

Other times, I couldn't wait to release my thoughts. I would drop my coat on the floor and rush to get my pen and journal. As I read some of the incidents I recorded years ago, I thought, "Wow, I forgot about that one." But I don't need a journal to refresh my memory for a lot of my calls.

Some were as simple as the dispatcher for an ambulance call telling us, "Your patient is suffering from a severe nosebleed, and is on nose thinner." She immediately corrected herself and said, "Blood thinner."

I learned long ago that you have to laugh at the smallest things, or you'll end up crying. So a strange sense of humor is found around any emergency services organization.

Many people would find it appalling to know we return from a call and say, "Wow, that was a good call!"

That doesn't necessarily mean it went well, or even had a good outcome, it means the call was quite interesting and challenging, to put it nicely. But you have to have this strange sense of humor to deal with life and death situations on a routine basis, and remain sane.

Most people would be disgusted at the nicknames we gave patients or a DOA. "Pizza Face," "Popper," "Crispy Critter," "Hang Man," "Blue Bonnet," "Sinker Sam," or "Frequent Flier." I don't expect an outsider to understand this. I only know it's one means of how we cope with challenging, and often, grossly disturbing calls.

Laughter is the music of the soul. To keep our souls functioning, we need to laugh.

Today's experiences are tomorrows' memories. The beauty of writing and keeping a journal is that it can be read over and over. It's like ivy on a garden trellis; our lives are inescapably entwined with the past; and our hopes for the future.

Nobody sees what we see. Nobody touches or smells the things we experience. On rare occasions, we get to see people at one of their happiest moments, such as a successful, emergency childbirth. However, most times, a call for an ambulance or a coroner has the family members and friends in a panic mode.

We are trained to be models of calmness and professionalism. We see sick, and dead, children. We see torn flesh and broken bones. We see amputations from car accidents.

Imagine undressing a dead, five-month-old baby, and checking for any trauma on his tiny body. His parents watched my every move, as they sobbed uncontrollably. I examined him, re-dressed him, and packaged his tiny body for removal to the morgue, while praying that I wouldn't shake too much and drop his little body. How can you not be driven to your knees in sadness and despair?

We think we must contain our feelings, and not let our emotions show. So what should we do with our emotions? We don't want to appear weak, and we feel we must be the stoic caregiver.

Well, I can tell you, I have cried many times. I have to release my emotions, in order to continue my jobs. When we've worked so hard to save a life, and find our efforts have failed, there is a tremendous letdown. A feeling of failure and frustration. No one can go from such an adrenaline rush, to total despair, without feeling emotions.

But I have learned to suffuse these incidents, even the most negative and heinous, with my own brand of enlightened compassion. Suffering and anguish, for the most part, seem to move through my body, coming out the other side in the form of kindness and caring.

October 2, in the Nickel Mines Amish schoolhouse, spurred me to write my book now, rather than waiting until my retirement. While it meant re-visiting the anxiety and memories experienced during my journey, it was therapeutic in my emotional growth to find myself. To find the person I thought I had left inside the schoolhouse on that day.

The same question kept arising, "What would the title be?"

One day at lunch, I thought of a title that I liked, "Tossed Salad." How appropriate! My book was a little of this, and a little of that. When I think of a tossed salad, I tend to think earthly nature—the many sides of "nature" that I have seen. Life and death are nature's cycle.

Hiding behind trees to eliminate the urine I can no longer hold, because I'm stuck in a park with locked bathrooms, on a coroner call. Sitting, looking at the nearby Susquehanna River, didn't help matters. "Tossed Salad" seemed to fit perfectly.

I've lost count of the clothes that I've had to toss out, because they were "earthly." They were covered with "schmutz" that just wouldn't come out. If you don't know what schmutz is, count your blessings. Schmutz is "our" term for the yucky stuff that comes out of bodies, dead or alive. The yucky stuff is nasty.

I thought of all the times I've sat on the ground; railroad tracks; a lane of the Pennsylvania turnpike (which had been closed because of a violent, motor vehicle accident); perched on a tombstone, and praying for forgiveness for using a tombstone as my "desk." The times I sat in fields and yards, filling out reports, preparing toe tags, making phone calls, just sitting. It doesn't get much more down to earth. "Tossed Salad" seemed perfect.

Don't get me wrong, probably more of my clothes were tossed out because they were saturated in blood, feces, or other bodily fluids, that I was not able to remove. I found myself cringing as I threw away a pair of my favorite, good fitting pants. But you can't do this work and not have those experiences. If you do, you're doing something wrong, or not doing anything.

I made a commitment to myself, "When a person dials 911, they are, in their opinion, having one of the worst days of their life. Despite how trivial, or how significant, I will approach everyone involved, with the attitude that they are thinking, "why me?" It truly is, to them, one of the worst days of their lives. My clothes can be replaced, but the feelings they are experiencing can't."

Sometime during my writing, "Tossed Salad" seemed too nice of a title. Tossed salads are good. Nature is generally good. These are good, God-given gifts. My life has been filled with good and bad.

So many times, after a call, I would be crying inside, "What about me?"

Am I supposed to go on like I just purchased items to prepare a tossed salad? Am I to go home, calmly sit down and eat a nice tossed salad? Some lettuce, topped with loads of Ranch dressing, turns my salad from a healthy meal, into a little bit of lettuce with a lot of high calorie dressing.

It just wasn't right. It can't be that nice. It isn't that nice. While a lot of calls turn out nicely, a lot of them don't. I can't glamorize my book by giving it a nice title. So midway through my writing, I decided "Tossed Salad" just didn't work.

I couldn't find a title that expressed the depth of sadness that overwhelms me during, and after, so many calls. I considered, "What About Me?"

The many times I wasn't certain I would make it to my driveway. The times I finally made it to my driveway, didn't even turn off my Jeep, and broke down and cried, "What about me? Who is going to take care of me? I've taken care of everyone else, now who is going to take care of me?"

The anguish of pulling into my driveway, and wondering how I was going to drag my drained body inside, to the comfort zone of my home. The wondering of how I even made it to my driveway.

Then the realization that no one but myself is going to take care of me. Even if there was someone inside my house, they are not going to understand what I've just been through.

Many of my peers tell me their significant other prefers them to leave their anguish, and the need to talk, inside their car. Don't bring it inside the house!

It's like we're carrying a contagious disease. We're not. We have just given as much compassion and caring as we can pull from our souls. Now our souls need tended to. But there's no one to help us.

We're just doing our job. Yes, jobs we chose. Someone has to do them. When I think of the times people ask me, "How can you do that kind of work?" and I casually answer, "Someone has to do it." But inside I'm crying, "What about me?" You say what people want to hear. That has become an unfortunate routine in my life.

"What About Me?" seemed too selfish. That is not my nature. But I know many other providers leave a scene asking the same question, "What about me?"

I continued to ponder the title as I wrote my book. Why was it so difficult to come up with a title that suited me? I was browsing through one of the monthly journals I receive, when I read an article titled, "Trauma Junkie." Why couldn't I have come up with a title like that?

Angie, my ambulance partner, suggested, "Addicted to Life & Death." As she said, "You're addicted to it; we're all addicted to it. Despite all of the gruesome things we see, we keep going back for more. But you're not only addicted to saving lives, you're addicted to dead people, too!" She had a valid point.

I am addicted to life and death.

"Death" is a cold, harsh word, one that we do our best to avoid. It is mankind's ultimate enemy, the one foe that we've not been able to conquer. At the point of death, ones wealth, prestige and power all diminish to nothingness, revealing the truth . . . we are totally impotent in the face of that one unconquerable foe.

When one speaks of death, a very grim picture is painted. I don't view death as an end, but rather, as a beginning of a new life.

I have learned to respect life and death. It's like nature; you need to respect its powers. Death is similar to nature in the fact that you need the rain to have the rainbow. Sometimes people need to experience the death of a loved one to evaluate their own lives.

I have saved lives as an EMT, and I have seen death as a deputy coroner.

I try to live by the philosophy that true bliss is being as satisfied with what I have, as with what I don't have. I don't believe that life is a spelling bee, where one mistake wipes out all of the right things someone has done. But I've come to accept the fact that many people don't see life from this perspective. So often it breaks my heart when I see things that others have, and they feel they have nothing. But I can't do anything about it, especially if they're already dead.

While my hands may be small, they're mine. No one else has felt some of the things my hands have felt. My eyes are my own. No one else has seen a lot of what my eyes have seen. As long as my heart remains large enough to carry my body, I will continue to do this work.

I truly believe that our happiness is greatest when we contribute to the happiness of others. Being an EMT has provided me the opportunity to relieve people of their suffering, offer reassurance, and give the greatest gift of all, a second chance at life. Armed with skill and compassion, I reach into the void between comfort and pain, hope and fear, life and death. Then I try to sleep, get up the next day, and do it all over again.

I believe in going the extra mile, it's never crowded. Although it's imperative not to get into the stress lane! While we're taught the necessary precautions to protect ourselves physically, so little is mentioned about protecting ourselves mentally.

Try to imagine going on a call, and having no idea what you're going to see, touch, or smell. It's scary. The dark cloud of anticipated pain is threatening. Through the dark, you struggle to find the radiance of light.

I've learned not to question everything, but rather to find the good and run with it. To accomplish this you need to stay strong and healthy, both physically and mentally. It's so much easier to say than to do.

I've read about "compassion fatigue" and I know I've experienced it many times. I've read about "post-traumatic stress syndrome" and I know I've experienced it. But it never ceases to amaze me how people think we're immune to experiencing emotions. We're not.

We are people, just like you, except we've decided, yes, we made the decision to try to help people experiencing one of the worst days of their lives. I will never regret any moment of my life that I've been able to help people.

I am saddened that some people, who are important to me in my life, don't have a clue as to my feelings. So many times following a call, I wanted to scream; "Does anyone know I'm here? Does anyone know how much I'm hurting? Does anybody care?" Then I remind myself that it's not all about me.

Sometimes I feel like I am the one whose life has been shattered. But I'm the caregiver, the comforter, and the carrier of kindness and compassion. I'm the first step towards healing for a lot of families. I respect that role tremendously.

As I delve further into my book, I'll venture into the deep, deep sadness that has been locked inside a special room in my mind. It's a room I've constructed, inside my brain, to put the nasty, horrifying images that I can't bear to look at anymore.

I try to put them in the room, and then quickly close and lock the door. Now and then some of the images manage to escape from the room. I haven't figured out how they do this. I always lock the door.

But I deal with each image, as it somehow emerges from the room, then put it back in the room, and re-lock the door. I can't throw away the key, or how would I open it to put the images from the days ahead of me into the room?

I've also learned that some times things are hidden in plain sight. I just needed to open my eyes.

There are many calls that I relish in the comfort I've given. I've made a difference. I helped someone through one of the worst days of his or her lives. So many other times, I've wished that I'd just disappear from the scene, and some other being would take over. Let me go home to my comfort zone. Leave me alone. I didn't expect this. I don't want to be here!

There are thoughts and vivid images that I wish I had somewhere other than my self-constructed "room" to put them in. Somewhere I could be certain I'd never see them again. But I know that's not possible. So you accept that these thoughts, distinct smells and images are permanent fixtures in your life.

I have experienced, firsthand, what it feels and smells like to pick up the bones of skeletal remains, and place them in a body bag. To dig further with my small hands, trying to find more bones. To have more bugs surface as I continue digging, and trying to keep them out of my face and hair.

I've experienced, more times than I can count, moving a body that has been decomposing for weeks, in 95 degree, hot, humid weather.

Moving bodies into body bags, knowing that one small touch will cause the "schmutz" to begin squirting, while the rookie police officer sat with his head hanging out an open window, because he couldn't handle the smell.

I've put many bodies into body bags, as the "schmutz" squirted on my clothes, in my hair, and on my body. It's gross and disgusting.

I believe that every person has his or her intended place on earth, and each of us has a gift. Don't ask me to be a dental hygienist! There's not enough money to pay me to do the jobs that many other people do. Each person is important. Don't ever underestimate the value of your worth. I couldn't do your job, so don't give me any credit for doing a job you couldn't do.

I would guess that nearly everyone returns from his or her day at work with a feeling of exhaustion. Why would the saying, "Thank goodness it's Friday," be so popular? Although for many of us, our jobs don't end at 5:00 on Friday afternoon.

Others who have experienced this type of work know exactly what I'm talking about. My wish is that those who have never experienced it would understand that it's not "All in a day's work."

It consumes your entire body and being. The images and smells play havoc with your brain. You try your hardest to appear normal, but you know you're not. Often you don't know when you will feel normal again. Some days you think you'll never feel normal again.

But people expect you to be normal, so you put on the forced, happy face. You say hello, ask how they are doing, and respond to their same question with what they want to hear, "I'm good, too."

While inside you're crying, "What about me? Don't you know about the tragic call I was on yesterday? Can't you imagine how much I'm suffering?" But people don't want to hear that, so you give them what they want to hear.

My responses had been well rehearsed, and I felt confident I could handle anything thrown my way. I was wrong.

On Monday, October 2, 2006, I was the primary deputy coroner on call for Lancaster County. I received a call from our county dispatcher, saying I was to respond to Bart Township, for a "hostage situation with multiple, deceased pediatrics." The information given to me at that time was limited, as the information our county dispatchers had received was still limited.

Little did I know, that following that day, I would turn to writing my book now, as a form of mental therapy, and knowing that others would relate to my feelings. Many would find comfort in knowing that they are not alone, even when crying, "What about me?"

If this book helps one person, other than myself, it was worth every character typed, and retyped. You are not alone. You're addicted, just like me.

Many days you want to throw in the towel, and not be subjected to the torture anymore. But you know you have good to offer, so you keep giving. Giving makes you feel good.

It's like people playing lottery tickets or gambling. They get some sort of high from playing, and expecting to win, so they keep giving their money, in hopes of winning.

We keep giving of ourselves, not hoping to win, just hoping to experience that high, but knowing all along, we have to go through the lowest of lows to get to the high, and it's not always an uphill battle.

Still, despite all the madness and sadness, we get to enjoy vast rewards, like being able to revive someone from the brink of death. The highs are few and the lows are high. But we keep going back for more.

Chapter 2

Rescue Me

When I received the phone call that my application to Ephrata Rescue had been approved, it was received with joy, coupled with anxiety. What was I really getting in to? I was told to be at the station on Thursday at 6:45 p.m.

When I joined, there were two other "active" female members. The active members responded to calls, and were expected to know how to use the equipment. The rescue truck carried the "Jaws of Life"; air bags; wood pieces for cribbing a vehicle; throw bags and ice squalls for water rescues; a stokes basket; come-along chains; rope rescue kits. Anything you could think of that would be needed for any type of rescue was on the truck.

They had a large number of social members, who undertook the tasks of fundraisers and administrative duties.

I will never forget my first night of training. I was shown all of the "Heavy Rescue" equipment, and instructed on how to use each piece. Needless to say, this was a bit overwhelming, but I tried to absorb as much as possible, knowing all along, I was not really retaining a large portion of it.

Following the training, I was fitted for "turnout gear" and I was given a pager, which would alert me to a call. I was issued gear to use until mine arrived, as most of the turnout gear was sized for men. The boots I was given were too large, so I put several pairs of socks inside my boots, so they wouldn't fall off.

I had my own "locker," which was a large, wooden cubicle made by one of the members. I was given a helmet, gloves, and safety goggles. I was directed to my "locker." With great excitement, I neatly arranged all of my "gear" in my locker.

The next day, I proudly wore my pager on my jeans as I went shopping for more personal gear. I wanted my own protective goggles; reflective stickers for my helmet; a Velcro holder to secure my gloves to my turnout coat. I had a huge list of things I wanted. But there is a fine line between enough stuff and too much stuff. Crossing that line moves you into the category known as a "whacker." A whacker is someone who flaunts his position by having too much stuff. I didn't want to be a whacker, but I wanted more stuff!

Kevin Wolf was our chief. He seemed nice enough; he had hooked me up with my gear and a locker. I didn't know it then, but Kevin would later become a person who I have the utmost respect for. Soon after I joined, Kevin resigned as chief, and Fred Fivecoat assumed the position. He was just as nice, and he seemed genuinely interested in helping me learn the "ropes."

Our Thursday night training became the evening I looked forward to. As grueling as the trainings were, I could barely wait from one Thursday until the following Thursday. The other two females and I quickly formed a bond. They taught me so much.

Some of the trainings proved very difficult for me. Knots. I have always been directionally challenged, so learning the knots proved extremely challenging. But I knew if I was going to do this, I had to master the knots. So I took a large piece of rope along home one evening, and practiced for hours and hours. I finally mastered the knots.

Following extensive training, I was informed that I would be able to ride along on calls.

I had my clothing laid out; my shoes and socks ready; my car keys ready; everything in its place, so when a call came, I could be out my door and at the station within four minutes. If you didn't make it in time, you wouldn't be on the truck. So I had everything ready. I've I always been a bit of an organizational freak, so this wasn't too difficult for me to accomplish.

The anticipation of that first call was beyond comprehension. Every time I took a shower, I worried that my pager would start beeping and I would miss the call.

One evening, while making dinner, my pager opened up for a vehicle accident, with entrapment. I thought I had everything ready. I had my material items ready, but my mind was scrambling. There are no words to describe the thoughts that flood your mind when your pager goes off. It's a combination of, "Oh my gosh, what if it's really bad," to, "Oh, what if we get recalled before we even get to the scene."

This happens when police arrive on scene, prior to our arrival, and inform our county dispatcher that rescue efforts are not needed. If we're not needed, we turn around and go back to the station, with a feeling of letdown that we weren't needed, but at the same time, a sense of gratefulness that the accident wasn't really that bad.

I made it to the station in time to throw on my turnout gear and hop into the truck. My mind was swirling. We found a car, smashed into a pole. The young, blonde, female driver was screaming, "Get me out of here! Hurry!" Her door was pushed in, and she couldn't get out. From a distance, she didn't appear to have any serious medical injuries, but being stuck inside a car, with a pole against the driver's door, must have been scary.

That's where the extrication process that I'd trained for was needed. I was assigned to the generator for the Jaws of Life. As I watched the generator, and watched the ambulance crew helping the woman, I longed to be helping her in a more direct way, rather than tending to the generator. I didn't give it anymore thought. I did what I was assigned to do, the patient was extricated, and other than the demolished car, the outcome was good.

After returning to our station, we had to clean our equipment. As we were doing this, one of the assistant chiefs, who had been in command during the call, began critiquing the call. "What went right? What went wrong? Was there anything we could have done differently or better?"

I thought, "Wow, this guy is good!" It was Gene Ferrari. Gene also volunteered with Ephrata Ambulance, and after I joined ambulance, Gene and I began running calls together. I've come to respect Gene's knowledge, and appreciate his friendship. Gene is "good people."

Gene and I later began the annual tradition of taking an ambulance in the "Make A Wish Truck Convoy." The event is held every year, on Mother's Day. In 2003, 288 trucks participated in the convoy, stretching over a distance of 38.6 km, breaking the Guinness World Record.

All of the proceeds help make a terminally ill child's dream come true. It is my favorite day of the year. When I think times are tough for me, I remember the faces of these children, who have such small desires. It all began with one child's final wish of wanting to ride in a "big truck."

Each year there is a truck displaying names of our "fallen angels," the children who have died since last year. People line the sides of the route, cheering, waving, giving thumbs up, to the Make A Wish children riding in trucks. The more lights, sirens and noise, the better! If this event doesn't put a lump in your throat, and a tear in your eye, there's something out of perspective in your life.

After several years with Ephrata Rescue, I made the decision to take advanced medical classes. I signed up for the next "emergency medical technician," (EMT) class. I registered to take the class in Columbia, which is quite a drive from Ephrata. The classes in Columbia were two nights a week, Tuesdays and Fridays. The classes being offered in Ephrata fell on Monday and Thursday evenings. I was not going to miss my Thursday night rescue training.

When my chief learned about this, he pulled me aside and strongly encouraged me to take the class at Ephrata, rather than driving to Columbia. He told me I would be excused from our rescue training during this time period, because I would be attending EMT classes. So I somewhat reluctantly changed my registration to the classes in Ephrata.

I had no clue what I was getting into. The EMT classes were extremely intense. It was like I would envision boot camp. There was so much studying that needed done between Mondays and Thursdays. My group began with many more students than it ended with.

I made a lot of new friends, and I had hooked up with a great partner, Karen, to practice our skills. Karen worked at Ephrata Community Hospital, and it was going well.

Our instructor, Joe Haas, was the best instructor one could wish for. He was thorough, patient, and kind, but strict when necessary. In 1999, Joe was named, "State Emergency Medical Instructor of the Year" by the Pennsylvania Emergency Health Service Council. The council acknowledged that Haas' students consistently tested at the top in regional exams. In a tribute to him by our local newspaper, Joe was quoted as saying, "I never wanted to be anything other than a paramedic, and the reason is simple, I like to help people."

EMT classes were well underway, and our state testing was approaching. Then our rescue chief ordered all responders who were not certified in VRT (Vehicle Rescue Technician) to attend the upcoming VRT classes. The classes were held one night a week, each class being four hours long. And they were four, long, hours.

They were also intense, and I had so much studying to do. It seemed nearly impossible, at the time, preparing for my EMT testing, and trying to comprehend everything being taught in the VRT classes.

One of the other female members, Jessica, was not certified in VRT, so we sat together. She obviously did not want to be there. Our instructor, Jim Lingg, was a great instructor. Jim had a way of making boring information fun to learn. He'd come pulling into the parking lot, in his way cool fancy truck, with his way cool music blaring. He was always upbeat. In the middle of class, he'd suddenly say, "Smoke 'em if ya got them."

Jim's easygoing manner led Jessica to believe his kindness was a sign of weakness. One evening, she had her head down on her arms, and Jim yelled to her, "You . . . the girl sleeping . . . you will stay awake, and you will learn what I'm teaching, and you will like it!" I learned years ago that kindness is not necessarily a sign of weakness. Jessica learned it that evening, and she didn't sleep during class again.

At home I drew pictures of a car, and tried to figure out where the A post needed cut, where the B post needed cut, and thought, "I'm never going to understand this." By the end of the class, I knew how to cut a car apart without any diagrams. I knew how to do a dash push; I knew how to take out a windshield. I was amazed at what Jim had taught me.

VRT was a necessary class to perform the primary function of Ephrata Rescue, vehicle extrication. We were given junk cars to practice on. We practiced for hours on vehicle stabilization, cribbing, using the struts to stabilize, the Jaws of Life, the spreaders, all of the equipment we had. "Lift an inch, crib an inch," when using the air bags, became engrained in my mind. It was a tedious process, but one that needed to be done properly for patient protection.

Many nights it was pouring rain, storming, or hot and humid, and we were out there ripping a car apart. One member asked our chief, "Why must we train in the rain and mud? We just end up returning to the station and spending hours cleaning the equipment!" Our chief explained it very simply, "Accidents don't only happen on nice, sunny days."

With my VRT course completed, my EMT testing was less than a month away. Karen and I were doing well, and I enjoyed her friendship.

I walked into class one evening, sat down next to Karen, and thought, "We have it made, we work so well together." Just then she looked at me and said, "Tonight's my last night." At first I thought she was joking, then I realized she was serious. She explained that as we started our practical skills, actually putting each other on backboards, splinting, practicing actual patient care, she realized this was not for her. I tried to convince her to not give up at this point. Not after all the months and months of intense studying. We were so close to our testing. Her mind was made up. That was Karen's last night of class.

On the day of our state practical testing, I was assigned to a partner whom I'd never met before. Fortunately, we both did well, and passed the written and practical tests on our first attempt. I still run into Karen now and then at the hospital. She never says if she regrets having dropped out so close to the end.

I knew from the start of EMT classes that I wanted to volunteer with Ephrata Ambulance. I also knew I had to take a break. Having passed VRT class, I felt I should continue running with rescue, and in the near future, I'd join Ephrata Ambulance. My plans were to run with both volunteer companies, each requiring many hours of training and being on call. But for the time being, I would focus on rescue, and sharpening my new VRT skills.

So I continued taking every rescue course that was offered. In February of 1998, I took a two-day course in "Ice Safety." I've always loved the water. Again, I was fortunate to have two great instructors, Greg and George. They turned the misery of training in extremely cold, frozen, water into a tolerable, learning experience.

In April of 1998, I somehow passed the Pennsylvania State Fire Academy course, "Respiratory Protection", taught by Jim. The class was on a Saturday and Sunday. It was two, excruciating, long days.

We had to wear SCBA (self-contained breathing apparatus) equipment, climb to the second floor of the training building, and pull a huge bale of hay through the window. Then drag it across the room, to the rear of the building, and lower it to the ground. Now that may not seem too difficult, but for females wearing male-sized gloves, it was extremely difficult. The next step was to find your way back down the steps, go outside, and pick up an axe.

You had to make twenty chops on a piece of wood, but it seemed like two hundred. The axe had to be above your head before each chop. I thought, "I have to think of something I really hate to get the strength to do this," but I couldn't think of anything that I disliked that much.

Then the thought of not passing the test entered my mind. I chopped like there was no tomorrow. You were given a specific number of minutes in which to complete the entire course, and if you spent too much time on one challenge, that took precious minutes away from the others.

I made it through that, and knew I only had one more challenge to defeat—climbing underneath our rescue squad, and exiting on the other side. That again, might sound easy, but I was wearing full, cumbersome, turnout gear; gloves that were too large; and breathing through a now clouded face piece. Then fatigue attacked me. I took a moment to compose myself, knowing the clock was ticking.

I crawled underneath the truck. With an air tank on my back, in order to crawl underneath the squad, I had to lie on my side, and drag my air pack along with me. I confidently started crawling underneath the squad. Then I realized that I had no clue in which direction I was headed.

At one point I actually thought, "Just quit now, I'm never going to do this." I was so tired, it was a hot and humid day, and I was drained. I didn't have the energy to continue pulling myself, and I was lost underneath our truck. That's not my nature, but I was exhausted and confused. I could barely breath. I was ready to accept defeat.

Then I heard a voice saying, "Come towards me."

I've heard the saying, "The light at the end of the tunnel." There was the light at the end of this tunnel! Ok, I can do this. So I dragged my body and gear a little more.

I heard the voice saying, "Over here." I followed the voice and finally emerged on the other side. I knew I didn't have any seconds to waste. I got up, went to the finish line, and heard a few people clapping and cheering.

At that point I probably should have collapsed, but I was so thrilled that I had completed the course, my second or third wind kicked in. I calmly took off my gear, got some water, and watched the others finish.

There were more intense trainings ahead, but I now had the self-confidence that I could do whatever I chose to do.

I took additional classes, in different phases of water rescue, enjoying each one. One evening George announced that he would be teaching an all-day training class on Jet Ski/stokes basket rescue. I immediately signed up. The theory was to maneuver a Jet Ski with one hand, rescue a victim from the water with your other hand, and place the victim into the attached stokes basket. Sounded fun and easy. I was wrong on both counts.

While I'm not an extremely muscular person, I always felt I could carry my own weight, so to speak. I could always muster whatever energy was needed. Our training was held on a bitterly cold, windy day, in a frigid river. We put on our wet suits, went into the water with our partner and Jet Ski, and began practicing.

Maneuvering the Jet Ski wasn't too bad, but trying to do it with one hand, and using the other hand to rescue your victim, was challenging. I couldn't decide which hand to steer with, and which one to rescue my victim with. We practiced until lunchtime.

For lunch, we changed into our street clothes and went to a nearby restaurant. To be warm, sitting, and eating a cheeseburger felt so good. Ok, maybe this wasn't so bad. Then George said, "Ten minutes and we're leaving to go back, so if you need to use the bathroom, do it now."

Just the thought of going back into the freezing water brought thoughts to my mind, "Am I getting sick? Do I feel too sick to finish the afternoon of training?" But again, from somewhere deep inside, I found the stamina to continue. We changed into our now wet and cold wet suits, and went back in the river.

The testing finally arrived, and we all passed. George told us we were the first in the state of Pennsylvania to complete this course, and he was very proud of us. George was a great instructor. Despite being bitterly cold and exhausted, we felt a great sense of accomplishment.

Then came the long-awaited calls in which I could participate on a more advanced level. In May of 1998, we were dispatched for a "assist police department" call.

By now I was carrying a duffel bag of assorted clothes. Long- and short-sleeved tops, extra jeans, socks, shoes, you name it, and it was in my bag.

On Monday, May 18th, 1998, the dead body of Heather Greth had been found floating in the Cocalico Creek. On Tuesday, the body of her boyfriend, Craig Bowers, 22 years old, was also found, dead in the same creek.

On Monday evening, Thomas Chapman, age 19, confessed to the murder of Heather. Chapman's information was unsubstantiated, and the evidence did not match with the confession given by Chapman.

We were called to comb the surrounding areas, looking for any additional pieces of evidence. I looked at the wooded area we were to search. I thought about the heat and humidity index, and opted to wear one of my long-sleeved tee shirts. The others laughed and joked, "It's 95 degrees and you're wearing a long-sleeved tee shirt?" Yep.

The next day we were dispatched to continue searching, and the others arrived, all in great discomfort from the poison ivy they had gotten the day before. My arms were fine. I told them I figured I was going to be sweating profusely anyway, I didn't need to combine it with the poison ivy discomfort they were now experiencing. They agreed, and wished they had taken me seriously, as they watched me put on a long-sleeved shirt again.

Our efforts did not produce anything of significance, and the drownings were ruled accidental. Another lesson learned, go with your gut feeling. I walked away from the two-day search without any poison ivy, itching, redness, or bruises.

As I continued running calls, I began dreading the motor vehicle accidents on Route 222. It is a four-lane highway, where people think something is wrong with you if you drive within the speed limit.

An early morning call in August was to Route 222. A man from Reading, Pa., was killed as the result of a crash involving two cars, and two tractor-trailer trucks. Lee Hess was driving a tractor-trailer truck, northbound on Route 222. He attempted to pass a slower moving tractor-trailer truck. Karen Fitch was traveling in the left lane of Route 222 north, as Hess began to pass the other truck. Hess was driving about 63 miles per hour, when he moved into the left lane. But Fitch's car was already there.

Fitch saw the truck moving into her lane, and swerved left, into a grass strip.

After she thought the truck had passed her, she tried to get back onto the highway. She merged right, but she clipped the rear, left side of Hess's truck. Her Pathfinder, spinning out of control, went across the grass strip, and into the southbound lanes of Route 222. Her car smashed head-on into a blue Ford Taurus, then rolled onto its side.

It was a gruesome sight. I prayed that my legs wouldn't turn into "noodle legs," as I prepared to use our Jaws of Life. They didn't. Both cars were mangled; our rescue crew tore the roofs off of both vehicles to remove the drivers. Graff was flown, by helicopter, to Lancaster General Hospital, where he was pronounced dead on arrival. Fitch was also taken, by ambulance, to a local hospital.

Hess pulled off the road unscathed.

On a Friday in August, my pager opened up for a fire call. It was 2:30 in the morning.

My immediate reaction, as I was heading out my door, was, "Something's wrong with this picture. They must have dispatched us by mistake. They probably meant to dispatch a fire company." Jessica and I were in the back of the truck. We both mumbled the same thing, "We'll be recalled any minute now, we don't respond to fires." But we put on our turnout gear and air packs. We pulled up in front of a house and saw a large portion of the home had burned.

We were more puzzled than before.

Finally the word spread to us. A driver had lost control of his vehicle, crossed over the opposite lane of traffic, and ended up inside a boy's bedroom. The car burst into flames, killing both the sleeping boy and the driver.

From the outside, you couldn't tell there was a car inside the house. We shored up the entrance to the bedroom, and then waited hours as the police reconstruction team did their field investigation.

Some of us slept on the road, using our bunker coats as pillows. We found woods to use as a bathroom. It was a hot night, and a local fire company had requested their ladies auxiliary to prepare food and cold drinks. We took turns riding down to their station for some long awaited relief.

Then we had the grisly task of pulling the car out of the house, and extricating the bodies.

The sight of dead bodies, burned to a crisp, and the smell of the corpses, brewing in the heat for hours, produced sights and smells you never forget. Because the bodies were already dead, our chief said the rookies should use the tools for extrication. Most of them performed flawlessly, while a few had to walk away from the scene. We were told to put the "crispy critters" in body bags for the undertakers. I was assigned to holding the head of the driver.

The average human head weighs between 17 and 22 pounds. But this head looked like a giant marshmallow left over a grill too long. I figured it couldn't weigh that much, so I wasn't too concerned. Then an officer said, "Whoever has the head, be very careful that it doesn't come off of the body." I became concerned.

My gear was covered with a coat of black dust. My nose was filled with a disgusting smell of burnt flesh. The smell permeated my body. My hair reeked of the same odor. My clothing under my turnout gear was drenched with sweat. But we got the bodies into the bags.

We returned to our station to finish cleaning our equipment. It was twelve hours after we had been dispatched. Most of us went home to take a shower and go to our jobs. It's so difficult to leave a scene, emotionally and physically drained, and then go to your job, wearing your happy face. But that's what you do.

I have always begged, "Employers, please let your employees leave for emergency calls. Whether it's fire, rescue, or any volunteer organization dedicated to saving lives and properties, don't wait until it's you or your family member, trapped inside a vehicle, and the truck can't leave the station because they don't have a full crew."

Too often it takes a personal experience for an employer to realize the value of volunteers. What paper work, or line work, is more important than saving a life?

How would you feel if you dialed 911, and no one responded?

It was a weekday afternoon. I happened to have the day off. My pager opened up for a "mass casualty incident involving a school bus." I went down to the station to find only three other members there. Each of us watched, in a different direction, for someone else to show up, knowing our four-minute window to go responding was closing. No one else showed up. We headed out, not having any idea of what we were going to find.

We only knew it was an accident involving a school bus and a pickup truck. We arrived to find the bus loaded with students from Ephrata middle and senior high schools.

There was no hysteria. The students all remained calm and in their seats. Some appeared to be in shock, but fortunately, there were no serious injuries.

As a precautionary measure, we cribbed the bus for stability, and assisted the students into a transport vehicle, to be taken to Ephrata Community Hospital for examination. The driver of the truck was also taken, by ambulance, to the hospital for a minor neck injury.

Showers had fallen shortly before the accident occurred.

I used to think that bad weather always brought bad calls, but I've learned there is no rhyme or reason as to what triggers calls.

Our Route 222 has become infamous for the number of nasty accidents that occur on it. One evening we were alerted to a vehicle accident, with entrapment. The driver used his cell phone to dial 911, but he was uncertain where he was, other than somewhere along Route 222.

The road conditions were treacherous. We cautiously searched the sides of Route 222, trying to find the crash. We saw some near accidents, but we couldn't find the accident that we were dispatched to. A passing driver had witnessed the vehicle sliding off the road, rolling down an embankment, and dialed 911. But he also couldn't provide a location, other than "Along Route 222."

We finally saw tire tracks in the snow, going off the side of the highway. We pulled over, and using our large flashlights, we saw a car about 200 feet down the embankment. The car was hanging over the edge of a small creek. We held our breath and called for assistance. Then we began dragging all our equipment down the embankment. The driver was alert, but was unable to get out of his car.

A ladder was placed on the ground and I was told to climb up and calm the driver until his car could be stabilized.

His first question, "What time is it?" caught me by surprise. When I told him the time, he said, "I've been down here nearly two hours waiting for you!"

I felt like screaming to him, "It's not my fault!" But I reassured him that we were there now, and everything would be okay. His car was stabilized; he was removed and taken to the hospital with minor injuries.

In late 1998 we began receiving a printed rescue training schedule. It listed the date, the type of training, and if it was a mandatory training. I loved the phrase that was handwritten on the bottom, "SUBJECT TO CHANGE FOR ANY REASON." That is so true of life in general.

When Doug Lynch and Belle Reed's Lancaster Township home was gutted by fire, they didn't realize, at first, that the firefighters, who spent long, sweaty hours, at their home, weren't getting paid. While some firefighters were fighting the fire, others were saving emotionally irreplaceable items, a family photo album and some sentimental artwork pieces. Reed was quoted as saying, "We are incredibly grateful to them, a heaven-sent. You don't invite something like a fire, but in many ways we feel blessed, thanks to the firefighters' response."

Like many Lancaster County residents, Lynch and Reed didn't know how the 81 volunteer fire companies operate. All they knew was they needed them when disaster struck, and they came to help them. The companies are facing more obstacles these days, just to get to the fires they fight. The reasons are varied, but they revolve around the same two key areas—money and manpower. With many Lancaster Countians not realizing that all but one of Lancaster's units are volunteers, two out of three fund drive requests are unanswered.

Volunteers continue having to hold fund drives, festivals, Christmas tree sales, and raffles. This is in addition to the many hours spent training and doing equipment maintenance.

The headline of an article in our local newspaper summed it up. "Christmas Day? Your child's birthday? If you're a volunteer and there's a call, it doesn't matter—you leave."

On a cold, Tuesday evening in December, I was getting ready for bed and my tones opened up for a vehicle accident with entrapment.

We were directed to a car where an elderly man and woman were both trapped in the front of their car. As we carried our tools towards the wreckage, we looked at the car, and all said the same thing, "Holy crap!"

A husband and wife were both heavily entrapped in their vehicle. A tractor-trailer was traveling west on Rothsville Road, when it collided with the eastbound car. Mr. and Mrs. Robert Jacobs were trapped in their car for about 40 minutes. A third vehicle was involved, when debris from the Jacobs' vehicle struck an eastbound pickup truck. Mr. Jacobs was the last to be extricated. His wife, Patricia, was extricated, taken to the hospital, and was in critical condition.

Over ten years later, it seems like the accident happened last evening. I vividly remember the medics yelling, "Bob, hang in there." Bob had the dash pushed tight against his lower extremities, but was conscious and trying to talk to us as we worked to free him. After the dash was pushed off of him, he took a quick dive, downhill. The dash had been keeping blood flowing to his heart. Bob died, just as we freed his body from the wreckage.

Ephrata Rescue's logo is, "We volunteer because we care."

One evening, after selling Easter flowers all day, I was hot, hungry and exhausted. But we had made close to $100.00 in profit. I looked at our logo, and thought, "If one more person had cared, and not thrown away their fund drive card, but mailed it with a check for $100.00, we wouldn't have had to spend weeks preparing for this event, and the entire day selling these flowers!"

During the time selling flowers, we also had to remain available to run calls. I think people feel a small donation isn't worth sending. It is. Small donations count, it's like saving change, it adds up. It helps lessen the already heavy load of every volunteer organization. Think about it.

Rescue training continued. I particularly enjoyed the farm rescue training. We had a large John Deere tractor, with a mock patient, trapped underneath the tractor. Our airbags were used to gently crib, and then lift the tractor off of the patient. I was intrigued by all of the hazards posed on a farm.

Then it happened, my first call with Rescue, for a patient that I knew.

It was a beautiful, clear day, April 16th. We were dispatched to the intersection of Route 272 and Fulton Street, in Akron, for a three-vehicle accident. A car, traveling north on 272, struck the rear of a vehicle, driven by Roxanne Bentzel, of Ephrata. The collision then caused Bentzel's car to strike a tractor-trailer in the opposite lane.

When I got to the car, I realized it was Roxanne. She felt a sense of relief that someone was there who she knew. This was another turning point in my life, when I realized I wanted to be able to help people in a more intense, medical way. I assisted with Roxanne's extrication, and later saw her on a frequent basis, and was able to learn the outcome of her injuries.

September of 1999 brought Hurricane Floyd to Lancaster County. Four to eight inches of rain was dumped on drought-stricken ground in a short period of time. As usual with sudden, severe flooding, the water rescues began.

I am continuously amazed at the number of people that comment, "The water didn't look that deep so I drove through it." Or the people who actually get out of their vehicles and move the barricades, which are put up to block cars from driving through the high water, so they can drive through.

The water often rises quickly, and people don't realize how deep it is and how fast it can be moving. Many of these same people ended up clinging to trees until retrieved by a rescue boat. Some ended up not as fortunate.

One of my favorite water rescue calls was for a young man who tried to drive through high water, his car stalled, and he was rescued and sitting in the back of our ambulance. He was fortunate and not injured.

Of course he was able to keep his cell phone from being damaged, and called for his father to pick him up. I couldn't help but overhear the apparent quarrelling between the two.

"But dad, I really didn't do anything that bad! The police didn't have barricades up yet, so I won't be arrested for moving any barricades. The towing company is close, so it shouldn't cost that much to tow the car."

His repeated attempts to convince his father that it wasn't really that bad were unsuccessful. The father told him he had his cell phone, so he should call a friend to come and get him.

Tough love, you have to love it.

In 2001, Ephrata Area Rescue Services, Inc. announced the purchase of a new station located at 609 North State Street in Ephrata. We were all very excited. This venture was a giant step for our organization.

We had put over six years of research into finding a suitable building to house the rescue truck, squad, boats and other equipment under one roof. It also had room for administrative and operational office space, training areas, storage space, as well as room for rescue volunteers to standby during extreme weather conditions. That meant we could actually sleep on sofas or cots, rather than on the hard floor in sleeping bags!

It was a huge undertaking.

Our volunteers felt we could do a lot of the work ourselves, so we forged ahead with a great deal of confidence, coupled with the anxiety of being able to afford the new building and renovations.

Volunteers began transforming the former car dealership building into our rescue station. Work parties were held nearly every day. I couldn't figure out why they were called "parties," when they were far from a party, but certainly involved a lot of work.

One evening, the guys were hanging dry wall. I said, "I can do that!" So I was given a huge piece of dry wall, and shown where it needed to fit. I was also given a quick lesson in hanging dry wall. After picking up the piece of dry wall, I realized this was not nearly as easy as it appeared. But, after many hours, I had cut and hung my piece of dry wall. I was so proud of the results.

I mentioned to the guys, "That was fun, why do dry wall hangers make such good money?" One guy answered, "They get paid by the piece, not by the hour. At the rate it took you to hang one piece of dry wall, you would owe your employer money!"

Several weeks after we began working on our new building, someone wrote a Letter to the Editor of our local newspaper. Portions of the letter read: "There are so many organizations out there which are solely run by volunteers, like the fire company, rescue station, to name a few. My definition of a volunteer means giving freely and unselfishly of yourself and of your own time, without any expectation of monetary or payment of any kind. Knowing the fact that he or she may just have helped save a life is payment enough.

"It's amazing how many people take these organizations for granted. In this case I'm talking about one in particular, Ephrata Area Rescue Services. The time and energy they put into the station, training, paperwork, meetings, fund-raisers and the 2 a.m. pager calls for vehicle entrapments are things people don't know anything about. I have seen first hand, literally, the blood, sweat and tears these people go through. If I ever need emergency services I'm glad they're there. They truly are the men and women of 'unsung heroes.'"

We appreciated her letter. "Thank you" are words we don't hear too often.

I am convinced that there's no given, as to time, weather, full moon, heat and humidity, or weather conditions that trigger calls. The days you expect nothing to happen, something happens. It was 1:00 in the afternoon on a beautiful, sunny, clear day. My tones opened up for a vehicle accident, with entrapment. It sounded bad, and it was bad.

A Pontiac Grand Am hit a house with so much force, Ronald Davis said it sounded like a bomb went off. Bricks littered the front yard, and the driver was heavily trapped in his seat.

Carrying a tool, I approached the remains of the Pontiac Grand Am. I stared at the driver.

Jagged white bones protruded from what looked like steamship rounds of beef. 76-year-old Barry had been driving for hours, having left his house in Virginia, and was trying to find his way back. He thought he saw his driveway, which was actually a driveway in Ephrata, and drove directly into the Davis' home.

The confused, old man was so heavily entrapped that his slippers were still in his car, on the pedals, after extrication. The petrified Davis family found Barry's upper and lower dentures inside their house. His glasses were lying on the ground, twenty yards away from the car.

I was pretty much the "gopher" on this call. After the extrication was complete, and he was on his way to the hospital, I was told that a small tip I had brought for a piece of equipment was missing. "Okay, I'll find it," I told our chief.

I searched in vain inside the demolished car. I crawled underneath the car, looking for the tip. I couldn't find it. I was exhausted. I began begging. "Can't we just buy another piece?" They told me that we could, but what would happen if we were dispatched for another accident before we got a new piece. I continued searching, as the others cleaned the equipment.

While underneath the car, I questioned myself, "When will I know it's time to stop driving? Why was this man driving? How did he end up in a different state? Will someone tell me when I have to stop driving, or will they just take my Jeep away from me?" I stopped thinking, because I didn't have answers, and I continued hunting for the missing tip.

It was a gruesome task. There was so much blood, broken glass and debris strewn everywhere. I gave it my best shot, but I couldn't find it.

One hand felt like a loser, but the other hand realized that I wasn't the one who had lost the tip, someone else had. I had only brought the tip over to the guy using the tool. I was just the "gopher." It was never found. We stopped on the way back to the station and bought a new tip.

One person I came to rely on heavily for guidance at Ephrata Rescue, was Tom Hoffman. Tom is a caring, dedicated, good person. People with Tom's qualities are a rare breed.

Tom was 24 years old, and a volunteer firefighter with Akron Fire Department, when he climbed through a bathroom window, and entered a burning house. He was focused on rescuing an 18-year-old girl, trapped inside. Her screams had just quieted, as she lapsed into unconsciousness. Tom searched through the dark, smoke-filled house until he found her. He carried her out to the ambulance, where she was treated and made a complete recovery.

So why would a volunteer put himself in harm's way? Tom answered that question perfectly, "It's the satisfaction of helping people. I never wanted to be a hero, but I have learned to put my fears aside." Tom, like an estimated 50 percent of Lancaster County's volunteer firefighters, had a volunteer firefighter as his father.

Tom, his brother, Tim, and I took our EMT class together. We joined Ephrata Ambulance at the same time. No member of Ephrata Ambulance will ever forget, or was ever able to adequately express, the deep sorrow that we felt following one evening that Tom was on call with Ephrata Ambulance. Our tones opened up for unconscious person, AED, meaning the person was in full cardiac arrest, and CPR was in progress.

The terrifying part was the address. It was Tom's parents' address.

Tom was on call with the ambulance crew that night, and immediately realized the call was to his parents' home. They found his father in full cardiac arrest, and despite their efforts, he didn't make it. These are the calls that truly make you, or break you. Tom returned to running ambulance. Today, Tom is a paid firefighter with Lancaster City Fire Department. As Tom puts it, "A dream come true." Granted, there are a lot of caring, compassionate firefighters and EMTs. In my humble little world, it takes a lot for me to label someone as "good people." Tom is "good people."

In August of 2001, I was a member of the "RIT" team at the Bowmansville General Store fire. A "RIT" team is a rapid intervention team. We stood by, to relieve overworked, exhausted teams fighting the fire. We got to the fire and were told we probably wouldn't be needed for several hours.

This fire was huge! Several guys began asking, "Who has cigarettes?" I certainly was not going to admit that I did, but then one or two guys saw me smoking. So I started keeping track of whom I had given a cigarette to. I realized I was running out of cigarettes.

As I stood watching them fight the fire, some man asked me if there's anything he can do, or anything that we need. I sort of jokingly said, "Well, yes, a lot of guys would like some cigarettes."

The man gave me a look I'll never forget, and said, "Well, that is my store that's burning, and I had racks and racks of cigarettes, but I think they've burned. But you can take any you find that can still be used." His comments made me re-evaluate my priorities.

Many occasions—a wedding, a child's birth, a family tragedy—are so compelling that the details are forever etched in memory. Few events define all of us.

September 11, 2001, did.

Fear, shock and anger resonated across our nation.

It was a day I wished had never existed. As ignorant as it may sound, I just wanted to wake up and have it all have been a nightmare. Only twice in my years of service did I ever wish for that to happen. Both times it didn't happen.

So much sadness and controversy followed that day. It was reported there were serious communication problems with fire department radios in the towers and barely any communication at all between the police and fire departments.

It was heartbreaking. We constructed a memorial inside our new rescue building, in honor of our 343 "brothers" who had sacrificed their lives, to save others, as the World Trade Center towers collapsed.

Recently, I was on scene of a mass casualty incident on the Pennsylvania Turnpike. EMS command was being turned over to my unit, and a comment was made, "You know, we learned a lot after 9-11, but nothing has really changed." It's often scary. But again, someone's got to do it.

Chapter 3

What Seems to Be, Is Not Always What Seems to Be

I have learned that too often, "What seems to be, is not always what seems to be."

While I wrote this book with what appears as confidence, and the ability to walk away from each incident unaffected, that truly is not the case. Many emotions are left unattended.

But I don't want anyone to think, "Oh, she's just doing her job." It's never like that. In one sense, you have a job to do, but to think it doesn't affect us emotionally and physically, is not near the world "we" live in.

We learned to cope, and to somehow deal with what we witnessed.

Don't think we're not as human as you are.

Don't think our lives are not distraught by what we see.

Don't think there aren't calls, during or after, that we don't think, "Why am I doing this? Will this be my last call? Will I be able to sleep tonight?" I've seen people come and go, because they can't handle what we see.

When I am asked why I continue to do the work I do, I always say the same thing, "Someone has to do it, and I feel I was given the ability to do it, and still remain sane."

Only those involved in emergency services, nursing, or hospital arenas, can share and appreciate our sense of humor. I think how disgusted some people would be if they ever overheard us talking after a call.

This is not in disrespect, but rather, our only way of finding something other than somber and sadness in many calls.

The acronyms I wouldn't even share with my parents. Ask a firefighter or EMT what "fubar" means. That's your first clue as to their level of experience, or lack thereof.

One of the hardest things for me to do is to return to an empty house. I've been given suggestions of ways to cope with this. Leave a radio playing, so you don't walk into a quiet house. Leave lights on. Get a pet.

I have a light on a timer, so I always return to a lighted room in the evening. I have lots of nightlights. I don't leave a radio on. I have a pet.

My stuffed dog, "Bif," is on my bed. He's the perfect pet. Very low maintenance, always listens to me, never interrupts me, and he's always there.

Bif's name has more meaning than just being his name. I was on a window-shopping spree one afternoon, after an extremely trying day. I saw him sitting on a shelf, it was like he was saying, "Take me home with you, rescue me!" So I did. Earlier in the day, I had tried to tune out the foul ramblings of a co-worker, whose name started with a B. Hence the name BIF. Bill Is Foul.

By now I had applied to Ephrata Ambulance. I was so eager to use my new medical knowledge. I worried I would cross the line and become a "whacker."

My application was approved. It was one of the most rewarding decisions I have ever made.

When you begin at Ephrata Ambulance, you are a "Trainee." I have made so many friends at Ephrata Ambulance. I can't imagine my life without it. I signed up to run whenever I could. They have paid crew on during the day, from 6 AM until 6 PM. Volunteers run from 6 PM until 6 AM, in addition to weekends and paid crew holidays.

I began to understand why they often said to us, "This is the way you would do it for the test, but this is the way you would actually do it on a call." I learned there is no textbook standard in the life of an EMT.

I was blessed to have a crew chief, Deb, take me under her wings. She showed me, with unrelenting patience, how to do trip sheet reports, and all of the tricks of the trade. Deb reinforced that what seems to be, is not always what seems to be. She taught me to look and think outside of the box.

Although Deb is no longer a volunteer at ambulance, I still saw her now and then. But on October 2nd, 2006, I saw Deb at a place I never imagined I would see her. She was in Bart Township, at the Amish schoolhouse murders. She walked up to me, and it took me a minute or two to realize it was Deb.

That day, everything was so out of proportion. It still is, in a lot of ways.

Often our ambulance crew arrives to hear the same question, "What took you so long?" I'm certain this question is asked by many of the same people that fail to pull over for my blue light, while I'm attempting to get to the station for an emergency call. Or the same people who have their radios so loud they don't hear the sirens from our rescue vehicles, or they're in too much of a hurry to get where they're going that they just ignore us.

What seems to be forever, isn't always what seems to be.

Then there are calls that seemingly should be a relatively, easy call. My tones went for an emergency transport from our local hospital to another hospital. I was hurrying too much to hear the other hospital.

I pulled into the ambulance parking lot, and was met by a guy going off duty. He told me, "You might want to put your windows up. Do you know where you're going?"

I said, "No, I only know it's an emergency transfer." He told me that it was to John Hopkins Hospital, in Baltimore, Maryland. I put my windows up. Okay, so this will be a longer call than I expected.

We loaded our patient and headed towards Maryland. Our patient had received a kidney transplant there, and they needed her to return, due to complications she had developed.

As we got closer to John Hopkins, our driver, Mike, asked if one of us could read the directions to him. I agreed to do this. As I was climbing from the back of the rig to the front, passenger seat, I heard Mike mumble something about the rig not running right. As the minutes ticked away, he appeared more concerned with the engine noises. I wasn't hearing them. I was only hearing our sirens, and seeing too many cars for my comfort.

As we got near the hospital, Mike said, "Unload the patient, and I'll stay outside, with the rig running."

We pleaded to him, "No, we wanted to look around a little. No, we wanted to have a cigarette. No, we needed to use the bathroom." He emphatically denied our pleas. We transported the patient to her assigned room, and returned to the rig. The patient was in her room, now we wanted to stop somewhere, get a snack, have a cigarette, and use a bathroom.

It was a hot and humid evening. Mike said that once we were outside of the city, we would stop at a convenience store. We got out of the city, and we were on some interstate highway, with nothing in sight except highway and open grass.

We're fussing that we should have stopped back where there were stores. Mike's not saying a word. Suddenly, we noticed we're pulling over, but we don't see a store. We were pulling over because the rig had just lost its power! There we sat.

Mike made a few calls to our executive board members. They decided to have our local towing company come down and tow the truck home.

We were to find a family member to come and pick us up. We were to strip the rig of the most valuable items, the AED, suction unit, the expensive items, and bring those home with us. We were able to contact Mindy's husband, who agreed to come and pick us up, but it would be several hours until he, and the towing company, would get to us, then several hours to return home.

So we locked the rig and started walking.

Fortunately, there was a small convenience store not too far up the road. The employee was kind enough to let us use the bathroom. Then we realized we didn't have much money with us. Mindy had her debit card, so she ended up paying for our snacks.

After that day, I began carrying money with me whenever I go on a call.

Mindy's husband, and the towing truck, arrived at the same time. We loaded our equipment into his car, but still leaving room for us to sit. We headed back to Ephrata.

We needed to drop off Dana, a nurse who had gone with us, at the hospital. By now her shift was over. By now we had all bonded. We were calling each other, "sister," and still do. It was the longest emergency transfer I was ever on.

I had gotten into the habit of wearing a baseball cap when I was not at my full time job. I liked to wear it backwards. I still have not figured out how, or why, this became a routine for me, but that was my way of wearing a baseball cap. Only certain caps fit well, and I would stick with the same few caps.

One day, while visiting my grandmother, she asked me why I wear a baseball cap. She said, "Girls shouldn't wear baseball caps." So I gave her my word that I would try to break the habit. I told her I would "try to break the habit." I didn't make any promises to her, thank goodness. But I liked wearing them. Especially my Pittsburgh Steelers cap.

One evening I attended a course on Life Lion helicopter landing zone safety. There were many people in attendance. I had my baseball cap on, but not backwards. Through the back opening, I had pulled my hair out. It seemed to be just another class. But it certainly wasn't what it seemed to be.

The following week our local paper featured coverage of the class.

There, on the front page, was a color photo of our training, with the back of my head in the picture, wearing my baseball cap! As you can imagine, I received a phone from my grandmother, asking what happened to the "not wearing a baseball cap anymore discussion." I didn't have an answer.

In our society, we are conditioned to believe that anything less than winning or being right, is failure. The ultimate decision is sometimes not ours to make. The load is not always for us to bear.

A swift and heroic response to an emergency call doesn't mean everything always ends well.

What seems to be, is not always what seems to be.

Then came the long-awaited Millennium. We stationed in quarters, in preparation for what would occur at midnight, January 1st, in the year 2000. We had portable generators, extra food, clothing, candles, everything; we were prepared.

Midnight approached. We went outside to wait for the lights to go out, the sirens to begin blaring, and the mass confusion. Nothing happened. We continued waiting. Nothing happened.

About 3 a.m., one guy said, "This was the biggest, non-event, event we've ever experienced!" But, as the saying goes, "Better to have it and not need it, than to need it and not have it."

In April, I received a call on the Saturday before Easter Sunday, "What are your plans for Easter Sunday?" I asked my chief why he was asking. I've learned to always ask why before answering.

"Well, there was a man who was seen jumping off the Wrights-Ferry Bridge about 10 days ago. They have taken into account the water temperature and other variables, and they feel that tomorrow will be the day his body would surface," he explained, "so water rescue crews were requested to assist in searching the Susquehanna River on Easter." It didn't take me much time to decide. I'd be there in the morning.

With our rescue squad, crew and boats, we headed to Columbia. We geared up, and joined several other water rescue companies in searching the river.

We took turns looking through the binoculars and steering the boat. We searched for hours, to no avail. There was a raw, cold bite in the air. The current was rapid. Our chief officer made the decision in the afternoon, that we would discontinue searching, due to the weather hazards that were increasing.

I returned home and I couldn't decide which I needed to take care of first, my tiredness, my coldness or my hunger. I chose warming up, eating and then sleeping. That was one of those days I returned from a call feeling like I'd never feel normal again.

The body didn't surface until ten days after Easter.

In February of 2000, I learned a lesson that has proven true, too many times. The Pennsylvania Turnpike does everything it can to prevent lane closures. On February 21st there was a bad accident on the turnpike.

Five cars were involved in the chain reaction crash. Vehicle debris was lying everywhere. One young man was heavily trapped in his driver's seat. Cars were smashed like pancakes. Walking wounded patients were everywhere. It was like a war zone. You didn't know where to go first. Everyone was screaming, "Help me first!"

We needed a medic helicopter to land and transport a patient to Lancaster General Hospital. We don't call for a chopper unless it's a very serious injury, or an extended extrication is anticipated.

As we worked, cars continued to zoom by, often within inches of us. I was scared. I wanted to scream, "Please close down this section of the turnpike!"

The turnpike strives to keep at least one lane of traffic flowing at all times. This sometimes causes a precarious situation. Generally, in Lancaster County, when you request a road be closed due to an auto accident or other incident, it's done immediately, without any questioning.

I realize the travelers on the turnpike are paying tolls and they expect to keep moving. But then you have the "rubber neckers," who gawk out their windows, trying to see what is going on, and occasionally causing another accident.

Sometimes they will close both lanes to permit the landing of a medic chopper. I have been on enough accidents on the turnpike that I dread driving on the turnpike.

I cringe when I'm sent to the turnpike for an accident. I learned you have to watch your own back, as no one else is going to watch it for you.

One morning, around 3:30 a.m., in April of 2000, I went to a vehicle accident on a relatively straight section of road in Brecknock Township. We learned a 24-year-old male may have fallen asleep, because there were no indications that he had tried to avoid having his truck slam into a barn.

A passing motorist discovered the accident. As he drove by the barn, he saw the rear end of the truck sticking out from the barn. He walked over to check it out. He found the driver had been decapitated. So we had one dead man and one emotionally distraught man to deal with.

A deputy coroner pronounced the truck driver dead at the scene. We waited and waited for the coroner to arrive. It seemed to be forever. I have a vague recollection of thinking to myself, "Wow, that would be an interesting job, but I don't know if I could do that."

Several weeks later we were dispatched for a vehicle accident with entrapment. It sounded like a fairly routine call, until we were jumping into our gear and a member mentioned he heard it on his scanner, and thought it was one of our police officers who was trapped. My heart stopped beating for a few seconds, hoping he was wrong. He was right.

It was later reported, "Ephrata Borough Police Fred Sprecher underwent five hours of surgery for a torn aorta after a fleeing vehicle crashed into his cruiser Friday night in Ephrata Township.

"Sprecher remains in serious condition as of Wednesday morning, after he was upgraded from critical to serious Monday at LGH, where he was taken after being extricated from his police cruiser. A Toyota driven by an 18-year-old Ephrata male allegedly attempted to hit two other officers prior to the crash.

"Police said they believe the crash into Sprecher's vehicle was intentional.

"The crash trapped the 12-year veteran, causing the need for extrication by Ephrata Rescue. Using a new device, called the Hurst Extrication Cutter, Ephrata Rescue needed just 18 minutes to get Sprecher out from the time they arrived."

Fred's brother, Ed, was the chief of police in New Holland Borough, and commented, "He went in and they found out he had a torn aorta, then he went into a five-hour operation, suffering rib and other injuries as well. It's by the grace of God that he's still living. How they kept that from bleeding so much . . . somehow the blood was stopped."

Chief Ed Sprecher continued, "The rescue and ambulance crews did an outstanding job. Our family is very grateful for their work. What would we do without the volunteers?"

Fred has since made a complete recovery and is back on the force.

Ephrata is a relatively small town, and almost everyone knows everyone, or a relative of someone. Due to our increasing population, new police officers are constantly being hired.

But everyone knows Fred. He's the guy who's always there to help. If it's winter, and the walkway to a home is covered with snow, he'll have the shoveling started before the ambulance arrives. He's one officer you don't have to hesitate to ask for help. He's one of a kind. Every time I see him on an ambulance call, even after all of these years, I thank someone above for watching over him that evening.

2001 brought its share of rescue calls, but now I was trying to decide what I wanted to do, as far as volunteer work. Both rescue and ambulance required a significant amount of training.

Ambulance required constant re-certifications and updates for my EMT certification. Then there were fund drives, and the house duties. So much time was required with each organization. I was leaning heavily towards leaving rescue, and only running with ambulance. One beautiful afternoon, I happened to be at the rescue station when our rescue tones went off for a "water rescue, boater in distress." I had signed up to run with ambulance that afternoon.

I thought to myself, "Why can't I do both?" But I couldn't. I had to stay behind for any ambulance calls.

I stood in the driveway and watched the rescue squad pull out with the boats. I heard one guy yell, "See, that's why I only run with one company!"

I decided to give this some serious thought. It didn't take a lot of thinking. The pre-hospital emergency care as an EMT was definitely my favorite. But for the time being, I continued running with both companies.

A week later a vehicle accident, with entrapment, came in around lunchtime, on a clear afternoon. Two vehicles had collided at the intersection of South 7th Street and North Conestoga View Drive. It seemed the extrication went well, both drivers were transported to local hospitals for injuries; it seemed to be a "routine call."

Several days later I saw the obituary of the one driver, stating he died from injuries suffered in an auto accident. I was shocked and saddened. I read he had been married for 49 years, enjoyed tinkering with cars, hard work and sports. He was a retired Swiss cheese maker, and had worked for Sugarcreek Dairy in Sugarcreek, Ohio, for many years. I've never met a cheese maker.

Then I wondered, "Was the family planning a 50th wedding anniversary party? How was his wife doing? What were the internal injuries that we were unaware of?"

But you have to turn your mind off sometimes, and accept what you know, and not question what you don't know.

I think about the commercial, "Life comes at you fast!" When I stare at these people, either in critical condition, or dead, I can only pray that life came at them fast, that they never had a clue, or suffered any pain.

Tomorrow is not promised to anyone. Life is so fragile. We are aware that all of us will eventually die, we see lingering deaths, and many have watched a loved one slip away from a lengthy illness.

But often we forget how life can suddenly, and often violently, be taken away. So many bright futures are tragically cut short. We tend to take life for granted.

But life offers no guarantees, other than death.

I saved an article, "How to die in 0.7 Seconds."

A car going 55 miles per hour hits a solid object.

In the first tenth of the second, the front bumper and grille collapse.

In the second tenth, the hood crumbles, rises, and strikes the windshield as simultaneously, fenders begin wrapping themselves around the solid object, and although the car's frame has been halted, the REST OF THE DRIVER'S CAR IS STILL GOING 55 MILES PER HOUR. Instinct causes the driver to stiffen his legs against the crash, and they snap at the knees.

During the third tenth of the second, the steering wheel starts to disintegrate and the steering column aims for the driver's chest.

The fourth tenth finds two feet of the car's front end wrecked, while the rear end still moves at 35 miles per hour, and the driver's body is still traveling at 55 miles per hour.

In the fifth tenth the driver is impaled on the steering column, and blood rushes to his lungs.

The sixth tenth finds the impact built up to the extent that feet are ripped out of tightly laces shoes. The brake pedal snaps off. The car frame buckles in the middle, and the driver's head bangs into the windshield, as the rear wheels, still spinning, fall back to the ground.

In the seventh tenth, hinges rip loose, doors open, and the seat breaks free, striking the driver from behind. BUT HE DOESN'T MIND BECAUSE HE IS ALREADY DEAD, and the last three tenths of a second mean nothing to him.

NOW WILL YOU BUCKLE YOUR SEAT BELT?

So often people involved in crashes say, "It just happened so fast." Yes, it does. The above reactions take place in less than one second.

Two elderly sisters were traveling a back road in Adamstown, when their car briefly left the road, and struck a small tree. The vehicle then spun and flipped onto its roof. The passenger was killed instantly, and the driver was flown to Brandywine Hospital. As I fixated on the petite, plainly dressed, elderly dead woman, I wondered, "Did life come at her that fast?"

It seems many accidents occur on the way to work, or on the way home from work. Some days I'm just casually driving along and I panic. What if another car crosses over and hits my Jeep head-on? Will I be trapped in my Jeep, or will I be dead within one second.

I try to push these thoughts out of my mind.

On a cold, January morning, our tones opened for a vehicle accident with entrapment. A 54-year-old man was on his way to work. He lost control of his car, skidded across both lanes, and smashed head-on into a pole. The skid marks measured 170 feet long. It was determined that his speeding had caused the accident.

Neighbors heard the sound of the car's skidding tires, just before hearing a "bang." Looking outside, they saw a dark blue car, wrapped around the pole, with the driver still inside.

He wasn't moving. He didn't have any traumatic injuries on his body, but his neck had snapped and he was dead.

Our rescue unit extricated the victim, and he was pronounced dead at the scene. He looked like he was sleeping, not like he had just crashed into a pole.

As I looked at the wreckage and the dead man, I couldn't stop thinking, "Why not leave a little earlier to go to work? Isn't it better to be a few minutes late, rather than to not make it at all?"

But it seems our society has become so fast paced. Everything seems so rushed. People get upset if they have to wait. My grandfather's aunt once told me that in her days they were always busy, but it was a different kind of busy. They still had time to respect each other. They made time at the end of the day to just sit and visit. It is a shame that we have lost so much of that character.

I'm constantly amazed at some of the scenes we go to, and find the vehicles smashed beyond recognition of what make of car or truck they are, but the drivers are fine. What seems to be, isn't always what seems to be.

Then again, often people are just in the wrong place at the wrong time. The outcome is not always good. What seems to be is not always what seems to be. Sometimes we never understand "why?"

Our ambulance was dispatched for an unconscious person. We arrived to find a neatly dressed lady, sitting outside on a picnic table, with several suitcases packed and stacked next to her. She promptly informed us that she was no longer unconscious. Really? Her suitcases were packed, and she wanted to take a trip to the hospital. That's when you count to ten.

A class 3 call for an injured person. Class 3 calls are the lowest priority calls. We don't use lights and sirens, but we are still required to respond within the allotted time frame. Our dispatcher had told us that the patient had cut his finger while chopping onions. Okay, that didn't sound too bad.

We entered the home to find 43-year-old Paulus, sitting calmly at his kitchen table, with blood saturating the table-cloth. Paulus told us that he loved cooking, and he had bought a new set of knives the night before. While chopping onions into homemade tomato sauce, he accidentally chopped off "the tip of his thumb."

He kept apologizing for his clumsiness, blaming it on his not being familiar with using these new knives, which were much sharper than his old ones. I politely asked him to stop apologizing.

We asked to look at his hand. Paulus had used duct tape to try to control the bleeding. I'm a firm believer that duct tape is a necessity in life, but not to bandage your hand to control the bleeding. As my partner and I unwound the duct tape, we saw his entire thumb was missing!

Oops.

"Would your thumb be in the sauce?" we asked him.

"Yes, I guess so, if it's not on my hand," he answered.

I offered to dig through the sauce, while my partner tried to control the bleeding and applied sterile dressings. Suddenly Paulus said, "I feel like I'm going to pass out."

Looking at the tomato sauce, it was difficult to tell how much of it was blood, and how much of it was sauce. As I continued my search, I quickly did my usual routine to prepare myself, just in case he does become unconsciousness.

"Do you take any medications? Are you allergic to any medicines? Do you have any significant past medical history?"

With the last question, the answers changed from, "No" to "Does having full-blown AIDS and Hepatitis C count?" Hmm, yes!

I quickly assessed the situation. I was digging through the sauce, not being able to tell an onion from a thumb, and I just learned my patient has full-blown AIDS and Hepatitis C. I told my partner, "This call has just become a load and go. I'll load the container of sauce, and we'll go to the hospital. They can search for the thumb at the hospital."

As much as I try not to judge a person, and to give them the greatest care possible, I realized we were jeopardizing our lives. With this patient in the final stages of AIDS and having Hepatitis C, what good would one thumb be? He still had his nine other fingers. So I made the decision. He was a load and go, along with the container of spaghetti sauce. It's another one of those calls where what seems to be, is not what always what it actually is.

Several years later I was on a call in Lancaster Township. The lady was a DOA. She had lived with her sister. I questioned her as to the date of birth of her deceased sister. The sister firmly stated, "No one ever really knew hold old she was." I tactfully asked, "Why was that?"

"Well, she never wanted anyone to know how old she really was!" she answered, with a tinge of bitterness in her voice.

I looked at her driver's license. According to her driver's license, she would have been 86 years old. Her sister insisted that was not correct. While waiting for the undertakers, I offered to help the surviving sister go through some documents. Sure enough, buried under lots of other papers, was a graduation diploma from a local college. I quickly did the math.

The deceased, at some point in time, began adding ten years to her date of birth. This made her appear, on paper, to be ten years younger than she was. I couldn't find fault with the deceased.

I was raised to believe you never go through a female's purse, and you never ask a female her age. But for official purposes, I had to document, "age uncertain." I felt she would have been satisfied with that.

As I was leaving, her sister yelled to me, "I knew she was older than me!"

Another coroner call certainly wasn't what seemed to be as it had been dispatched. Fire companies were dispatched for a brush fire one afternoon in April.

An elderly man told his wife that he was going out back to burn some wood in their field, something he had routinely done. After some time, she happened to look out the back window, and saw their field was on fire. She dialed 911 and said they needed a fire truck to put out the fire in their field.

The firefighters arrived, and as they were putting out the fire, they found her husband, lying dead, near where he had started burning wood.

This caused great concern to other firefighters, listening to the call on their scanners. Firemen fighting a relatively small brush fire and suddenly medics are dispatched to the scene, followed by a request for a coroner.

The widow invited me inside their home. She offered me some lemonade, and a seat at the "good table." She reminded me of my grandmother. She spoke of the good life they had lived, despite her husband's heart problems, and she was grateful for the years they had together. Her husband had died of sudden, cardiac arrest, but she was at peace with his death.

Then another ambulance call for an unconscious person. Was I wrong to have thought that this call would actually result in finding an unconscious person? So many times, while responding to an "unconscious person call," the dispatcher informs us the patient is now conscious, and breathing normally.

This woman was definitely unconscious, lying in the middle of a beautifully decorated living room. Everything seemed to be in place, other than the elderly, unconscious woman, lying on the living room floor. I rolled her over and began deciding my next move.

As I rolled her, I noticed a piece of an apple lying on the floor. It seemed out of place. I asked the family, who was watching every move we made, "What is this piece of apple doing here on the floor?"

"Oh," they recalled, "she was eating an apple when she fell over."

Okay, now we have something, possibly and hopefully, in our favor. I rolled her again and did a finger sweep. Low and behold, a piece of apple emerged from her mouth! She immediately began breathing, and regained consciousness.

She looked up and asked, "Why are all of these people here looking at me? I have things to do, will you please leave?"

The following day, at 3:30 in the morning, my pager woke me for a carbon monoxide poisoning. The firefighters went in first, to obtain air readings. There was no carbon monoxide in the home. The elderly homeowner insisted the firemen were wrong.

We tried to convince her, "Go to bed, everything is ok."

She said, "I haven't slept in days, because there is carbon monoxide in my home! If there wasn't, why would my son have installed that detector?"

I've learned that life throws you curves. I suppose that is the whole meaning behind, "What seems to be, is not always what seems to be."

I have spent many years learning to dodge or deal with the curves. I have categorized these years as, "years of growing my roots." Roots that run very deep; roots that held me up during the most grueling experiences.

One afternoon we were sent to an address I was familiar with, for an unconscious person. Driving to the address, we were told that our patient was now conscious, to enter from the rear, and go to the second floor. I knew the steps were probably less than twelve inches wide and it would be taxing to carry a patient down them. But it didn't matter. We had been told that our patient was now conscious.

As we pulled into the parking lot, a young guy ran towards us, screaming, "Hurry, hurry, Larry had a heart attack and I think he's dead!"

We told him, "Calm down, it's ok. We were told he's conscious. We'll take care of him." We carried our bags up the winding, narrow stairs, stepped inside the apartment, and saw Larry, lying unresponsive, unconscious, in the middle of the floor.

I checked for a pulse, found none, and began CPR, as my partner prepared the AED. We shocked the patient, and I continued CPR down the narrow steps and into our rig. CPR was continued until we arrived at the hospital. Larry was dead.

Another unconscious person on Route 222. A passerby had supposedly seen a person, lying unconscious, on the side of the road. The beauty of cell phones. You can call 911, but you don't have to stop and see if help is needed. It's a love/hate relationship I have developed for cell phones. We drove along the highway. I was on the passenger side, so I used the floodlight to look for the "unconscious person." After an extensive search, I spotted something white lying on the side of the road. We pulled over. It was a deer!

That must have been what the driver had seen. I asked my partner if I could use our AED to try shocking the deer back to life.

He immediately said, "No!"

I asked him why I couldn't at least give it a try. He reminded me of the protocols for using the AED.

Then he asked me, "How will you explain the fur on the AED patches?" Okay, he was right. We informed the road crew of our finding, so the deer could be removed. I still wonder if the AED would have saved the deer. But rules are rules.

Then a firefighter's greatest nightmare, a call for a fire in a residence, with entrapment. As we responded, we were told there was confirmed entrapment.

As we approached the house, we saw smoke coming out of the windows. Now we were really scared. Yes, we get scared.

We quickly organized our plans. Firetrucks blocked the entrance, so we parked away from the actual scene. I walked up the steep hill, carrying as many bags as I could. My partner was close behind me bringing additional bags and a litter.

I heard a female screaming, "My babies are inside, get my babies out!" My heart stopped beating for a few seconds. I desperately tried to calm her down, to find out exactly where, and how many babies, were inside the residence.

She started counting on her fingers. My heart sank.

Then she told me how many are in which cage, and in which room. Which cage?

She hysterically answered, "We don't let them out of their cages at night!"

I asked her, "Why are your babies in cages?"

She looked at me, like something was wrong with me, and said, "Birds live in cages, don't you know that!"

I refocused my questioning. I asked if there were any children or people inside the home. She emphatically answered, "No, just my babies!" Her baby birds were all successfully rescued.

A wise man once told me, "If it looks like a duck, waddles like a duck, quacks like a duck, it's not a swan, but it's not always a duck." I've learned the hard way, that what appears to be, isn't always what appears to be. Just because it looks like a duck, doesn't always mean it's a duck.

Our ambulance was dispatched for a drug overdose. The patient displayed all of the symptoms of an overdose. We loaded the patient, and on the way to the hospital, he began projectile vomiting. Vomit was everywhere. I couldn't stand the sight or the smell of it. It was disgusting.

I was annoyed that his vomit landed in my hair, but my shift was soon ending, and I could go home and shower. We unloaded the patient at the hospital. He hadn't overdosed; he had suffered a massive heart attack. He was 37 years old. He died the following day.

When I learned he had died, I was filled with guilt for being upset with him vomiting in my hair. But I knew we had given him the best medical treatment we could. I had to accept the fact that his time was up. It's so much easier said than done.

Then there are happy endings. We were dispatched for a residential rescue. We were told that a 4-year-old girl was mangled in her bike. I'm thinking the worst. I'm preparing for the worst. We pulled up to find a tiny, dark-haired girl, with her foot caught in the spokes of her bike. She was talking a mile a minute. She was on her new "Barbie" bike. I looked her square in the eyes and began talking a mile a minute back to her.

During this time, our fire department arrived, and they were bending the spokes of her wheel. It only took a few minutes, but it seemed like hours. I kept talking to her. They finally were able to remove her foot. I told her it might hurt, but it wouldn't hurt for very long. She asked me, "How long is 'long'?"

I thought, "She's way too smart for a four year old!"

Her foot was extricated from the spokes, and everyone started clapping and cheering. I thought to myself, "This is a Kodak moment." I carried her into our rig to assess her and her foot. My assessment was good. I felt she was able to go back to her mother, who was waiting outside of our rig. I gave her a teddy bear and told her I'd take her back outside to her mother.

She looked at me and asked, "But what about my bike?"

I told her that the bike may not be able to be fixed, but her foot was ok. She wasn't happy with that answer. She had refused to name her teddy bear, because she was upset over her new bike being broken.

What we didn't know was that while we were inside the ambulance, the firefighters had repaired all of the bent spokes, and her bike was as good as new. She insisted on limping over to see it for herself.

Suddenly she came back to me and announced that she had named her teddy bear. His name was "B." "Because you were so nice to me. Because they fixed my bike. Because my foot isn't broken. Because my mom is not mad!" Maturity beyond many of the adults we treat!

Some endings are not good, and certainly not what they seemed to be. I was sent to a house fire in which 46-year-old Jim had perished. Initially police and the fire marshal believed that Jim, who was now the charred resemblance of a body, had died from smoke inhalation. But when we moved his body, a .22-caliber Ruger pistol was found under his hand. X-rays revealed a gunshot wound to his head.

Jim had started a fire near the fireplace, at the opposite end of his home. That gave him time to go to his bedroom, crawl into bed, shoot himself, and have it appear he died from the fire. Jim's family insisted that he always slept with a gun in bed because his home was in a rural, secluded area. What Jim didn't know was that we would do a full body x-ray following his death. His plan didn't work.

I was still running with Ephrata Rescue, and had just finished a night of training on vehicle stabilization, using 2 x 4s. An ambulance call came in for an injured person at McDonalds. We found a man, seated on a chair, inside the restaurant, with a laceration on his head. I asked Dan, my partner, to hand me a two by four. He gave me confused look, but without saying a word, Dan pulled out a four by four bandage, and some sterile water.

We transported the patient, and then Dan left me have it, "What were you going to do with a two by four, hit him over the head?"

I tried to explain that I had just finished a cribbing class, where I was continuously asking for a two by four and that was stuck in my head. In humor, Dan continued to heckle me about my mistake.

I returned home, went to my basement, and cut off the end of a two by four. I took a marker and wrote on the wooden block, "In case you ever need a 2 x 4!" I placed it in Dan's mailbox at the ambulance building.

As I was leaving the station, I realized I was being pulled in too many directions. I had to decide which organization to devote my time to. I couldn't keep running with both of them. I had to make a gut-wrenching, heartbreaking decision.

Chapter 4

The Ambulance Awaits

With a lump in my throat, and tears swelling in my eyes, I turned in my equipment to my rescue chief. I was going to devote my volunteer energies to the ambulance association.

I can't say, "I never looked back." I did look back, but I knew I had to give up something. I was putting my heart, soul and many hours into both organizations, in addition to working full time.

So the roller coaster in the ambulance began.

Ephrata Ambulance provides you with the opportunity to run a lot of calls. With three ambulances, three transport vans, and one squad, we're kept very busy. In 2007 we responded to over 6,000 calls.

One evening, we were sent to a patient in seizures. Jimmy came out of his seizures on the way to the hospital, and he began telling us about his recent engagement to Rebecca. He told us they were going to wait at least two years before marrying, to be certain they were doing the right thing.

We all knew Rebecca. She worked as a cashier at a local store. She was physically challenged, but that never stopped her from doing a good job, and being polite and caring. We were happy for them.

The next day we were dispatched to Rebecca's residence for an unconscious AED call. Rebecca didn't make it. We were devastated, and again thought, "Too often life just doesn't seem fair."

September brings our annual Ephrata Fair. Billed as the largest street fair in Pennsylvania, we expect, and prepare for a large turnout. Nearly 50,000 people come out Wednesday night, to watch the parade.

We expect and prepare for many calls during the fair. This is in addition to doing routine transports from nursing homes to doctor appointments, and running other emergency calls. It is quite a challenge for our illustrious EMS manager, Kevin Wolf. Kevin truly is the soul of Ephrata Ambulance. He's always upbeat, easy going, ready to listen to any concerns, but runs a tight ship.

He is always on top of everything. He co-ordinates the van transports. He ends up calling (begging) people to fill in the gaps on weekends. It's not uncommon to go to the station for a second or third ambulance call, in the middle of the night, and find him there. If there can be another unsung hero, it must be Kevin. He is another person I call "good people."

We have our "traditions" at some of the Ephrata Fair events. Mine include the "Tug of War" standby, where teams challenge each other by tugging on a rope, until one team pulls the other across a line on the ball field.

Another one is the "Pig Chase." It's pretty much exactly what it's called. Various age groups chase greased pigs, catching them, and carrying them to the pigpen. One year a group of people showed up at the Pig Chase, wearing "Official Observer" shirts. We noticed extra police combing the area. For a pig chase?

We learned this group was there to see if any cruelty was being done to the pigs. Nothing happened, and they didn't return the next year, so I suppose they were satisfied that the pigs weren't being harmed.

I used to save a week's vacation and help out, days and nights, the week of the fair. One Friday evening, I was begging anyone to run my Saturday shift for me.

When I started offering to pay them, I knew it was bad. I finally made a deal with Bonnie. I paid Bonnie's husband, Dan, a quarter, for him to babysit their children, so Bonnie could run my Saturday shift. That's when I knew I wouldn't be signing up for that many hours again during the week of the fair.

One fair year an unusual and scary call happened. The call was during the middle of the night. Our patient displayed general, flu-like symptoms, so we figured he had the flu. The following morning I arrived at our fair first aid trailer. Kevin came in to the trailer and asked if I was on that call the night before. I told him I was, and I had already completed my trip sheet.

He asked me to step outside with him. I was nervous. I started replaying the call in my mind, "Had I done something wrong?"

Kevin told me our patient had tested positive for bacterial meningitis. Whew, I actually felt a sense of relief. Then reality kicked in. We had all been exposed! Kevin took me to the hospital for the required preventative dose of antibiotics. The others were also going to be taken for treatment. The petite nurse giving me the antibiotic said, "Well, hopefully you'll be lucky and the patient will not test positive." Kevin tactfully told her it was too late for luck.

I kept busy the next few days with ambulance calls and eating fair food, to keep my mind off of the illness. Weeks passed; none of us got sick and I finally stopped worrying about it.

Our fair night traditions included Elva Stauffer, Angie Sensenig and I as a crew for standbys. We looked forward to these annual events. The weather would range from a winter-like evening, to a sweltering summer-like sizzle.

One year, during the tug of war event, it began pouring. This event is held on the dirt baseball field, which quickly turned into a mud field. But there we were, cheering for our favorite team, in the pouring rain. I knew then that both these people were going to be lifelong friends.

Angie became my "rock" through my years as a deputy coroner. I'd call her for directions when I was lost, which was a lot of times. I'd call her and cry, when I needed to cry and have someone listen to me. True friends are one of life's greatest blessings; I am blessed to have her as my friend.

Elva invited me to her home for holiday dinners. One Christmas, she had 54 people in her home for dinner. As she was preparing her dinner, she pulled me aside and gave me a present. It was a beautiful knitted cap and scarf set. I was so touched by her act of kindness. She is truly an amazing person.

The fair brings out the best and the worst in people.

One evening, my partner and I were walking down the midway to get something to eat. A young girl was lying on the street, with her purse dumped out on the ground. I went over, kneeled down, and asked her if she was okay. She slurred, "NO!" She told me she was hunting through her purse for something she could use to kill herself. We called the police and she was transported to the hospital.

I was told I had to go to the hospital to sign the commitment form, as I was the one she told she was going to kill herself. We went to the hospital, I signed the form, and as we were standing at the entrance, we heard banging, coming from the hospital's "quiet room." The "quiet room" is for patients who might be a danger to themselves or others. I asked a police officer, "What is she doing?" He answered, "Getting a sore hand!"

Every spring our ambulance holds a fund raising auction. Jesse Roberts, a paid crewmember, organizes the event. He is another great guy. If something needs done at the ambulance station, just ask Jesse and it will get done.

Paid crew and volunteers spend many hours, in between calls, going to businesses to collect donations. Volunteers are the auction runners. Pete, Elva, Angie and I always went together in one rig. Pete and I were runners, Elva was the organizer of items to be auctioned, and Angie was the dedicated spender.

One year there was an old fashioned, tall, horrible green colored vase. It depended on whom you talked to as to how pretty, or how ugly, it is. We somewhat reluctantly put it up for auction. To our surprise, Kevin purchased it for a few dollars. We asked him why he bought that hideous vase. He said he was going to collect donations in it. Sure enough, by the end of the auction, he had quite a few dollar bills and a nice hand full of change in it.

The following year we arrived at the auction site to find the same, ugly vase there again. Kevin had donated it back to be re-auctioned. Immediately we all knew the destination of the vase. An ambulance member buys it each year, and brings it back the following year, to be purchased by another member. It was dedicated as our "traveling vase."

Elva's husband, Aaron, had been ill for some time. In September of 1999 he passed away. As I read the service bulletin insert, it seemed like he was telling Elva to continue managing their diner, and remain involved with ambulance and their church.

"Then you must not grieve so sorely, for I love you dearly still; try to look beyond earth's shadows, pray to trust our Father's Will. There is work still waiting for you, so you must not idly stand; do it now, while life remaineth—you shall rest in Jesus' land. When that work is completed, He will gently call you home."

A lot of classes and new practices were put into effect following 9-11. I honestly don't know how our response would be in the event of a major catastrophe. I want to think that it would be superior. I want to think we will never have to find out. But I want to be as prepared as I can.

Now I'm concerned about a pandemic. Some say it's not a matter of, "if" anymore, it's a matter of, "when." So I started reading and taking courses to prepare myself in the event "when" happens during my lifetime. My findings were startling.

The average workplace will lose 40% of their employees. You won't be able to order supplies. You'll have to make do with what you have. A lot of articles suggested stockpiling extra supplies now. Most people I know aren't considering a pandemic a possibility. I hope they are right.

One day in August, we had a motorcyclist who was seriously injured in a car versus motorcycle crash. The car won. The motorcyclist had multiple, exposed fractures of both legs. I needed to have his clothing removed before our arrival at the trauma center.

I knew he had to be in excruciating pain, and my head reeled as I tried to drown out his screaming and wade through the blood to get to his injuries. Then he began screaming, at the top of his lungs, "Don't cut my good biker jeans! I paid good money for them! Don't you dare cut them!"

I tried yelling back, over his voice, "Sorry, I'll try my best to cut along the seams so they can be repaired." We normally do this anyway, but it was amazing how someone, in so much pain, could be concerned about his pants.

Often we arrive for an emergency ambulance call, only to be told by the patient, "You'll have to wait until I change into nicer clothes before I go to the hospital." Patience is a virtue.

We are blessed to have a wonderful group of volunteers and paid members who are dedicated to saving people's lives, and show true compassion and caring for their patients.

I often joke with my friends, saying, "Patience is so over-rated." "Sleep is so over-rated." But you need patience to be a good EMT. A good sense of humor is another requirement, but there's a time and place for it.

I was on a call for an elderly, sick woman. She obviously was confused, due to either her age or her illness. I had a trainee with me. As I was taking vitals, I asked the trainee to see what she could learn from the patient, about the woman's pain. I stopped dead in my tracks, as I heard the trainee say to the patient, "So you're not sick, then why on earth would you call for an ambulance, we have other things to do, you know!" The trainee was removed from our volunteer roster.

A fourteen-year-old girl was eight months pregnant, and lived with her mother, from whom she had been hiding her pregnancy. She was in labor, and the pain was too much to bear without screaming. Her mother woke up, and was in total disbelief and denial that this was happening.

I needed to call the hospital, giving them basic information about our patient, so they would be ready for us when we arrived there. The teenager was screaming so loudly, I wasn't certain if the doctor heard my report. We pulled up to the hospital emergency entrance, where security was waiting to take us to the delivery room. As we moved our patient from our litter to the delivery room bed, she delivered a stillborn baby.

The girl's mother had stayed at home, angry with her daughter. Our patient had called a girlfriend, who was waiting in the lobby. She saw me and asked, "Did she have her baby yet? Is it a boy or a girl?" With a heavy heart, I told her I could not release any information.

I try not to judge other people. I believe that one never knows how he or she would react until they are in that situation.

A woman in East Cocalico Township shot and killed her 8-year-old daughter, and then turned the gun on herself. Our ambulance crew, along with a flight paramedic, worked desperately to save the mother's life. This scene was caught on camera, and plastered on the front page of our newspaper. The mother died hours later at the hospital.

I found myself questioning how I would respond to a call like that. Would I be able to remain as focused as they did? Would my legs turn to noodles, and I'd just stand there, unable to walk?

This was always one of my biggest fears. Noodle legs. Then my share of traumatic calls started, and I realized I could do it. My legs didn't turn to noodles. Fright accompanied me to a lot of scenes, but once we arrived, my fright was left inside the rig.

One call was for an eight-year-old child who had been burned by hot water. That's all we knew. We found a cute little girl, with second and third degree burns on her chest and arms. The mother was more distraught than the daughter was.

She'd been cooking chicken on the stove, went to move the kettle, and the daughter got caught in between. The boiling chicken broth splashed on the daughter. After we stabilized and loaded the daughter, I tried explaining to her mother that it was an accident, these things happen. Right now we needed to remain calm and take care of the daughter's wounds. The mother wouldn't calm down.

She blurted out, "Oh, great! I finally just got visitation rights to see my daughter, and then this happens. I will probably never get to see her again!"

What do you say? So often you can't find the right words, so you come up with something to say and you hope it works.

Don't think for one minute there aren't days when I question myself, "Why I am doing this?" Don't think there aren't many times when I say to myself, "Okay, I'll run the rest of my shift, then that's it."

Being an EMT is not always easy, and life's not always fair. Sometimes I'd think of a million places that I'd rather be, other than where I was. I believe we all have those days.

One Christmas day proved to be one of those days when I felt like just throwing in the towel. Paid staff has off on holidays, so I signed up to be crew chief from 6 a.m. until 6 p.m. It was a Tuesday. I know it was a Tuesday because my last call came in shortly before 6 p.m., when the evening volunteers go on duty. Pete, who runs Tuesday nights, was coming on. He knew it had been a long day, and he offered to take the call for me. Stubborn, thickheaded me, said, "Thanks, but no thanks, I'll take it. It's not 6:00 yet."

That call was the last call I ran that Christmas, and it was the last Christmas for our patient. He was a 55-year-old man, who was shoveling snow, after having eaten a large holiday meal. Neighbors witnessed him fall over, and one immediately began CPR.

I generally wear my stethoscope around my neck, but as I looked at him, lying in a pile of snow, I knew we had to move him into our rig, while continuing CPR. I yanked my stethoscope off and threw it on the ground, so it wouldn't be in my way. After we returned to our station, I realized I didn't have my stethoscope. We drove back to the house and dug through the snow piles. We never found it. But as I weighed the loss of my stethoscope against the loss of this father and husband, my stethoscope seemed meaningless.

Earlier in the day it had started snowing. The flakes were large and it was a very heavy snow. It was only my driver and I. We had calls all day long.

One was for a lonely man who had attempted suicide. He was distraught because none of his family came to visit or called him that Christmas day. He decided to kill himself, but he couldn't figure out how to do that. He said, "I'm just a total loser."

A distraught pregnant woman was afraid her husband would get stuck in the snow while driving her to the hospital, for her impending delivery. So she called for a ride in our ambulance.

Then a fire, during the snowstorm, near the Ephrata Park. Our rig, which weighs five tons, got stuck in the snow several times. You need a large motor to pull our rig out of a lot of snow. We were returning to the station and got stuck trying to go up an incline near the station. A few guys in a SUV offered to pull us out. My driver told them the weight of our rig. They said, "No problem," and proceeded to pull us out of the snow! I never got to thank them, but it rekindled my belief that there are caring people!

One of our calls that Christmas day was for a sick person. We found the address, and saw a young guy standing outside, waiting for us. He walked himself into the rig, sat down on the litter, and said, "I just feel yucky." After questioning him on various health issues, I finally asked him if he had done any illegal drugs.

He hesitated before answering. We often need to convince people that we are not the police; we are medics, just trying to help them. He finally said, "Well, I hadn't done any last night, but then today I thought maybe that's why I was feeling so yucky, so I shot up. But I still felt yucky so I thought I better go to the hospital."

He began acting a little bizarre. I'm getting nervous; it's just him and I in the back of the rig. I leaned forward to see where we were at, only to see we were at the exact same place as when we arrived. I asked my driver, "What's up? Why aren't you driving to the hospital?"

He said, "We're stuck again." I not so calmly told him, "I don't care who you have to call, or what you have to do, but you get us out of here, now!" We finally started moving. My patient was calm during the trip to the hospital. Much calmer than I was!

We got back to the station to find we had no electricity. We have electric door openers, and both of us had left our keys inside the building. Could it get any worse? Luckily, another member was driving by, saw us sitting outside, and stopped to unlock the side door. We manually pushed up the bay door. Mike, my driver, climbed on top of the rig to pull down the string to close the bay door. No sooner had Mike climbed down from the top of the rig and our tones went again! He quickly climbed back up and opened the bay door, so we could go to our next call.

The next day presented what is so typical for us. We returned to our paying jobs, and everyone asks how your holiday was. Our routine response is, "Nice, how was yours?" People want to hear what they want to hear, so that's what you say.

Only after counseling in 2006 did I learn, and accept, that it is ok to say, "Well, it could have been better."

Ephrata Ambulance has a "1,000 Hour" recognition board. If a volunteer runs over 1,000 hours in one year, they are given a plaque, engraved with the year and number of hours you ran. In 2001, I ran 1,294 hours. Had I realized I was six hours shy of 1,300 hours, I would have squeezed in six more hours, just to make it an even number. I had figured I needed to average 83 hours a month to attain the 1,000 hours. So I ran and ran. I kept a record each month, to be certain I was on track. By the end of 2001, I had a new appreciation for volunteers who routinely put in over 1,000 hours a year. It's exhausting. But I wanted to do it one time in my lifetime. Once was enough.

One Sunday evening, we "dumped the station." That means all three rigs are called for at the same time. I ended up on the second rig, with just a driver, but he's a good driver and an excellent EMT. Tim, my partner, told me that we were going to the unconscious person. No, I didn't want to go to the unconscious person; I wanted to go to the vehicle accident. But I knew our obligation was the priority patient, the unconscious person. So we headed to a trailer park for the unconscious person.

The dispatcher had not gotten a trailer number, so we slowly drove around the trailer park, looking for someone waiting for us. I noticed a woman standing at her door, waving, as if saying, "Hello." I waved back. We circled the trailer park again, finding nothing. We went back to the woman who was doing the soft and gentle, hello wave.

I rolled my window down and asked her, "Did you by chance call for an ambulance, or do you know who did?"

"Yes," she said, "I did. I think my husband is sick."

Tim went in first, as I pulled our bags out of the rig. As I was going up the narrow steps to the door, I heard Tim yell, "Get the AED and suction, now!" I threw the bags inside the door, ran and grabbed our AED and suction unit, and took them inside. I saw her husband, lying on the floor, in cardiac arrest. Tim prepared the AED, as I was getting the suction ready, and contacting a dispatcher to have a company dispatched for lifting assistance.

We continued working on the man, and got him onto a backboard.

I slid back the little clip on the bottom of the screen door, so the door would stay open, for us to carry him out to our rig. Every time I looked at the door, it was closed. Then I noticed the wife was closing it! I tried to remain calm as I asked her to please leave it open so we could get her husband out and to the hospital.

She was extremely upset with this idea, and she didn't hesitate to tell me, "We never leave that door open, the flies will come in!" I explained to her that we needed the door open, and I was sorry if any flies come inside her home. She reluctantly agreed and left it open.

We did everything possible to save her husband, but he died. Nearly every time I pass that mobile home park, I wonder if any flies came in and annoyed his wife. Then I try to convince myself she didn't realize how seriously ill her husband was. We try to be as professional and respectful as possible when we are in other people's homes. But there are times you just have to do what you have to do.

During one call, I was moving furniture to make a path to take our patient out of her home, and I knocked down an Easter arrangement. Fortunately, none of the beautiful pieces broke, and none of the family seemed to mind. Some family members actually think ahead, and will clear a path for you.

Now if only everyone would get the neon numbered signs for outside their homes. Imagine the frustration of going on a call for an unconscious or choking child, and you can't find the house because the numbers are decorative type numbers. They look nice, but you can barely see them at night, or they are hidden underneath a door wreath.

The only ambulance call that I've been subpoenaed to court for, was one of the calls we dread the most, ones involving children. It was dispatched as an emergency transfer from Ephrata Community Hospital to Hershey Medical Center.

As we drove to the Ephrata hospital, my partner said, "It's probably for some pregnant lady, we're probably going to have to wait for them to get her ready, so I'm waiting outside and smoking a cigarette. You can go in and see what equipment we need."

It was a chilly evening for June.

I stepped inside the emergency entrance and was met by several staff members, including a doctor. They told me we were transporting a three-month-old child to the Hershey Medical Center pediatric trauma unit; to bring in a pediatric backboard; head stabilizer; and to do it now!

I ran outside and told my partner to start the rig and to make sure the heat was on. I grabbed our equipment, returned inside, and saw this cute little boy, lying on a hospital bed. We were told he had an internal head bleed, to keep his head stationary and administer "blow by" oxygen. "Blow by" method is where we take a pediatric facemask, with oxygen coming out of it, and gently blow it by their face, giving them additional oxygen, but not frightening them by securing the mask to their face.

The infant's 23-year-old father rode with us, seated in the front passenger seat. He carried on a routine conversation with my driver, almost like we were going on a social trip. At Hershey, we were met by security, who took us directly to their pediatric trauma room, where a host of doctors and nurses were waiting.

The next morning I was contacted by our local police for a statement of what I had observed while the child was in my care. After hearing myself say out loud what I had seen and heard, I began to seriously doubt the father's statement that he had tripped while carrying the baby, and the baby hit a bureau edge. Several days later the headline appeared, "Ephrata man charged with shaking infant." Eighteen months later, jury selection began in the trial of the father, Mr. Smith, who was charged with severely shaking his infant son, causing permanent paralysis.

My partner and I sat in the courthouse waiting room for two days, going home both days to read about the trial in the paper. Smith admitted shaking the infant when he became angry with the child for crying. He was babysitting their two children, while their mother worked, and he couldn't control his anger. When he realized the baby was injured, Smith called their pediatrician, who told him to immediately take the infant to the hospital. Smith later admitted, "I shook him around about 12 times." Smith's defense was that it was society's fault that he shook his son. He claimed he was never told not to shake your baby.

Before the trial ended, Smith pleaded guilty to one count of aggravated assault for abusing his infant son by shaking him. We were dismissed, and the next day I read that sentencing would follow at a later date. I never read the sentencing.

Seeing the infant in the courtroom, a year and a half later, in a wheelchair, was devastating. I believe that someone much greater and higher than us will decide on the ultimate punishment.

Speaking of punishment, the weather can challenge even the most seasoned responders and dispatchers. Some days I feel like I'm being punished, for not appreciating more often, the beautiful days we have.

I went to the station for a call, and ran the call with Kevin. It felt like a winter storm was brewing, but nothing was happening, just one of those feelings you get. We returned to the station, and when I went outside to get in my Jeep, I found the ground was a sheet of solid ice. I cautiously slid back inside the station, knowing our pagers were going to be lighting up like 4th of July fireworks.

We ran calls with all three ambulances, non-stop from 10:00 a.m. until about 2:00 p.m. Our Lancaster County dispatch center noted that during those four hours, they had received and dispatched, over 200 vehicle accidents. Their dispatch board was nearing the 1,000th call mark by the end of the day. An average day's dispatch, during that year, would be between 300 and 400 calls in a 24-hour period.

Ambulances were all over the county. We were sent to areas far from our home area, because all of the ambulances were very busy. A lot of stations only have one ambulance, so our three ambulances went wherever needed. I don't remember where all we were that day. I remember it was treacherous walking, sliding, and getting the patients to the rig. I was glad Kevin was my driver.

Severe weather brings out the best, and the worst, in people. During a snowstorm, it's not uncommon to hear, "My knee has been hurting for days now, and I'm afraid if it keeps snowing, I won't be able to drive to my doctor appointment tomorrow, so I called for an ambulance to take me now." Or the pregnant female, who worries she may go into labor during the snowstorm, so she calls an ambulance to assure she's at the hospital, just in case she goes into labor during the storm.

It also brings out the people who help shovel paths to the doors for our crews. The police officers, who are available, help us by carrying our equipment through the snow. Then the snow becomes covered with a sheet of ice, and the sledding accidents begin. Some of those are nasty.

A local park is a prime area for sledding. The park is filled with long, sloping hills, strewn with large trees that are not nice landing objects, if you lose control of your sled. A lot of the trees are down in the park, at places where our ambulances can't travel. So we carry all of our equipment down to the patient, then carry the litter, with the patient on it, up to our ambulance. Finally we began requesting assistance from a nearby fire company, on any sledding injury calls that happened in their park. They rigged up systems to assist in patient removal, in addition to securing large hay bales around the trees most frequently hit. This tre-mendously lessened the severity of injuries.

Sudden, severe snowstorms reek havoc on everyone. Ambu-lances are probably one of the worst emergency vehicles to drive in the snow. Blizzards throw a whole new dimension into our operations. We have three crews stationed in quarters, with the crews rotating calls. That gives you a little time to sleep, warm up, and eat after a call, before you have to go out on another call.

I learned the hard way, you can never pack too much extra clothes. You find your "waterproof" boots are, in fact, not water-proof. Your "waterproof" gloves are not "waterproof." After run-ning a snowstorm weekend in wet, cold socks, pants, and boots, I began carrying several changes of clothes with me during the winter months.

During one snowstorm, a van filled with five children, ages one to twelve, slid on ice and crashed into a tree. The mother was taking them home from an evening church service. This call was outside of our response area, but all of the closer ambulances were on other calls.

The children and mother had all been taken inside a nearby house to wait for the ambulance. Upon our initial examina-tion, none of their injuries appeared to be serious. We decided to transport all of them together, rather than risk another am-bulance coming out on the icy roads. We treated and stabilized them, before securing them in the back of our rig. Some seemed nervous. That was to be expected.

One young girl was secured on a bench seat, lying on her side. She began complaining that her stomach hurt. I quietly asked her mother, "Is she the type to normally be nervous and com-plain?" Her mother said, "No, of all of my children, she would be the least likely to complain." Now I was concerned. She began projectile vomiting. Her vomit was everywhere. I tried to grab blankets to shield the other children from the vomit. A large amount of vomit landed in my hair. I quickly grabbed a towel for my head, and peaked out the window.

We were close to the hospital, thank goodness. I advised the staff that the toughest child seemed to be the sickest child. I had started my shift at 4:00 that afternoon. We had calls all evening. I walked into my house at 11:56 p.m. I was exhausted, mentally and physically, cold, tired and hungry. The hot shower was the first place I went. As I was heating up some leftover food, our tones went for an emergency transfer from ECH to Hershey Medical Center. I immediately had this gut feeling that it was my "tough" girl from the accident. The emergency transfer was for her. She had ruptured her spleen in the accident.

On a beautiful late afternoon in June, I headed to my parents' place for a cookout. I had just passed Green Mountain Cyclery, when I heard a loud bang, looked in my rear view mirror, and saw cars spinning all over both lanes of traffic. I pulled over and ran to the scene.

No one was seriously injured, but there were multiple, "walking wounded." I waited with the injured until our ambulances arrived. I found out that Floyd Landis' wife, Amber, was stopped in traffic, waiting to turn left into the cycle shop, when her vehicle was hit from behind, sending it into the other lane of traffic, where it hit another vehicle. Floyd Landis grew up in Farmersville. His initial win in the Tour De' France bike race put Farmersville, Pennsylvania, on the map. He bought his first bike at Green Mountain, and had remained friends with the owner of the shop. Floyd was in the area doing book signings, along with his wife, who was by herself that afternoon. I'm not a bike-racing fan, but Farmersville is in my backyard, so I followed Landis' story.

Ephrata has a Wal-Mart store. When the development was proposed, there was much controversy over taking farmland to build a store, coupled with the issues of increased traffic. The developers assured us we would have an intersection that surpassed "excellence in safety designs." That intersection has had more accidents than I can count! I believe it's because our drivers are not used to having five or six lanes of traffic combined at one intersection.

One call to that intersection was for an "injured person from a vehicle accident." An employee took one of his company's brand new cars for a test drive. He approached the intersection at Wal-Mart and became confused by the many lanes of traffic. As he attempted to make a turn, he collided with another vehicle, and totaled the brand new company car. Not a good way to start the workday.

Then there are the three Hs. Hot, Hazy, and Humid. I believe there is something about that combination that causes people to act in bizarre ways. Other people swear a full moon does it. But definitely, hot, hazy and humid days make people a little crazy. Especially when you have several of them in a row.

Do people, without air conditioning, go hang out at Wal-Mart and places that are air-conditioned? Do they drink more cold beverages, a lot of them containing alcohol, which causes increased dehydration? Don't people realize you can't be working on a roof all day when it's 100 degrees, and the humidity level is 95%? Do people just get so tired of being hot and miserable that they do strange things? I don't know. I do know "cabin fever" is a mild trigger of calls during the winter months, but it's nothing compared to the calls during the hot, hazy days of summer.

One hot and humid evening we were dispatched for an accident involving several people. A car missed a curve, went off of the roadway, and sheared off a pole. We arrived to find all three occupants of the vehicle up and walking around. There were three people in the car, but none of them admitted to being the driver.

According to them, they were all passengers!

None of them knew what happened to the driver, or even the name of the driver. One of the "passengers" had just been released from jail, and they were out celebrating. Celebrating a little too much. We never learned who the driver was. It was on that call that I began adopting the phrase, "whatever," to use when I was frustrated or totally confused. "Whatever." It's proven to be a great stress reliever for me many times.

Ephrata has an annual, "Firecracker Run," which is a 5-mile run that winds through the town on the 4th of July. It begins at 8:30 a.m. Normally, over 400 runners participate in this event. One 4th of July the temperature was in the 90s at 8:30; the humidity was extremely high, and of course, to round out the three Hs, it was hazy.

Before the race began, the volunteers talked all about "us." How hot we were in our uniforms, how hot we'd be just sitting in, or near, our rigs, watching the runners in their lightly clad outfits run by, with the fire company positioned to spray water on them to cool them, pretty much about just how miserable we'd be.

It didn't take long for those thoughts to abandon our minds. Gene and I were stationed at an intersection about halfway through the course. No sooner had the runners started passing us, then someone yelled, "A runner is down, come and help him!" We grabbed our bags and ran up the street. We couldn't find any runner down. We were told that he had gotten up, and returned to the race.

We treated and transported so many sick people that day. It was decided earlier, before the race, each downed runner would be a load and go. We would load, treat, stabilize the patient, and go to the hospital as quickly as possibly, dropping them off, so we could return for another patient.

That 4th of July event was grueling for everyone involved. Many people were taken to the hospital for heat exhaustion or heat stroke, and several with heat stroke induced seizures. We dropped off a patient, returned to the field, stepped out of the rig, and heard people yelling, "Over here, over here, help me, help him!"

We were inundated with collapsed runners.

We called for additional ambulances to assist us. We prioritized. The runners were spread out along the route, all over the field, in cars, everywhere. As you went to help someone, you'd pass another runner vomiting, while his friend begged for you to stop and help. I have never seen so many people vomit in such a short period of time.

After the race was over, and all of the patients recuperated, the discussion began, "Should the race have been postponed or cancelled? Didn't the organizers realize that it was a dangerous situation, with the heat and humidity so high the few days before the race, and no signs of any relief in sight?"

Then the flip side, "These runners knew the risks of running in this weather; they made the decision to run, no one forced them into running." I just hope that we never have another day like that one. The organization that sponsors the run gives each ambulance volunteer a tee shirt. I have a nice collection of tee shirts from these runs. That year we certainly earned our free shirt.

Soon after the race, our tones went for an "emotional problem." We found a British lady, who appeared dressed for a White House reception, standing at the top of the steps, with luggage by her side. She told us she needed to go to the hospital, because she'd been having thoughts of killing herself.

After dropping her off at the hospital, we all questioned our own sanity, "Why had we agreed to run all day?" But now we had a break, and we could get something to eat. That didn't happen.

We were sent to the opposite end of town for a young guy who had been "horsing around" with a young girl. She had been riding on the back of his trunk as he drove through a trailer park. A friend dared him to "gun it." He did, and she flew off of the trunk and landed on the road, suffering massive head injuries. The driver was so upset that he couldn't even look at her head. We took her to LGH, and returned to our station just as our shift ended. We asked each other, "Did we eat today?" None of us remembered. It didn't matter.

Another, hot, hazy, and humid day. A call for a baby girl, in a locked vehicle, with the windows rolled up. Neighbors noticed the baby in the car, but they didn't know if the baby was dead or alive. They didn't know where her parents were.

These are the calls that truly test your ability to remain calm under pressure. You start thinking, while driving to the scene, "What if the baby is not conscious? What if the baby is dead? What if the baby is in cardiac arrest?" You can't seem to get there fast enough. We finally arrived, to find the mother had been located, unlocked the car, and removed the now crying infant. She said that she had just run inside an apartment to drop something off, and she had left the baby, sleeping in the car. Okay, now my heart was beating normally again, so I could prepare for our next call. But I wanted to scream at the mother for leaving her baby, unattended, in a hot car.

Several weeks later, I went on a call that resulted in my attending counseling. It was a beautiful spring day. It was early evening, and my tones opened for a vehicle accident involving a motorcycle. A father and his 8-year-old daughter were on a motorcycle. The daughter was wearing a helmet, but it was an adult size helmet, on a small child's head.

The father lost control, causing the girl to be thrown off of the cycle and go flying through the air. She flew over the top of a van that was following them. Her helmet came off, and she landed on the road. Her father had tried laying the bike, to stop it, but ending up crushed against a stone wall at the entrance to a farm.

Witnesses were extremely distraught by what they had seen. We arrived to find organized chaos. I was first directed to the little girl, who looked like a rag doll, lying in the middle of the road, unresponsive, with many broken bones, and in a huge pool of her own blood. I was told a helicopter had been called to transport her.

I had finished packaging her for the helicopter, when someone yelled that they needed an interpreter. I asked, "For what language?" Sign language. I know sign language. So I turned over the girl's care to another EMT, and went to the person needing assistance by sign language. After that was resolved, I was directed to the young girl's father. We were to transport him, in our rig, to a trauma center.

I was with our third ambulance, so I was in jeans, brand new jeans. Jeans that I loved. I hate shopping for jeans. I get so frustrated. Every time I go shopping for jeans, I think to myself, "They can put men on the moon, but they can't make jeans that fit all figures?" I finally had found a pair that I liked, and later realized that I should have bought more than one pair.

The father bled all over my jeans. I was filled with anger towards him. Anger for hurting his daughter, and anger for getting blood all over my new jeans. But I remained calm and professional.

I don't think there was an area on his body that didn't have major injuries. I've tried not to get too technical in my writing, but this man had so many injuries, that I just have to share some of them. He suffered from right upper, middle and lower lobe pulmonary contusions; fracture of the trochlear groove in his right knee; fracture of the right tibia plateau medially, which was open; lateral malleolus fractures of his right ankle with displacement; subtalar complete dislocation of the left foot; oblique fracture of the right distal fibula with widened ankle mortis, also displaced; fracture of the right medial aspect of medial femoral condyle, which was open; anterior dislocation of the right shoulder; extensive lacerations to his entire body; contusion to cecum and along the greater curvature of stomach with hematoma; avulsion laceration of the rectus abdominis muscle from pubis; traumatic disruption of right lateral abdominal wall: scrotal lacerations with exposed right testicle; extensive lacerations with a degloving injury to his right knee; laceration on left proximal thigh with contusion; and extensive lacerations on his left knee.

As we say, he was "FUBAR!" He was discharged to his home approximately 20 days later. I heard rumors that he was seen with his daughter, several months later at a local restaurant, both of them in wheelchairs.

I came home and tried my hardest to get the blood out of my jeans. Usually peroxide works well to remove schmutz and blood, but this time it didn't. I finally threw them out, along with a lot of anger.

The crash happened on a Thursday. I went down to the station the following day and another EMT, who had also been on the call, was there. She asked me if the call had affected me. I said, "Yes, I am so angry, but fortunately I have today off, so I didn't have to put on my forced, happy face."

She told me she had called off of work; she hadn't slept the night before; and was continuing to call Hershey Medical Center to check on the condition of the girl. I told her I was there for her if she wanted to talk more. What can you say? It was a difficult call. I'm not a counselor. I didn't know what to say.

Then sadness took anger's place. I started to think of all of the people who suffer because of other people's actions. I felt so badly for her and myself. Why do we subject ourselves to this?

Sunday evening I received a phone call from one of our executive board members, "Some of the local fire company's guys are having nightmares, trouble eating, sleeping, and they are putting together a debriefing (counseling session). It will be on Monday evening, at the fire station, do you want to attend?" I immediately answered, "Yes."

I went somewhat hesitantly, not knowing what to expect from a debriefing. Everyone gathered in one room, and you sat in a big circle. The counselors introduced themselves and told us, "If you get up to go to the bathroom or have a smoke, one of us will be going with you. It's our way of making certain you are okay." I liked that idea.

Then they made certain that everyone in the room was actually on scene, no outsiders. Okay, we understood the rules, now what? They randomly picked one person to start with, and we went around the circle, saying who we were, if you wanted to, and what our role was on the call. Then we went around the circle again, this time saying anything we wanted to say. I said how angry I was at the father. I listened to the others. I sat on the edge of my seat waiting to hear other people's feelings.

At one point I wanted to step outside and smoke a cigarette, but I also didn't want to miss anything. The counselors explained the stages of post-traumatic stress syndrome. They gave us brochures with symptoms to watch for, what is normal, and what isn't normal.

One firefighter said he didn't think he needed the counseling session, but since all of the other guys were going, he thought he'd go. Then he realized it had helped him. At the end you went around the circle again, and could give any final comments. I said that I was surprised to hear the younger firefighters saying they really didn't do anything except crowd control, or act as fire police and closing the intersections. I told them they had helped more than they realized. If they hadn't been there to set up the landing zone and secure the scene so we could work without distraction, our jobs would have been harder than they already were. Every person on scene that day played a crucial part in the outcome of the patients. Don't ever underestimate your worth.

It was a rainy, dark evening. My pager opened up for a "person struck." A 76-year-old lady had just visited the bank across the street from her home, along busy Route 272. She commented to the teller, "I'll be lucky to make it back home alive with the rain and the traffic." She wasn't lucky.

She must have thought it was clear to cross, and stepped

directly in front of a van, driven by a father taking his daughter to a Chinese restaurant. She was killed instantly.

I stared at this petite woman, lying directly on the centerline of the highway. I didn't stare too long before we were told the driver was having trouble breathing. He and his daughter had been taken inside the bank to wait for a ride. We went inside and gave oxygen to the driver. Their ride arrived and we felt they were okay to leave.

I read in her obituary that the dead lady was a cafeteria work- er at a local elementary school, a wife, and she enjoyed crossword puzzles, reading and gardening. Life comes at you fast.

Earthly again, in a sad way. It was a hot, summer Tuesday. We were dispatched for a barn fire. The family was eating dinner, when their 13-year-old son heard the cattle squealing. The family rushed out of the house, to find cows trying to break out of a barn. Within two minutes, the barn was engulfed in flames. Of the 42 head of cattle, more than 20 perished. The cattle that weren't killed escaped into 45 acres of cornfield surrounding the barn.

A neighboring farmer had come over to help, and was rammed and run over by one of the burned and half-blinded dairy cows. All we heard was shouting, "Help! Help!"

Through the corn, we couldn't see anyone; we could only hear the cries for help. We trenched through the corn until we found the patient. We stabilized him; and then carried our litter and equipment through the corn, to the man. We were covered in mud, dirt, and corn shalks, but you don't think about those things when you have an injured person lying in front of you. The neighbor had suffered broken ribs when the cow stepped on him.

My crew remained on scene the entire time. After the fire was extinguished, they used a front-end loader to overturn the charred and burned remains, to make sure there weren't any hid- den hot spots of fire. As they turned over the remains, dead cows dropped from the loader to the ground. It was sad. The family was also sad, but grateful that no human lives were lost. Broken ribs hurt, but they will heal.

Patience. A powerful word, and while it is difficult to always practice, it is definitely needed on so many calls.

Our patience was tested on an early morning call for difficulty breathing, at a mobile home park. The dispatcher advised us that the call came in from police on scene for a possible burglary attempt, and the resident was having trouble breathing. We arrived at the address to find a trailer with no lights on. I confirmed the address with the dispatcher, and told him that no police were there, and it was totally dark. He contacted the police, who said to tell us that it was probably okay for us to enter the home, and the patient was mentally challenged.

It was "Probably okay to enter?" Remove the word "probably" and I would have been more comfortable. But I had Gene and Keith with me, so I felt a tad safe. We knocked on the door. An outside light came on. We entered the trailer and found a large man lying on the floor in the living room.

He told us he was having trouble breathing. His vitals were immediately obtained. His pulse ox level was low, so we put oxygen on him. We told him we needed to take him to the hospital. He asked for his pants, shoes and cologne from his bedroom. He asked us to put cat food and water in the cat dishes. He told us his dirty plate and glass needed placed in the sink, so the cats couldn't get near them. His container of iced tea needed to go back in the refrigerator. He needed his comb to fix his hair. Then he asked us to turn on a specific channel on his television, so it would be ready for him to watch when he returned from the hospital.

My patience was running out.

As I walked towards his bedroom to get his requested items, I noticed a large oxygen tank. I questioned him about it. He answered, "Oh, it's not mine, a friend gave it to me, so once in a while I use it." I calmly said, "Friends don't let friends not breath." It took a while for my crew to find any humor in my saying.

Angie volunteers Tuesday evenings. She was pregnant with twin boys when a vehicle accident with entrapment was dispatched. The initial call reported 5 young people trapped in the car. Multiple ambulances, medic units and rescues were dispatched. We pulled up to the scene and saw a car, literally wrapped around a pole, up an embankment. We heard so many voices screaming, "Get me out!" "Help me!" "I'm dying."

Angie obviously could not be climbing up the embankment, so she became the gopher. Go get more backboards, and I'll be right down for them. Go get more heavy blankets, and someone will be down for them. This continued until all the patients were extricated. During the extrication process, EMS command asked for a helicopter, then a second one, and then a third one.

The horrific images etched in my mind, from the time of our arrival, until the last patient was loaded, are sights I will never forget. The rescue crews did an excellent job. Everyone worked together. The car was wrapped so tightly around the pole, we couldn't tell how many patients were in the car. They just kept extricating one after another.

The screaming continued. It was dark, but rescue trucks had set up lighting. Pete had his magna flashlight on his forehead. As often as we tease Pete about carrying everything under the sun when he runs ambulance, that night we were indebted to him for carrying his flashlight.

Forever imbedded in my mind is hearing the voice of the last male to be extricated. He was conscious enough to realize that his foot was no longer attached to his leg. He kept screaming, "Put my foot back before you move me any farther."

I knew this couldn't be done, but what do you say?

The patients were extricated, and on their way to hospitals. My driver, Ken, and I were left without a patient. We looked at the car in awe, amazed that no one was dead upon our arrival. We returned to station, our clothes muddy and saturated with blood.

But the sounds of the screaming outweighed the concern for my clothing. We were left not knowing the outcome of the kids.

That is one of the hardest parts of running with ambulance. You treat the patient, and transport to a hospital facility. Unless you personally follow up on your patient, you never know the outcome of your treatment. You're left wondering, and knowing that you provided the best care possible.

We later learned PP&L (our supplier of electricity) had been advised that there was a safety hazard at this scene. Live wires were on the ground and car. Their response when asked for an ETA (estimated time of arrival) was, "As fast as the truck can go, legally." As we looked at pictures taken of the car, we noticed the wires. We hadn't noticed them when we were at the scene. We counted our blessings that none of us touched one of the live wires.

One cold Saturday in January, I was getting ready to go to a holiday party. I was anxious to go. I had gone down to station for a second ambulance call, and had just returned home to continue getting ready for the party. Our tones went again, for another second due ambulance. This call was for a building fire. "Okay," I thought, "I might as well go back down and go to the building fire. They generally aren't much, and we usually aren't on scene very long." My partner and I had both caught the address of Church Avenue, but neither of us had caught the number. I was on the radio, contacting a dispatcher to get the exact address, as we turned onto Church Avenue.

Immediately we knew where it was by the huge billows of smoke coming from the apartment building on the next corner. I listened as the dispatcher gave us the address, then thought, "I don't think I'll be making the holiday party." We ended up being on scene from 4:00 p.m. until shortly after midnight.

Fire had ravaged through the Church Street Apartments, H&R Block and Dove Christian Fellowship buildings, started by a candle left unattended. We were starting to get our bags out of the rig, when we heard, "Get the medics to the front of the street, firefighter down!"

Your heart starts racing. You have no idea what is wrong. Did he fall through a floor; did a roof collapse on him? We grabbed as much equipment as we could, and made our way through the maze of firetrucks arriving, and the thick smoke. We reached the firefighter, and were relieved to see him sitting on a step of a neighboring porch. We transported him to the hospital, for smoke inhalation, and returned to the fire. Thankfully, all of the residents got out safely.

H&R Block's busiest tax season had just started. A call like this brings out the best in our community. A neighboring church opened its doors for use of its bathroom facilities, despite not having any electricity. They lit candles and the guys brought flashlights.

Area food establishments donated food and drinks for the over 100 volunteers on scene. Everyone pulled together with donations of support for the displaced residents of the apartments. The Ladies Auxiliary of the Ephrata Pioneer Fire Company helped serve the refreshments. I have the utmost pride in being a member of this community, and have always respected the leadership and abilities of our residents. Events like this engrave it deeper in my soul.

Events like this also engrave the power of candles. I love candles. In the dead of winter, the smell of a Yankee candle is one of my comfort smells. But I've come to respect the damage that can be done by leaving a candle unattended. I've come to respect fire. While you can't fear fire, you do need to respect it.

Ray and Doris Good owned the properties. They generously offered to prepare the tax returns for any volunteer who was on scene that evening. They have relocated their business to a beautiful building on Main Street. They allow our ambulance organization to use their parking lot as our command center, during the week of the fair. They even let us use their bathrooms! They are "good people."

Super Bowl Sunday. Not so super for some. Around 10:00 p.m. a male driver lost control of his vehicle, struck another vehicle, and continued, out of control. His car went up an embankment, and finally stopped, inside a church barn used for horse and buggies. Fortunately the barn was unoccupied, but the driver and his passenger were not so fortunate.

The driver was unconscious. We took him to the Lancaster General trauma center. On the way to the hospital, my partner began barking to me, "Janice, check for gag reflex; Janice, control that eye socket bleeding; Janice, start cutting his clothes off; Janice, start suctioning!"

I wanted to scream, "I am only one person and I can only do so much at one time!" But I kept my mouth shut and did the best I could do.

The driver suffered a TB/CHI; shear type brain injury; parenchymal hemorrhage; fluid within his left maxillary sinus; left nasal bone fracture; two fractured ribs; a small right pneumothorax with left pleural effusion; multiple lacerations including 1.5 cm lacerations on his right eye, medial aspect, left eyelid and forehead; and multiple contusions.

Another FUBAR. He was discharged to his home, fifteen days later. His passenger's injuries were not as serious.

The most trying calls are for patients who you know personally. One Sunday afternoon we were dispatched for an unconscious person, AED. I was busy collecting my thoughts, and organizing our plan, so I hadn't noticed what house we had arrived at. We went inside and saw a man, lying on the floor, with CPR being done by a police officer. I took over CPR.

Suddenly, as I was doing CPR, I noticed the man's crippled hands. I asked, "Is this Allen?" Someone answered, "Yes, do you know him?"

"Yes," I answered. I had known Allen for many years.

He was crippled from arthritis, but that didn't slow him down. He had the will and determination that most people only dream of. Many times I would pass his house and see him mowing his lawn, tending to the yard, and doing chores that we take for granted. But for Allen, they had to be difficult and painful.

Someone offered to take over CPR for me, but I insisted on continuing. I begged Allen not to give up, to hang in there, he'd been so strong all of his life; don't give up now. I continued CPR as we took him on the litter, through the yard and to the hospital.

I couldn't separate where my patient ended and where I began. I felt like I was a part of Allen. I couldn't let go. But I eventually had to let go.

He was pronounced dead at the hospital. I had to let go. Allen was no longer my patient, he was no longer a part of me. But a piece of me died that day, along with him. When I saw his family, it took every ounce of strength to not break down. I knew we had done everything humanly possible to save Allen. I had no doubts. But that doesn't make it any easier. When I see his family, I still go back in my mind to that cold winter day, working on him as we were going through the yard, begging him not to die.

Then there is the flip side. Another unconscious person, this time at Wal-Mart. It was the perfect scenario. The cardiac arrest was witnessed, an employee immediately dialed 911, and CPR was begun as soon as they realized he didn't have a pulse and wasn't breathing. A police officer arrived within three minutes, with his AED, and several shocks were delivered, restoring a normal heart rhythm.

For every minute that elapses after sudden cardiac arrest, the chances of survival diminish by seven to ten percent. If the victim can be shocked with an AED immediately, the chances for survival are close to 90 percent. The gentleman was transported to ECH and made a full recovery. The Wal-Mart employees involved, as well as the police officer, were honored for their fast thinking, which helped save a person's life.

Gene and I were now running Wednesday nights. Gene volunteers over 1,000 hours every year. Gene devotes three nights a week to doing van runs. We ran a lot of interesting calls together. One afternoon we took an elderly woman to Lancaster General Hospital, in one of our transport vans, so she could visit her dying son. We spent about three hours doing nothing, just hanging around outside, to give her time alone with her son.

Gene has a heart of gold, but he gets a little agitated with the middle of the night calls when he hears a patient say, "Well, let's see, my foot has been bothering me for about three weeks now, so I think it's time to get it checked out." I can read Gene's mind, knowing he will later mutter to me, "Okay, your frickin foot has been hurting for three weeks, and you decide at 3 in the morning to call for an ambulance!" But he never displays that in front of a patient.

As frustrating as it is, you learn to accept the "no patient found" calls. It was the middle of the night, and we were dispatched for a female, who had dialed 911, and told them she was going to kill herself. Other than that, all she said was that she's in a motel, before she hung up the phone. Along with the police department, we searched and searched, shining flashlights in every motel window. We found nothing. After nearly four hours of searching, we returned to station, where I completed a "no patient found" form.

Then a call for a "sick person." All we were told was that there was a female uptown, where kids hang out, and she needed an ambulance. We pulled up to a group of kids. "Did anyone call for an ambulance?" I asked the crowd.

"Oh, yeah," someone commented. "Some girl did, she's really sick."

"Where is this girl now?" I asked. No one seemed to know. None of her "friends" wanted to help us try to find her. We walked through the alleys, and around the block, trying to find her. We did this for over an hour, and again returned to station to complete the "no patient found" report.

A person, who routinely calls for an ambulance, is known to us as a "frequent flier." Frequent flier, Daniel, was playing in traffic, trying to get struck and killed. I had been to Daniel's residence numerous times, so he knew me on a first name basis. I asked him to get out of the road and come inside with me. He agreed, but only if he could play a song for me on his guitar, before we took him to the hospital. As my heart filled with sadness, I listened to him play his song, and then we took him to the hospital.

We see so much sadness, and there's often not a lot you can do about it. It's even sadder when your patients are children.

A grandmother was raising her granddaughter in a mobile home. The 8-year-old girl had a fever of 105 degrees for several days. The grandmother wanted to be able to go get more baby aspirin, but money was tight, so she waited it out, hoping the fever would break.

When the fever wouldn't break, the two of them headed towards Wal-Mart. While walking to the Wal-Mart, the girl went into seizures from her fever. We were dispatched for a child in seizures. It was a hot and humid day. We treated and transported the child to the hospital.

I kept thinking, "How do people get in these situations? Why isn't there more help for these children?" I've learned there is help available, but someone has to know how to find the help. Help just doesn't usually knock on your door. People in need of help have to find it, and for many, that's too difficult a chore. My only consolation is hoping that these children don't know that life isn't like that for every child.

Then there are the children who are well taken care of, but still have emergencies. We were dispatched for an eight-month-old infant, a possible poisoning. We were told that the infant had chewed on a tube of diaper rash ointment, and swallowed a large amount of it.

We found a frantic mother, holding her daughter, who was smiling through a mouth that was white, from eating the ointment. The baby appeared content, and was obviously not in any medical distress. We assessed her airway and everything was normal.

The mother was hysterical. It was like having two patients. She was ridden with guilt for letting the ointment in the play-pen with her daughter. We continued to reassure her that her daughter hadn't suffered any medical problems. She insisted that we take her baby to the hospital for evaluation. It goes from one extreme to the other.

Any call involving children is a trying call. Some are more trying than others are. We were dispatched for an emergency transfer from ECH to Hershey Medical Center. Our patient was ten-year-old Taylor, who was in the final stages of terminal cancer. We gave him a teddy bear, which he named "Cocoa." During the drive to Hershey, he told us story after story. He told us that he had met Jeff Gordon. That was his only wish, and it was granted by the Make A Wish Foundation. While I'm not a Jeff Gordon fan, that night I was a big fan of Jeff Gordon. That was the only thing that this little, intelligent boy wanted to do before he died. Meet Jeff Gordon.

Silently I said a thank you prayer to the Make A Wish Foundation. Silently I said a thank you prayer to Jeff Gordon, but I also told him that his kind deed wouldn't convert me into becoming one of his fans. The trip to Hershey took about thirty five minutes. But it seemed like forever. I kept listening to his stories. I kept wondering, "How many famous people would go the extra mile to grant a dying child's wish to meet them?"

Taylor remained stable and alert the entire trip, as we continued to assess his medical condition. So often life seems unfair. This cute little boy would soon be dead. On the way back, my driver asked me why I was so quiet. I told him that I was tired. I was tired, but more so, I was emotionally drained. I kept asking myself, "why?" and I know there is no answer to "why?"

Every time I watch a Nascar race, I think that Taylor is look-ing down and rooting for Jeff. Thanks, Jeff.

We stock teddy bears in all of our ambulances, and we give them to our pediatric patients. It helps comfort them. I've come up with a game for them. I give them five minutes to think of a name for their teddy bear, and then I'm going to ask them the name. This gives them something to do, other than dwelling on the reason they are in an ambulance.

I'm amazed at how many of the names begin with the let-ter "C." Some of the names included, "Cozy, Cutie, Cinnamon, Barbie, Duke, and Caramel." The most appropriate one was the name given to his bear by a seven-year-old involved in a motor vehicle accident. He named his teddy bear, "Crash."

It continues to amaze me at the difference in maturity of children the same age. Some thirteen-year-olds would be given a teddy bear, and they would love it. Other thirteen-year-olds, I wouldn't dream of asking if they wanted a teddy bear. One call on October 30th was for a thirteen-year-old boy who had funky, dyed orange, spiked hair. Tons of spiked silver jewelry, silver chains hanging all over him, and his body was pierced in places I'd never consider having pierced. My ears are pierced and that's enough for me. He had overdosed, and was semi-conscious upon our arrival. We treated and transported him. By the time we unloaded him, it was Octo-ber 31. I thought to myself, "How fitting, starting out Hal-loween with a person in costume," realizing, unfortunately, that was his normal attire.

I am extremely squeamish about two things in life. They are my eyes and mice. Both bother me tremendously. I've al-ways thought that if we ever have a call for an impaled object in someone's eye, I would have to call for additional crew, because I wouldn't be able to handle it. I know that and accept it.

Just as I know that if I saw a mouse, I would be on top of the closest piece of furniture I could climb on. I can handle amputations, dead people, and schmutz. But when it comes to eyes and mice, that's a whole different ballgame for me.

We were dispatched to Wal-Mart for an injured person. We were told that a male was unloading boxes of light bulbs, and one had fallen, broken open, and fragments of light bulbs were in his eyes. Okay, now what? Can I handle this call? I decided to give it a try.

I didn't mention my "eye fetish" to my driver. We arrived at Wal-Mart and my partner immediately stabilized our patient, while I found out what type of light bulbs they were. Fluorescent bulbs or regular bulbs, they needed to know that before we got to the hospital. By the time I found out this information, my partner had the patient packaged and ready to go. Whew. I made it through my "eye" call, and I hoped it was my last one.

I could probably write an entire chapter on obese patients, even morbidly obese. I read articles that vary so much as to why people become obese. Their eating habits? Their genetics? I don't know what I believe. I do know there are way too many obese people in our county.

We have calls for people, of all ages, that are so big, they rarely attempt to walk. Then when they try to walk, they end up falling and injuring themselves.

On obese patients, we can't use our regular blood pressure cuff, because it's not large enough. I ran a call with a trainee, and when we got there, we found an obese patient. How do you ask the trainee, in front of the patient, to go to the rig and get the "obese cuff?" It just isn't right.

While I will admit that I sometimes think badly towards these people for allowing themselves to become so obese, I still respect them. They are human beings. It's not in my place to judge them. It's my place to serve them.

I told my trainee, "Go out and get the other cuff." She gave me this look that I immediately recognized. She didn't know what I meant. Okay, let's try another tactic. I calmly asked her again to go bring in another cuff, as I described in detail, where the other cuffs are located, knowing in my mind that one is for pediatrics, and the other one is for obese people. She left the room and returned with both of them. I took both of them, put the pediatric one in my pocket, handed her the obese one, and asked her to get his blood pressure.

Todd, who was 18 years old, had been in his bed for over four months. Todd was huge. I couldn't even begin to guess his weight.

His feet were green. There were bugs all over him. It was disgusting! He was having trouble breathing. Imagine that!

I knew our litter's weight capacity is 500 pounds. His family told us that he might weigh over 500 pounds, they really didn't know, since he never got out of his bed. I also knew that our obese cuff wasn't large enough. He was a load and go, except for our waiting for lifting assistance to carry him down the steps and place him on our litter.

The firemen that responded to assist us had several EMTs with them. I asked the most experienced one about the weight capacity of our litter, and questioned him about Todd's weight. His only response was, "I guess you'll find out, good luck." Our litter managed to stand the test of his weight.

It's not only men who are overweight. We had a call for a woman who was gardening, fell, and had possibly broken her ankle. We found her in her backyard. She was very overweight, and she had broken both of her ankles. We stabilized both ankles and lifted her onto our litter. Is it any wonder that so many people in the pre-hospital emergency care suffer from back injuries? I made a vow to myself that this will never happen to me. If there is lifting that needs done, and is beyond my abilities, I'll be the first to call for a fire company to assist with lifting. If it's a life and death situation and we can't afford those extra minutes, yes, I'll lift beyond my means. But I'm not going to ruin my back if the call can wait a few minutes for additional help.

One of my favorite medics, Gwen, and I were on a vehicle accident with entrapment on the infamous Route 222. We were both inside the vehicle, one of us doing c-spine stabilization, while the other held a tarp to cover the driver's face during the removal of the windshield. We were talking with him when he interrupted us, and asked, "Where are my little girls, are they okay?" Gwen and I looked at each other and our hearts skipped several beats. "His little girls?" We were told he was our only patient.

"Okay, sir, tell us about your little girls," I asked, appearing to be calm. He told us they had been in the car with him, and he believed they were uninjured, and had been taken somewhere else until he was removed. I told Gwen I could manage with the tarp draping on us; she could go check on the little girls. It turned out the driver was right. The two little girls were uninjured, and were sitting inside a police car during the extrication of their father.

We later said we both experienced the same thoughts, "What if they had been ejected from the car and no one knew they were there? What if they were underneath the car?" But it ended well, once our hearts returned to their normal beat.

One ambulance call at Wal-Mart turned out to be more than I ever bargained for when I became an EMT. We were dispatched to Wal-Mart for an unconscious person. We walked in and saw a man lying on the floor in the check-out section. CPR was in progress. I took over CPR and continued it until our arrival at ECH. I didn't know whom I was doing CPR on. After the doctor pronounced the time of death, we went out to the snack area to get some much-needed cold beverages. We noticed distraught people mingling in the waiting area.

Then I recognized some of them. The man I had done CPR on was a friend of mine from years ago. Through family circumstances, I had gotten to know him, and his family, very well. While I had lost touch with his family, I always thought very highly of them.

I was now another one of the distraught people.

The family recognized me; they had recognized me at Wal-Mart, unbeknownst to me. They told me they had taken their father to Wal-Mart to do a little shopping, after visiting his wife, who was in ECH following a recent stroke, and he just dropped over in the store. This happened on February 27th. I kept in touch with the family as they made funeral arrangements. Then on March 3rd his wife died.

The funeral home was contacted to see if they could quickly arrange a double service. They pulled it off. I attended the service. The double funeral service was held on March 4th. They had been married for many years, and now they were spending forever together.

In a strange sense, it was peaceful to see the two of them, side by side, before their burial. I initially had thoughts of overwhelming sadness that we were unable to save him, but as I stared at the two caskets, I thought that perhaps it was meant to end the way it did. I found comfort in that thought.

We were called to do an emergency transfer from ECH to LGH. It was for a female lady who couldn't have been sweeter if she tried. She was just delightful. Our trip to LGH was pleasant, as we listened to her sharing her life's stories. She was a lady of grace and dignity.

She mentioned that she had been suffering from an earache for about four weeks. They had run tests, and felt she needed to be taken to LGH. We listened. Sometimes that's all you do. Listen.

We unloaded her at LGH, and on our return trip home, I looked through her paperwork. I came to the page that listed the specific reason for the emergency transfer. My body felt like someone had just twisted it like a soft pretzel.

She was diagnosed with a large, inoperable, cancerous tumor in her brain. She had been advised of the findings. I thought about our conversations, and the lightheartedness of them. My only rationalization was that it hadn't struck her yet. She was soon going to die. She died a few days later. Then again, perhaps she did realize her fate, and just accepted the fact that she had lived a full life, and now it was time for her to pass from this world to the eternal world.

Cancer is a word you never get used to hearing or saying. It's like a bad four-letter word, but with six letters. People try not to say it. We took a 50-year-old man to the hospital, in the final stage of his cancer. He had cancer of the mouth, and had seventy-five percent of his mouth removed. He was severely dehydrated. I thought to myself, "With seventy-five percent of your mouth gone, it would be difficult to eat or drink much." I also thought that I should quit smoking. As we were loading him onto our litter he asked us to stop for a minute, so he could look at the fourteen-point buck that was proudly mounted on the wall of his tiny apartment. It was as if he was saying goodbye to the deer. He died several days later.

We took him to the hospital, and didn't make it back to our station before our tones went for an "unconscious person, AED." We pulled up outside of the apartment, and were directed into the apartment by a female using hand signals. I wondered why this female wasn't talking to us. I assumed it was because she's very upset. We climbed up the steps to the apartment, where a male was lying in the middle of the living room, in cardiac arrest. As we were getting our equipment out, the young female said, "He speaks no English."

I thought, "Okay, what does it matter that he speaks no English? He's as close to dead as he can be, it doesn't matter!" But I remained professional, and thanked her for informing us of that fact. We treated and transported him, and he was still alive when we left the hospital, but certainly not speaking any English.

I wish there were a law that required people who live in the United States to learn English, within a certain amount of time, like one year. These people had lived here for seven years, and none of them spoke English. In my opinion, that is wrong. How are we to help people when they don't speak English? That call ended well, but I still feel that if you move to our country, you learn our language.

Billy and his father had gone four wheeling in a large, open area of ground, which was being leveled off for the construction of a building. Billy had gone to the top of one hill, thinking it continued, only to learn it dropped off sharply. He was thrown off of his four wheeler and suffered severe, traumatic injuries on his landing. Kevin, Keith and I responded.

The land was rocky and the going was rough to get our litter to him. We packaged him, put him on our litter, and headed towards the rig. He was screaming in pain. He had too many broken bones to count; a flail chest on the left; fractured and displaced ribs; fractured right scapula; fractured right distal clavicle, and numerous abrasions, contusions and large areas of avulsion on his body.

We knew the bumps in the ground weren't adding to his level of pain tolerance. Kevin looked at Keith and said, "How about we totally lower the litter and we just carry it to the rig?"

I'm carrying our bags, so I couldn't be of anymore help, but I thought, "Okay, I know Keith is very strong, and I'm certain Keith can carry the litter, with our patient on it, to our rig, but can Kevin?"

They didn't hesitate; they lowered the litter and carried it to our rig. That was one of the few times that I have been speechless. I was amazed at their abilities. I've always heard that you never know what strength you have, until you need it. That goes for physical, as well as emotional strength, and they proved that to be true.

Then you witness the strength of "beer muscles." Jared was at a party. He had driven his motorcycle to the party, and realized he was having too much to drink, so he decided to take his motorcycle home, and return to the party in his car.

Jared didn't make it out of the development before he crashed, and ended up underneath a parked truck. We pulled up, and he stood there, telling us he's not in any pain. One look at him told us he had to be in pain. We looked at his one leg, with multiple, open, displaced, fractured bones. There was blood everywhere. He was standing on that leg like nothing was wrong with it. As my crew was getting the litter, I asked him if his leg hurt. He calmly replied, "Nope, it's all good." I thought, "Nope, it's not all good."

Sometimes, you are just sick and tired of dealing with sick people. I would never show those feelings in front of a patient, but I do experience them. One day we had call after call for a "sick person." On the way to the last call on my shift, I said to my partner, "I'm sick of sick people!" But we responded to the call and put on our professional faces and attitudes.

This call was for a "sick female." Ruth had been vomiting for several days, and her sister felt she needed to go to the hospital. Ruth was crying hysterically. She finally told me that both of her parents had been taken to the hospital, years ago, and years apart, but both had died in the hospital. Ruth was scared to death that she was going to die in the hospital.

There was nothing I could say or do to make her stop crying. I gave her professional care and we transported her to our local hospital. I climbed back in the rig and said to my partner, "No more sick people for me today!" As sorry as I felt for Ruth and her feelings, I had my own feelings to deal with.

I was sick of the screaming; the hysteria; the sick people. But I had become addicted to it. The life you saved gave you the highest of highs. The ones you lost sent you to the lowest of low places. But I kept going back to the roller coaster ride, hoping for more of the highs.

I once read a piece on the creation of an EMT.

The Lord was busy working when an angel appeared and questioned why all the fiddling on this one person. The Lord asked if she's seen the specs on this order.

"He has to be able to lift three times his own weight; crawl into wrecked cars, with barely enough room to move. He has to console a grieving mother, as he is doing CPR on her baby; be in top mental condition at all times; run on no sleep, half eaten meals, and have six pairs of hands. He needs three pairs of eyes. One pair that sees open sores and blood, and asks if the patient may be HIV positive; one pair on the side of his head for his partner's safety; and another pair in front that can look reassuringly at a bleeding victim and say, "You'll be all right, sir.""

The angel circled the model very slowly then asked, "What is this, and can it think?" The Lord replied, "It's an EMT, and you bet it can think! It can tell you the symptoms of 300 plus illnesses, recite drug calculations in its sleep; intubate, defibrillate, medicate and continue CPR nonstop over terrain that any doctor would fear . . . and still keep its sense of humor.

"He can deal with a mass casualty incident; talk a frightened elderly person into unlocking their door; comfort a victim's family; and offer a chance for a stranger to live a little longer. He can carry a 250-pound cardiac patient down four flights of steps, and still calls it 'volunteering.' He makes tough choices during tough conditions. My volunteer EMT realizes his only pay is pride and the fact that he helped make a difference."

The angel bent over and ran her finger across the cheek of the EMT. "There's a leak," she pronounced. "I told you that you were trying to put too much into this model."

"That's not a leak," said The Lord. "It's a tear for bottled-up emotions, for patients they tried in vain to save, for commitment to hope that they will make a difference in a person's chance to survive, for life."

"You're a genius., said the angel. The Lord looked somber, and said, "I didn't put the tear there."

Chapter 5

Unpredicted and Unexpected

Certain events are predictable, while routine events can become unpredictable.

I've learned to never predict, and never expect anything; that minimizes the surprises.

In the middle of a hot, steamy night, our tones opened for another sick person. We had the address and we knew the street. As we entered the block, we couldn't find the house number. We found the number before it, and the house number after it, but not the number we had been given. I contacted a dispatcher to confirm the numerical address.

We searched again, to no avail. We contacted our dispatcher, and asked if someone could step outside, or turn a light on, do anything, to help us locate the house. Then we noticed a woman, standing at a sliding glass door, calmly waving to us. Okay, that must be the house. We climbed up the hill to the back of the house, where the woman was standing inside the door. As she left us into the house, we apologized for the delay in responding, and explained our difficulty in finding the house.

She said, with pride in her voice, "Yes, our house is the most difficult house to find, because we don't have the number out, and our front door is actually on the other street, even the mailmen have trouble finding it!" We tactfully tried to explain this could be a real concern in a life-threatening situation. That had made no impact, she was too proud of the fact that their house was the hardest one to find in her town.

It was a Monday night in January. I had decided to run from the ambulance station, rather than from my home, as it was beginning to sleet. I pulled into the station shortly before 9:00 p.m. and I noticed the temperature displayed at the business next to our station. It read 8 degrees when I pulled in, and I happened to be looking at it when it dropped to 7 degrees. "This is going to be a long, cold night," I thought to myself. But it turned out to be a quiet night, without any calls. It's so unpredictable.

Then the predictable occurs. It was another day of sleet and bitterly cold weather. I slid down to our station for a second due call. Vance was already there, and he hopped in the driver's seat. I would trust him with my life, and we headed out to a motor vehicle accident, again on Route 222.

Vance asked me if I had heard it on the scanner. I said, "Not really, only bits and pieces." He said he believed it might be for a police officer struck. My heart sank.

We were responding to the accident, as the second ambulance needed at the crash. We pulled up to the scene and saw Kevin, who was with the first ambulance. He pointed to a male, lying face down on the roadway and said, "He's your patient."

The police car had stopped to investigate another accident, when the police car was rear-ended by another car. The occupant of that car went through the windshield, and ended up face first on the highway. Kevin was there for the initial accident.

The police officer told us that our patient had severe head injuries, especially to his eye sockets. Now remember, I'm squeamish about eyes. But I had a job to do and I did it. There was so much blood on the road from our patient's face.

I yelled to one of the officers, "Go into our rig and grab as many towels as you can carry, and bring them to me." In the meantime, I'm talking to our patient, who is screaming in pain. When the towels arrived, I lifted his head, while Vance continued c-spine stabilization, and I literally packed his face with all of the towels. We put a collar on him, rolled him over, placed him on a backboard, and loaded him onto our litter.

On the way to Lancaster General Hospital's trauma center, he kept begging me to take the towels off of his face. He wanted me to look at his face. He wanted me to tell him if he would have scars on his face. I told him that I couldn't remove the towels, and that if he didn't want scars, he better stop trying to remove my packaging of his face. He finally agreed and stopped begging, but his screams of pain continued.

We arrived at LGH and took him to the trauma room. Once again, an angel appeared before me. I was leaving the trauma room, and there was Jane, a friend of mine, who worked at LGH. She noticed my blood-soaked jeans. I hadn't. She told me that I needed to take them off immediately, because who knew what was in the blood that was all over my jeans and socks.

I said, "Fine, but I don't have other clothes along, and it's freezing outside." She got me a set of scrubs, a hospital "wash up" kit, and directed me to the bathroom. I washed up and changed into the scrubs. I couldn't fit the slipper socks on with my boots, so I returned them to her, and told her I'd have to live dangerously. She took my jeans and told me that the hospital would clean them and she'd see that I got them back. She did. There were still stains on the jeans. Jane said the hospital had washed them several times, but they couldn't remove all the bloodstains. It was the thought that counts. I ended up throwing the jeans out, but it wasn't the first or last pair I've ever thrown out.

I generally don't go back to check on the outcome of a patient. I just happened to be on a call for another patient that we transported to LGH a few days later, and I begged my partner to give me a few minutes to see if my patient from the accident was still there. He agreed. I had ten minutes.

I learned my patient was still there. I was given his room number, and I rushed to his room. Many of his family members were in the room. What should I say? "Hello, I am one of the medics who scooped you up off of Route 222. I am the person who ended up throwing away a pair of my favorite jeans because you saturated them with your blood?"

I introduced myself as a member of Ephrata Ambulance, and I said that I was on the call the day of his accident. The family asked me if I had taken him to the hospital. With some hesitancy, I answered, "Yes." They began hugging me and thanking me for saving his eyesight. They chattered, in Spanish, to the patient, and I guessed they were talking about me.

His eyes were covered with dressings, but his face lit up with a smile I'll never forget, and he said, "Thanks so much." His family explained that the surgeon told them, if there would have been any movement to his eye sockets, even as small as a quarter of an inch, he would have lost his eyesight.

I thought back to questioning myself if I was doing the right thing on scene, then I knew I had done the right thing. I told them I just wanted to stop and say hello, but I left the room with a feeling of satisfaction that I just can't describe. It somehow helps make up for all of the sad feelings.

Then it was back to another day of emotions. I was at home when a third due call came in, for an injured person. It was cold outside, and the weather was a mixture of sleet and rain. I threw clothes on, not realizing I had grabbed another favorite pair of jeans, again, and headed down to the station.

I'm not a shopper, as you know. I can't stand shopping for jeans, or any clothing for that matter. I wear what's comfortable and I pray that my "comfortable" clothing won't be destroyed on a call. I pulled into the station and saw our third rig being pulled out. That was a good sign. That meant someone else was there. I hopped in and saw Kevin. He asked me if I had heard the additional given by county to the police. I hadn't heard anything except "an injured person." Kevin told me a young man had fallen about 15 to 20 feet off of a ladder.

I mumbled to Kevin, "I thought this call was for an injured person. I thought we'd make a quick trip to ECH and go home."

Kevin replied, "Nope. Nope. Nope."

The man was seriously injured. We were directed to the rear of the house, but we were told we could also enter through the front of the house. None of this was making any sense to me. We entered through the front of the house, and were directed by a nice woman to the rear of the house. She showed us a door that led onto a roof. I looked out the door and saw a guy, lying on his back, and bleeding profusely. Kevin was right behind me. I asked the nice woman what the man's name was, and she answered, "David."

So we have David, lying on the roof, in a huge pool of blood, and at least one police officer on the roof with him. I was glad the police were there to help us. I went outside, knelt down on the icy roof and immediately began c-spine stabilization. I asked the routine questions, "Do you remember what happened? Do you know what day it is? Are you allergic to any medications? Do you have any past medical history?"

David was so nice. He told me that he was a firefighter from the opposite end of the county, and he was here cleaning out the gutters. He said that this probably was not the best day to be doing that work. He said he understood why I was asking all of the questions, and he understood why he would have to have a collar put on him and be rolled onto a long board. I thought to myself, "Wow, if only more of our patients would be so cooperative!"

The police officer helped us to roll David onto the long board. As we were securing the straps to carry him inside, and out to our ambulance, other medics arrived. Someone told them to wait inside, but I had no idea why. I knew we could have used more help. Why did they have to wait inside? I said to myself, my favorite word, "whatever." We packaged David and carried him inside the house.

Now there were lots of people to help us. We loaded him into our rig. He had suffered a broken back, at T12. He was very lucky that there was an overhanging roof to break his fall, or David might have been paralyzed, or dead.

David was a trauma alert, you don't ask questions with a trauma alert, there is too much work to do. Like keeping him alive, and being certain he does not end up paralyzed. When David was safe and sound in the trauma room, I asked why they wouldn't let the other medics come out on the roof.

Kevin replied, "Didn't you notice all of the soft spots on the roof?"

"No," I answered, "I was busy taking care of David." Kevin told me that anymore weight, or even one of us walking in the wrong spot, could have sent us all spiraling to the ground. Sometimes it's better not to know what others know at the time.

I will never forget the words said by Ricky, following a vehicle accident. We had treated him and were taking him to a local hospital. Ricky reeked of alcohol, and it appeared he was greatly under the influence of the same. I asked Ricky to sign the HIPAA form, explaining that this means we will not sell, or give out, any of his information. Ricky tried his hardest to sign on the line. I then handed him the brochure that details the HIPAA law. By now he had become agitated, and I expected Ricky to throw the brochure at me. To my surprise he calmly said, "Thanks, I'll take this with me to jail to read."

People are just so unpredictable. Life is so unpredictable.

We were dispatched for an unconscious 80-year-old male patient. We arrived to find an obese person lying in bed. Our plan was for one of us to crawl across the bed, to the other side, and help lift, as space was limited in his bedroom. I was selected to crawl to the other side. As I'm cautiously working myself across his bed, our patient suddenly became very alert, and blurted out, "Come on girl, get in bed with me!"

Many times the unpredictable events leave you at a loss for words.

Like the call for Charles, who was sick, but not too sick to walk to our rig. He was walking slowly through the living room when he announced that he needed to pee in his cup before he could walk any farther. Okay, where's your cup? We got him his cup; he drops his pants and stands in the middle of the room and pees in the cup. As he's finishing, he said, as we smelled his words, "Oops, now my bowels have decided to move, too."

Again, we give the, "Do we laugh or do we cry?" look, but we remained professional, cleaned him up and transported him to the hospital.

The more calls you run, the more seasoned you become. By that I mean you learn to expect the unexpected and unpredicted. But watching the trainees is interesting. We had a call for an accident at the Wal-Mart intersection, involving a horse and buggy. I dreaded these calls, not knowing what you're going to find when you get there. On this one, none of the occupants were injured, however the horse was injured. A veterinarian was called to transport the horse. The buggy was lying, overturned, in the middle of the intersection.

I looked at the trainee and told her that we're going to have to take the buggy back to the shed, in the rear of the Wal-Mart parking lot. The buggy was heavier than I thought it would be, and we had quite a distance to go, but it needed to be done. As we pulled the buggy, it seemed to be getting heavier, even though I knew it wasn't the buggy getting heavier, it was us becoming more tired. She looked at me and said, "I don't remember this being in any of my EMT classes." I couldn't help laughing as I told her to trust me; this won't be the only thing she does that wasn't in any of her classes!

Then there are unexpected events that should have never occurred. One evening, there were four of us on crew. We were parked in the Ephrata hospital parking lot, preparing to return to our station. It was a cold night, and we were all anxious to get home.

Our driver, Tony, and I were in the front, chatting non-stop about the latest repairs my Jeep needed. I was unloading my frustrations on Tony. Sheri was in the back with Keith. Sheri said she had a paper she had forgotten to get from the hospital, and she was running back inside. We heard the rear door close. I was still complaining about my Jeep, when we heard the rear door close again. Sheri was back, so we can go.

We drove back to station. Tony opened the bay door and I yelled back to ask Keith if he would get out and hook up Snuffy. "Snuffy" is the hose that we connect to our exhaust pipe, to prevent exhaust fumes from entering the station. Keith didn't answer. I turned around, planning on begging Keith to hook up Snuffy.

Keith wasn't there! Sheri wasn't there!

I frantically told Tony that Keith and Sheri are not there! Tony thought I was joking. He said, "You've been running too many hours!" I got out and went in the back, like I'm going to find them hiding somewhere, knowing there is nowhere for them to hide. I told Tony again, "They're gone. Now what?"

We closed the bay door and drove back to the hospital. Keith was standing outside of the hospital, waiting for a ride. He told us Sheri had decided to walk back to the station, and she didn't seem very happy about it. By the time we returned to the station, Sheri was there.

We apologized to both, and then we re-enacted the events. Sheri had left the rig to go inside the hospital. Then Keith decided to run inside and get something to drink. Keith hadn't told us he was going inside. So when we heard the door the second time, we assumed it was Sheri getting back in.

Keith felt guilty for not having told us he was getting out. It was a chain of events that led to an unpredicted event. It seems when you drop the toast, the buttered side always lands face down.

Sadly, we have a lot of calls to the same residences, over and over. Most are for attention, more than medical necessity. These are the "frequent fliers."

While we have an obligation to respond to these calls, we're taking our rig out for a non-emergency call, and subjecting a true emergency call to waiting longer than necessary.

My favorite frequent flier was an elderly woman, Martha, who was truly confused all of the time. Martha and her husband, Victor, shared a home. One day Martha dialed 911, saying that Victor was dead. Victor wasn't dead. He was sleeping. Another time she called 911 and said that she was cutting her wrist, because she had lost her pulse, and she was trying to find it.

One day she dialed 911, saying she was sick. That's it, sick. We went inside, and she said, "I was sick when I dialed 911, but now I'm better." My driver tried explaining to her that she shouldn't dial 911, unless one of them is truly sick. He was getting nowhere fast.

I started looking around the room. I noticed a lot of bowling trophies amidst the collection of what appeared to be every piece of mail they had ever received. These were people who obviously never threw anything away.

I told Martha I was admiring all of the bowling trophies. I asked her who had won them. She said, "Nobody won them. We used to go around to yard sales, searching for trophies to impress people who come to our house!"

Calls for emotional problems generally involve patients suffering from emotional problems. Then there are the unpredicted calls. One call was for an emotional problem, on an extremely hot and humid day. We arrived to find a neatly dressed lady, with her suitcase packed, ready to go to the hospital. She said she didn't have air conditioning, and the heat was causing her to become upset, so she felt she should go to the hospital, where it would be nice and cool.

A lot of calls involve emotions running in high gear. We were dispatched for an unconscious person. As we approached the apartment, a woman opened the door, and yelled to us, "You can't come in unless you promise just to put my husband back in bed and then leave!"

So I promised her that is what we would do. I didn't have any other option.

As we're walking to the bedroom, she again said, "Jack fell out of bed. Just put him back in bed, because I need to get my sleep."

We walked into the bedroom and found Jack, lying unconscious on the floor. After stabilizing him, I told her that we needed to take him to the hospital, because he was very sick.

She jumped up and tried to block the doorway. She screamed, "If you take him to the hospital, you're all going to rot in hell!" We called for assistance from the police. In between her swearing, I asked her if she had a ride to the hospital. Without hesitating, she yelled, "I can tell you where your ride is going to be! You're going to hell in a hurry!" We left the police to deal with her while we took her husband to the hospital.

Then a good deed, turned deadly. I was dispatched for a coroner call. An elderly male was driving on a dark, back road when he suddenly came upon a horse, loose in the middle of the road. His rearview mirror clipped the horse. The man immediately stopped, put his emergency flashers on, and went to check on the horse.

He was told by a group of Amish children that the horse had gotten loose from the field, and they were trying to get it back into the field. The man offered to help them.

After getting the horse back into the field, with the children standing on the field bank, thanking him and waving goodbye, he turned to go back to his car. Just at that time a car came over the crest of the hill. He didn't have a chance.

The driver was not speeding, but the crest of the road, combined with the lack of lighting along the road, didn't give her a chance to prevent hitting him. He was struck so violently that his dentures were found several yards from his body. It was another sight I pictured happening, in my mind, as I drove home in the dark. A nice man helping Amish children and a horse. Children waving and thanking the nice man, going back to his car. The nice man is struck and killed by a car, as the children watched in horror.

When I read the small article about the accident, I was saddened. This man deserved more than a small paragraph stating he had been struck and killed. Why didn't they mention that he had possibly saved the horse's life? Why didn't they mention the good deed he had done, and sacrificed his life by doing so? Why do they seem to only print the horrific news? I was comforted only by the fact of knowing how the Amish would react. I'm certain they mentioned him in their prayers for many days to follow.

You just can't walk away from scenes without continuing to think about what happened, and what will continue to evolve following the incident. Will the children have nightmares? Will they become terrified the next time an animal becomes loose on the road? Will the ladies in the other car have nightmares? I'll never know the answers to these questions, but that doesn't stop the questions from going through my mind.

It was a beautiful spring day, and Gene and I were manning a booth at Wal-Mart's "Women's Health Day." We were to take blood pressures and hand out coloring books. It sounded like a fun day. Angie said she could stop by and help us, but she'd drive her personal vehicle to Wal-Mart.

Gene and I took our rig to Wal-Mart, and began doing our assigned tasks. Angie arrived, and told me I could take a break to look for a new watch. I found a Winnie the Pooh watch that was on sale, purchased it, and returned to our booth. I was beaming in delight of my new purchase. I was enjoying the day. Just then our tones opened up, "Vehicle accident involving entrapment and fire." Two of our ambulances were being called to the accident. Gene and I looked at each other, we both knew we needed to go. Angie looked at us and said, "Go, I'll stay here and finish."

The accident was on the turnpike. Thank goodness Gene was familiar with the turnpike and their emergency entrances. We arrived to find a tandem tractor-trailer truck had literally driven over a car. The car and truck cab had caught on fire. Several other cars were involved, as it was a chain reaction accident.

Other ambulances had transported the injured. After we were certain our services were not needed, we headed back, driving along the side of the turnpike, in the opposite direction of traffic. It was not fun.

We had just gotten off of the turnpike when we heard on our scanner, a request for county to contact us. They wanted us to return and provide rehab for the firefighters. So we headed back to the accident. Traffic was backed up for miles, but surprisingly, most people were very patient with their wait. They knew it had to be a bad accident. It was.

All we knew was that there had to be at least one person in the burned car, so the coroner was called to the scene. When he arrived, I told him that we would assist in any way needed. A large tow truck was brought in, and the cab was lifted off of the car. Everything in the car was burned beyond recognition. Our first look at the car didn't give us any clues as to how many bodies were in the car. There were some long, blonde strands of hair, dangling from the roof of the car that had been lifted up, along with the cab. I looked at the strands of hair and thought, "Oh, my gosh, this is just horrible."

The firefighters began cutting the car apart. There were three females in the car, a grandmother, daughter and granddaughter. We placed the two adult bodies on our long boards, and covered their bodies with blankets. We wrapped the small girl in a bag, and put all of the bodies together, to wait for the undertakers to arrive.

Driving back to our station, neither of us had much to say. We had just witnessed a horrific scene. A scene so horrific, a veteran firefighter became physically ill during the extrication of the three bodies. The sight of the small body, burned to a crisp, lying on the highway, was one none of us would ever forget. The scenes I would try to put in the special room in my brain, so I wouldn't have to keep seeing them, over and over.

When we returned to station, Gene asked me how we're going to clean our long boards. I said, "We're not; we're going to leave them for our paid crew to clean. I have no idea how to clean them; I don't even know what some of the stuff on them is."

I left the station and put on my happy face. Predictable Janice. Always smiling. Always happy. No, she's not. She's crying inside a lot of times when the smile is on her face. Sometimes I feel like I'm wearing a mask. A happy face mask. The face people expect and want to see.

Another unpredictable call with Gene. It was 5:30 in the morning. My pager opened up for a medical assist. On the way to the home, the dispatcher told us that an elderly man needed assistance getting back into bed, after he went to the bathroom, and couldn't get back into bed.

Gene ranted, "Why couldn't he have waited another half hour to go to the bathroom? Then paid crew could have taken the call!"

We entered the house and were directed up the steps by a gracious, petite lady. She's chattering on about how she always helps him get back into bed, but this morning she just couldn't get him into bed. I'm trying to reassure her, "It will be okay. We'll get him back into bed. I have Gene and Keith with me. Both are strong guys, your husband will be back in bed in no time." We climbed the steps. I saw her husband, his legs dangling off the side of the bed.

As Gene and Keith went into the bedroom to help the man back into bed, his wife continues her rambling. Then she made a statement that turned the whole call upside down, "He always answers me when I talk to him, today is the first time he didn't answer me. He won't even talk to me."

I darted into the room, asked for vitals to be taken, and quickly assessed her husband. He wasn't sleeping. He was unconscious! I'm trying to get oxygen ready, and questioning his wife about his past medical history. To get that information required a lot of patience. Every question was answered with, "Well, let me tell you . . ." and we went round and round on all sorts of other subjects before we finally got to the answer.

She wanted to show me the first three places that they had kept his medicines, each place not suiting her. I finally got her to show me his medicines. They were neatly arranged in one of the guest bathrooms, in a spot that she approved of. There it was. He was diabetic. His blood sugar reading was dangerously low. After we treated him, and on the way to the hospital, he became conscious and alert. As we moved him to the hospital bed, a nurse asked him if he experiences frequent problems with his diabetes. His answer was, "Well, let me tell you . . ." I had to walk out of the room.

Gene's comment on the way back to the station was cute, "If anyone tells you sugar is bad for you, tell them you saw it save a person's life, more than once." Thanks, Gene, but I'm trying to lose weight, so I'll continue to watch my sugar intake.

A healthy, twenty-five-year old male having severe chest pains is not normal and not expected. His grandparents took him to the nearest hospital, where he was examined and released. For six days he continued to complain of severe chest pains. For six days his grandmother told him to keep taking the medications he had gotten from the hospital.

He told her he was taking them faithfully, but they were not providing any relief. Six days after his hospital visit, his grandmother found him dead on the bathroom floor. Could his death have been prevented? Possibly. Or was it just his time to leave this life and continue on a new journey?

Another seemingly routine call for an injured person. A woman had caught her finger in her car door and would be sitting out in front of her residence, waiting for us. Again, this didn't seem like it should be too bad. We saw the woman sitting on her porch step, with many towels wrapped around her hand, each one saturated with blood. She calmly stated that she had been shopping, returned home, and as she closed her car door, her one finger became stuck in the car door.

We asked, "May we take a look at your finger?" It seemed like an awful lot of blood for a finger that was just jammed in her car door. She removed all of the towels that her neighbors had brought her, and we saw one finger was missing!

We quickly began to control the bleeding, and asked her where her car was parked. She pointed down the driveway and described her car. I went down to the car, and very carefully opened the car door. There was her finger! I removed her finger from the car door jam, took it to our rig, and put it in a sterile solution. We whisked her away to the hospital. We were so proud of the job we'd done. We had controlled her bleeding, the finger was neatly packaged in a sterile solution, and we got her to the hospital in a very timely manner.

As we were putting clean linens on our litter, one of the nurses came out and complimented us on our nice packaging. Before we had a chance to respond to her statement, she continued to tell us that due to the age of the patient, no attempts to re-attach the finger would be made. I wondered what they'd do with her finger. Just throw it away with the rest of their trash? I wondered if the lady would mind being short one finger. I found some comfort in knowing that she hadn't even realized she'd lost one of her fingers, so she most likely wouldn't be too upset over not having it back.

Sometimes your mind just can't blank out the thoughts. As we were returning to our station, I kept envisioning them just taking the entire container, with her finger in it, and throwing it away. At some point you have to stop yourself from thinking about things like this, or you'll drive yourself crazy. I was very careful that night when I closed my door!

Many times I've walked past the blood pressure machines in the local stores and thought how nice it is that they offer that service to their customers. You may have your blood pressure measured, free of charge.

One evening, the machine became a foe rather than a friend, to a female shopper. She had her six-month-old daughter seated in the front of the shopping cart, and decided to check her blood pressure. As the cuff was inflating, her daughter decided to climb out of the shopping cart. The mother was hysterical. She didn't realize there is an emergency release button on the machine, and the cuff engulfed her arm. She screamed for help as she watched her daughter climb over the handle of the shopping cart, fall down onto the floor, landing on her head.

Our ambulance crew arrived and took care of the injured infant, as well as the distraught mother. I thought to myself how such a good intention, checking your blood pressure, can lead to a totally unpredicted event of having your daughter end up in the hospital. Fortunately her injuries were not severe.

One hot summer day we were dispatched for a sick person. We found a 65-year-old female, who really didn't seem "sick." Her son told us that they lived together, and he can tell when his mother is sick, and that day she was sick. Okay, we can take her to the hospital for evaluation. As we're taking her vitals, the son made a strange comment, "I'm sick, too."

I looked at him and asked him what he meant. He answered, "I'm sick and tired of taking care of her. Maybe, if I'm lucky, she'll soon die." I had no reply to his comments. We transported his mother to the hospital. Two days later, I saw her obituary in the paper. I wondered if the son was sad, or actually happy, that his wish had come true. Life is so unpredictable.

As unpredictable as many events are, there are many events that are predictable. Lancaster County compiled results of motor vehicle accidents, and the time frame in which the most serious ones occurred.

While one might think New Year's Eve has the most accidents, it doesn't. People seem to stay home and off of the roads on New Year's Eve. There's a fear that every car on the road, on New Year's Eve, is being driven by a drunk driver.

I wasn't surprised to learn that the holiday with the most deadly accidents is Halloween. Revelers run amok. I suppose I'm considered a party pooper, but to me Halloween is just another day for commercial vendors to make a lot of money. But I know people get crazy on Halloween. I read all of the Halloween party invitations I receive, each promising a night you'll never forget. Perhaps a better term would be, "A night you'll never remember."

Close behind it is Thanksgiving, when a lot of college kids are returning home and in a partying mood, and hey, it's the beginning of the "holiday season," so enjoy it. A lot of people travel on Thanksgiving, to do the "family gatherings." That way they are done, out of the way, the self-imposed obligations have been met, and you have the rest of the holiday season to just enjoy yourself.

The third one surprised me, the last workday before Christmas. Statistics show that a lot of employees leave their work place inebriated, after partaking in Christmas celebrations.

The national average differs from our Lancaster County averages. The national numbers for deaths on a holiday ranks New

Year's Day as number one. Second is Super Bowl Sunday, which I easily believe.

I know so many people who arrange to be off of work the day after the Super Bowl. They have high hopes of their team playing in the Super Bowl. If that doesn't happen, hey, it's still the Super Bowl, which has become one of our country's largest celebrated events.

Running an overnight ambulance shift, one can predict having at least a few calls. What I never expected, was what happened following an ambulance call for a DOA. Gene and I arrived on scene, along with local police officers, to find a dead man who had been found by his son.

The son worked odd hours, and his father had not been answering the phone, so the son stopped by, after he finished working, around 3 a.m. He found his father, dead in his living room chair. I felt bad for the son. What a horrible thing to experience, walking in and finding your father dead. We agreed to wait at the home, with the son, until a coroner arrived. We waited and waited.

Finally a car pulled up, and out stepped a guy I knew. He runs with one of our local medic units. I asked him, "What are you doing here?" and he pointed to his cap, "Deputy Coroner." Somewhat in shock, I blurted out, "You're a deputy coroner?" He answered, "Yes, I am." I immediately told him I was interested in becoming one, too. He explained that the job is very unpredictable and you never know what to expect. It sounded just like running ambulance calls.

Don't ask what possessed me to tell him that I wanted to be a deputy coroner, I just knew it was something I wanted to do. After he finished his work, and the body had been removed, we went outside. I questioned him more about becoming a deputy coroner. He said he felt I had enough credentials to apply for a position, and he thought they were looking for additional deputies.

I emailed G. Gary Kirchner, M.D., our elected county coroner, the same day. Within a day I received a return email, arranging an interview with Dr. Kirchner. The interview was set and I became nervous. Five minutes into the initial interview, I realized that he was a nice, caring, intelligent individual. I had taken documentation of traumatic calls I had been on, and as much past medical background material that I could get together, to prove that I was capable of doing this work.

He laid out the requirements. He was kind, but strict. He expected you to follow the policies and procedures. The reports needed to be completed accurately, and in a timely manner. A good cell phone was a necessity. Attendance at the monthly training was mandatory. At all times, he was to be kept apprised of any calls we were dispatched to and I was to respect the command police officer's wishes.

I was impressed by Dr. Kirchner's dedication to his position. I assured him I would do everything in my power to represent him, and the office, in a professional manner. I convinced him that my being a female would not stop me from remaining professional on all calls.

Following a lengthy interview, I was told to contact Dr. Robert Good, a Senior Deputy Coroner, and arrange an interview with him. I wasted no time in doing this. I was so eager to be accepted, and to begin working. I never really stopped to analyze what I was getting in to. It was something I felt compelled to do.

The day before my interview with Dr. Good, a friend of mine was killed in a violent car accident. But I met with Dr. Good at my scheduled time, despite being directionally challenged and having to call his office for directions. Anyone who has no sense of direction, and cannot read a map book, understands what I mean. This defect in my system has caused me much frustration, but every time I am lost, I keep thinking, "It's okay, at least I'm alive and lost."

Instantly I liked Dr. Good. He seemed so sincere, and also so dedicated to his position. He began reciting statistics, which included the average number of annual calls for a coroner to a vehicle accident, which was approximately 50 per year, or one a week. The one for that week was my friend. Although I sometimes questioned how old those statistics were.

Dr. Good explained that he does the scheduling. He will email everyone for their available dates, and then create a schedule for the following month. Each shift begins at 8 a.m. and ends the following morning at 8 a.m. There is a primary coroner, as well as a secondary coroner, on call for each shift. The secondary will handle any calls that come in while the primary is busy with another call, or if the primary deputy coroner needs assistance on a call.

We reviewed all of the forms, the death certificates, the toe tags. At that time, most of the forms were transmitted via a fax machine. Today they are done on computers, and sent as email attachments. After that interview, I returned to the main office in Lancaster, completed the necessary paperwork, and picked up forms, toe tags, and a book listing funeral homes and contact information. I met with Sue, the administrative assistant. She was a blessing to me. She helped me so many times when I was confused or needed guidance. It was always a pleasure to stop in for more supplies and to chat with her.

I was given a laminated card; "ON CORONER BUSINESS", so I could park on some of the many narrow, crowded streets, and not have my Jeep towed away. I was told to contact Chuck McWilliams to obtain an official shirt and cap. A baseball cap! Needless to say I was excited to receive my cap.

Then I proceeded to the courthouse to have my picture taken and laminated on an identification badge. "Janice Ballenger, Deputy Coroner, County of Lancaster." Okay, I was getting closer. I received the current schedule and would shadow other deputies, until they felt comfortable that I could handle calls alone. I watched, as each deputy seemed to have his own routine. I purchased the perfect notebook. It zippered shut, for any nasty weather calls, and had plenty of pockets for examination gloves, toe tags, business cards, and extra pens. I bought inserts to hold my different forms. It even had a shoulder strap that worked out perfectly.

My friends have often told me that I'm too organized. I like to be organized. Things go much smoother when you know exactly where everything is located. I was now organized to my satisfaction, and I was ready to begin taking calls on my own.

While it's easy for me to say that my initial calls were relatively routine calls, for the surviving family members, every call was far from routine. I tried to put myself in their shoes, and treat every person as I would want my family to be treated.

In the beginning, it was similar to running ambulance calls, except the patient was dead. There were family members to deal with, gathering information on the deceased, and extending compassion to everyone present at the time I was there. I was, and continue to be, amazed at how many family members, friends and neighbors were on scene before I got there. This is largely due to so many people carrying cell phones.

I can't begin to count the number of ambulance patients we are attempting to treat, as they chat away on their cell phones. I must admit there have been many times when I just wanted to throw a cell phone out the window or into a yard. While I do like my cell phone for necessary purposes, I'm not on it constantly, like so many people I see. In my opinion, that's rude and an annoyance. Just imagine trying to obtain vitals on a patient and they ask you to wait a minute while they make a cell phone call, or answer a call. Excuse me, you've just had someone dial 911 for you, and you need to make a cell phone call? There's something wrong with that picture.

You always remember your first, solo coroner call. Mine was at 2:45 in the afternoon. Okay, this isn't too bad; it's the middle of the day, not like the middle of the night.

The call was for a 64-year-old lady, who appeared to be in the midst of her normal daily activities, sat down on the steps leading from the second floor to the first floor to catch her breath. She was still holding a container of fruit drink in her hand.

Family members stated she normally did this when breathing became difficult for her. Church members had stopped to visit her, found the door open, and she didn't answer, so they went inside. She was dead. She had an extensive past medical history and her death was not unexpected. I called Dr. Kirchner from the scene and informed him of my findings.

I extended my sincere sympathy to the friends and family members on scene. I began collecting her medication information. The medication report requires you to list the number of pills dispensed, the number of pills remaining, and the number of pills missing. Isn't that basic math? I waited on scene, until after her body was removed by the undertakers, and gave my name and number to the family members, in the event any questions would arise later.

I learned this would prove invaluable. Too often family members and friends are distraught at the time I am there, and they don't think of questions until after I leave the scene. I consider it an obligation as well as an honor to assist the deceased's family in any way I can. I left the scene with a good feeling, a feeling that I had helped people during a difficult time.

My second coroner call was not as predictable. I was told by our county dispatcher that the call was for a male, found dead in his home. Sometimes you get more information as to the nature of the call, other times you're left guessing. As I drove to the scene, I was hoping this was another natural death. I suppose I thought most of the calls that I would respond to, as a deputy coroner, would be predictable. Natural deaths. I learned there is nothing like a natural death to the family who survives the deceased.

I finally found the street and saw police cars in the driveway. I noticed the garage door was open, and police were in the garage. An officer met me and told me the immediate pertinent facts. Jack's companion had gone to work that morning, and she phoned him to remind him of a scheduled bank meeting. When Jack didn't show up for the meeting, his companion went to their home, found the house filled with a smoke type odor, and discovered his truck was running, while still parked inside the closed garage. Jack was dead from carbon monoxide poisoning. The firefighters provided ventilation of the garage and house. There was no past medical history.

He had never mentioned killing himself. I don't think I'll ever get used to saying or hearing, "killing himself."

According to his companion, her family was opposed to their upcoming wedding plans, but she didn't feel it had bothered him to the point of doing something like this. What do I say? I'm sorry? That doesn't seem like enough.

But I've learned that sometimes, too often, there just aren't words to describe the sorrow you're feeling for the surviving family and friends. You become engulfed in their despair. You want so badly to help them. But you don't have any answers. I can't change what has happened. I can only offer my sympathy and try to help in any way possible to ease the shock. But it just isn't enough.

The "natural" deaths continued and I had developed a sense of confidence that I could do this job. Someone has to do it. I felt I was given the ability to be able to do it with compassion and caring, while remaining sane.

Another one of my first coroner calls had me totally confused. I was sent to an Amish home and was told by the police that a volunteer from Hospice was there. Okay, we've been told that any person under the care of Hospice, and passes away, does not require a coroner to respond. They are terminally ill. There is a definite reason for their death. But I was told I needed to respond to the scene.

After I had arrived, and learned the details, I understood why I had been dispatched to this residence. An elderly woman had just been placed under the care of Hospice. The Hospice nurse arrived that morning, for her first visit with the woman, and she found the woman dead.

I'll never forget that day. It was in March, and it should have been cold outside. But it was 60 degrees and absolutely beautiful outside. I pronounced the lady dead, and asked if I could go outside to make my phone calls.

I walked outside, and found a set of concrete steps leading up to a field. I sat down, with my notes, on the steps. As I was about to make my call to Dr. Kirchner, the peacefulness overwhelmed me. Here I was, sitting outside of a home with a dead body inside, but it seemed so peaceful. I began wondering why the rest of the world can't be like this.

Clothes were hanging from the wash lines. There was a gentle breeze in the mild air. Horse and buggies were filling the driveway. The horses were making gentle noises, and appeared to be bowing their heads. I thought to myself, "Why can't I stay here forever?"

It was one of the most peaceful times I've ever experienced. I sat there way too long. The atmosphere consumed me. I felt like I was in a scene for the movie "Witness." I questioned myself as to my way of living. Was it wrong?

Finally, I forced myself to make my phone call to Dr. Kirchner. I only told him the facts. I didn't tell him that I was experiencing this desire to just stay in that same spot forever. With the business matters resolved, I went back inside the house. By this time, more relatives and friends had arrived. The men were seated on one side of the room, and the women on the opposite side. They were gracious. They told me they had cleared the "good table" in the middle of the room, for me to sit at. I felt like such an intrusion. But at the same time I kept thinking, "Ask me to stay here, ask me to join your way of life." But that didn't happen.

I left the scene and returned to my way of life. I think that day made me realize that I am not a part of their ways, but I am respectful of their ways. I can give something to others. I might not live the lifestyle they live, but I can still give and do good things for others. It is a day I will never forget, and I'm grateful for the experience, and all that I took with me when I left that day.

Then came the first call that challenged me to give it all up, a suicide by a young man. He had been arguing with his wife. She, and their infant baby, went to a relative's house for a "time out" to cool off. He didn't cool off.

He wrote a note, expressing his sorrow for being a bad husband and father. The note was neatly placed on an infant seat carrier, which was on top of an ottoman in front of the chair he was seated in. He took a 12-gauge shotgun, perched it between his legs, held the barrel with both hands, and shot himself under his chin. He had used his toe to pull the trigger.

He was seated underneath a running ceiling fan. Dogs ran loose in the house. We found parts of his body in rooms attached to the room he was in. I found teeth in the carpet. The police compared the note with a pen and tablet found nearby. We listened to the phone message, "Jim, pick up the phone, Jim I know you're there, Jim, we can work this out. Just pick up the phone and let's talk about it." It was the voice of his wife.

I went about collecting information for my reports. I saw baby things everywhere. I wondered how someone can become so distraught, and feel like such a failure as a husband and father, at the age of 26. His baby was only several months old. He had the rest of his life to be a better husband and father. What drives people to this point? The point of no return. I believe we all have a line, and a lot of people get close to the line, but they don't cross over the line. That night, Jim crossed over his line, leaving a wife, infant child and family to wonder what they could have done to prevent this tragedy.

The undertaker arrived. Yes, one person. He and I had the grim task of collecting all of the body parts and placing them into bags. We had to mark the bags, listing the contents and where they were found. Then he brought a body bag into the room. I was told that all "body matters" had to be collected, put into a bio-bag, and sent with the body.

I know the average adult brain weighs three pounds, but I swear I collected more than three pounds of brain matter. I finished collecting and marking the bags with what body parts I thought they were. It was a gruesome chore that I somehow managed to accomplish.

Then we went to move Jim from the chair into the body bag. As we lowered his body, the one remaining eyelid opened up. His eye was as blue as the sky. He seemed to be staring directly at me with his one eye. For many nights, I had images of him staring at me. We carried the body bag down and loaded it into the hearse.

By now the police had spoken with his wife and informed her of her loss. I noticed a truck pull up outside. I walked over to the truck and asked if I could help them. I saw a female driver, a baby in the middle, and a female on the passenger side of the truck. The female on the passenger side said, "This is my house and I need to go in to get some items for the baby."

There was no way I was allowing her to go inside and see the grisly mess. I was not going to let her see the blood, splattered on the baby pictures sitting proudly on shelves. The blood splattered on the infant seat. The huge amounts of blood everywhere. I asked her what she needed and where it was located. I went back inside and came out with all of the items. Through tears, she told me that it was her mother driving the truck, and her and the baby would be spending the next several days with her mother.

What should I say? I'm sorry? I've never found adequate words to express my sorrow. I never will. I just say exactly how I'm feeling, and I pray that what I say somehow brings comfort to those left behind.

I had taken care of cleaning up as best as I could, put more dog food and water in the dogs' dishes, helped load the body bag, and had expressed my sympathy to the widow.

Now I had a thirty-mile drive home, alone, in the pitch dark. What about me? Who is going to say to me that they're sorry for the feelings I'm experiencing? Who can I share my horrible, vivid image of Jim staring at me with his one sky blue eyeball? Am I supposed to just go on like I've just done a routine job? I was filled with sadness and despair. I felt like someone had taken my body and soul and put it in a washing machine, tossing and turning, wringing me out, and plopping me on the floor to dry out. Would I ever dry out? Would my soul ever be back inside my body?

Unable to concentrate on my reverse directions just provided me with more time to dwell on what I've just witnessed. As I drove aimlessly throughout the southern end of the county, I thought, "Can I really do this? Do I really want to do this?"

I also thought that the longer I remained lost, the less sleep I was going to get. I was hot, thirsty, and needed to use a bathroom. My cell phone rang and interrupted my thoughts. It was our county dispatcher calling. I was to respond to Lititz Borough for a natural death. The dispatcher put me through to a police officer on scene. The deceased had an extensive past medical history, but they were not able to contact a doctor to sign a death certificate. I wrote down the address and told him I was on my way.

I'm on my way? I have no clue where I am, I know I need to use a bathroom, I know it's the middle of the night, I'm thirsty, and I know there are people waiting for me in Lititz. I came to an intersection, with a bar, smack in the middle of the square. I parked my Jeep and I hurried inside. I said to the bartender, "I need to please use your bathroom, I need a soda or cold water to go, I need to figure out how to get from here to Lititz, and they can be in any order."

She, along with the men seated at the bar, stared at me like I was from another planet. At that point I felt like I was from another planet. But she rapidly fired back to me, where the bathroom was located, she'd get me a cold soda to go, and she'd find someone who could tell me how to get to Lititz, by the time I returned from the bathroom. Now that's service!

I returned from the bathroom, got my soda, and was shown who to talk to for directions. I gave the bartender a nice tip, and bought my direction coordinator a drink. You've heard it before "There's some things money just can't buy," but I think I bought what I needed that night, in that bar. I don't even know the town I was in, but perhaps, by chance, one day the bartender will read this and recognize herself. Your kind and caring manner helped turn the whole evening around for me. Thank you.

I found my way to Lititz and executed the death certificate. I found my way back home and began preparing my reports. Dawn was rapidly approaching. Again my cell phone startled me. Now what? I was to respond to a motor vehicle accident involving two tractor-trailers and one car, on Route 30. My first thought was of the bumper stickers that used to be around, "Pray for me, I drive on Route 30."

The dead man was going for kidney dialysis and never showed up. His mother was called and she knew immediately that something was wrong. She started on the route her son drives for his treatments, only to be met by a long backlog of traffic. At that moment, she knew this was not a good thing for her son. I suppose it's something mothers just know.

Her son had suffered a fatal heart attack while driving for his treatment. His car was demolished when it crossed the centerline, and ran into two tractor-trailers. She inched closer to the scene. A fire police officer told her that a Hyundai was involved in the accident and he believed the driver had been killed. She knew immediately it was her son.

I thought to myself, "This isn't the way life is supposed to be. Parents are to die before their children." But this has proven to be wrong over and over, although I still refuse to accept it. There is only one person in control of this, and I have to believe there is a reason. I firmly believe that if God brings you to it, He will bring you through it.

His mother made a comment that will stick with me forever. "All he wanted was to be a normal person, but it turned into a rough life."

Again I returned home to attempt completing my reports. I can find my way home from Route 30. I had just completed my reports and my cell phone rang. This time it was for another suicide in the absolute farthest end of the county from my home. I was fortunate in having the dispatcher give me good directions to the scene. It was a remote park. A beautiful park, that overlooks our Susquehanna River. A park where you could scream, "Run Forrest Run" at the top of your lungs, and it would just echo. This scene was so uniquely different from the earlier suicide.

Shawn had taken time to cover the car seats with multiple layers of blankets, to prevent any blood from messing up his car. He was seated in the driver's seat, dead, from a single gunshot to his chest. Everything was neat and tidy. He had even covered his back seats with blankets. His mind was made up, for a reason unknown to us, that he was going to end his life. He went to great lengths to preserve the dignity of his car. What about his dignity? He had crossed his line.

Having seen so many different situations in such a short period of time, I began questioning, "Why?" Why do people cross the line? Why don't they seek help? Perhaps they do, and it just doesn't help. I would never understand "Why?"

Every suicide call consumed my entire being. The devastation and guilt left behind for the survivors to live with. The horrific scenes witnessed by so many people. During my years as a deputy coroner and an EMT, I encountered so many suicide attempts, some successful and some unsuccessful, that I have devoted an entire chapter to them.

It is extremely difficult to remove yourself from what you've witnessed and return to the "normal world." To say hello to your friends as you see them. To answer, "I'm fine, how are you?" I don't want to pretend that I'm fine. I'm not having a good day. Why can't I say that?

Chapter 6

Deputy Coroner Demands

My deputy coroner demands were now running at full speed. I was seeing, touching, and smelling things I never knew existed. I experienced emotions I didn't know existed.

I pulled up in front of a row home in Columbia Borough. From the outside it looked like just another row home. Kids were crawling over the railings that were intended to separate the homes. I couldn't find a place to park on the narrow street, which is typical in congested towns with onstreet parking.

"I hate when I get in situations like this," I thought to myself in frustration. I finally just parked in the street, put my "On Coroner Duty" paper on my dash, and made certain my doors were locked.

A police officer greeted me, and I asked him about my Jeep. "Sure, it's okay where you parked," he replied. I respectfully drilled him, "You call leaving my Jeep in the middle of the street parking?" "Around here we do," he answered.

He took me inside the home, where an elderly male had passed away. After pronouncing the gentleman dead, and doing my investigative work, we waited for the undertakers to arrive.

One officer asked me, "Are you familiar with this house?" I thought a minute before I answered, "No, all I saw were piles of books and magazines he seemed to have saved forever, nothing to indicate anything suspicious." That wasn't what he meant. He showed me hidden doors, within the walls, with steps that led to an underground tunnel. The house had been a haven for slaves. He explained how a railroad car ran along the tunnel, dropping off slaves from the south. He showed me more doors, which blended in with the walls, fireplaces, any place one wouldn't suspect a door. I was amazed.

I began thinking, "What will become of this house? It holds so much of our country's history. It will probably be sold at a public auction and become just another house." It was evident that the dead man had great pride in his country and helping others. Would the new owners do the same? I doubted it.

One beautiful, summer morning I read our Sunday newspaper. On the front page was an article about the anticipated deadly effects of mixing Jagermeister, a strong alcohol, with Red Bull, a high-energy drink. If the article hadn't had a large picture of a can of Red Bull, I probably wouldn't have read the article. Local heart doctors stated concerns about the increase in "Jager bombs" (a mixture of the two), and a possible increase in death associated with them. The article said Jagermeister slows down the heart while Red Bull speeds up the heart. The two mixed together could be deadly. I learned something that day, never thinking it would have any impact on my life.

The following day I was sent to Conoy Township. I was told a young male was found dead at a picnic table, outside of a camper. As I walked towards the camper, I saw groups of young people wandering around. Many were talking on cell phones and crying. One person pointed to the picnic table and said, "There's Jim, he's dead."

I saw Jim, seated with his head faced down on the picnic table, outside the camper. One girl, whose eyes were filled with tears, told me, "We had been out drinking yesterday and came back to play cards." A young man added, "We were doing Jager bombs and we thought Jim had too many drinks and passed out. We put a blanket over him and went inside the camper to sleep."

The female jumped back into the conversation; "It seemed weird though, because Jim can really hold his alcohol, better than most of us, and we were surprised when he passed out."

She explained that in the morning, the first person to go outside noticed Jim was still in the same spot at the picnic table. Something didn't seem right with Jim, so she dialed 911. Something wasn't right, Jim was dead.

As I spoke with them, I learned they had continued making their own Jager bombs after returning to the camper. I looked inside of the trashcans. I found a large, empty bottle of Jagermeister and many empty cans of Red Bull. The newspaper article hit close to home. Too close to home for Jim. When I am out, and I hear someone order a "Jager bomb," I cringe, but remain silent.

While I'll be the first to admit I enjoy a beer, I'm continuously amazed at the amount of alcohol some people can consume. I should say, "consume and survive." They don't always survive.

I was sent to Lancaster City for a dead female. Mary and her companion had been drinking since morning. There were twelve, half-gallon bottles of alcohol, all empty, in the small apartment. After spending the day drinking, they decided to take naps. There was only a sofa in the apartment, no bed, so he chose to nap on the sofa, while Mary agreed to nap on the floor. An hour later, he woke up and thought she was still sleeping. So he walked to a neighbor's house for a few more drinks. When he returned, he saw Mary, still in the same spot. He tried to wake her but he couldn't.

When I arrived he was outside, probably drinking more alcohol. I did my work, put a toe tag on her, and decided to move Mary into a body bag before the undertakers arrived.

Mary was 43 years old when her obsession with alcohol took her life. Mary was a big woman. It's amazing how the police suddenly have to leave for another call when the time comes to move a large body. This call required moving her from one point on the floor, and into the body bag. I was left alone in the apartment, as officers disappeared, but one remained behind. He stayed outside talking to her companion.

When you're moving a dead body, you have to be careful. You don't want to induce any trauma by moving the body. So I began slowly moving each body part a little closer to the body bag. Mary was three hundred pounds of dead weight. I finally got her into the bag. I was hot and exhausted.

The undertakers arrived. Their first comment was, "Wow, you've already packaged her!" I didn't quite share in their joy. I gathered my belongings, took one final look around, and thought, "I'm so grateful that I don't live in conditions like this, having to choose between sleeping on the sofa or the floor." But I realized that we don't know what the future holds. One day I might have to make a decision like that. I pray I don't have to.

Often people who partake in excessive alcohol consumption are thought to have passed out. I was sent to Lancaster City, again, for a 44-year-old dead female. The address was in an apartment development. I drove in circles looking for a police car and trying to find the apartment. I prayed that I'd be able to find my way out of the complex without driving in circles. I finally noticed a police car and found the apartment.

Jill had moved in with her niece, after Jill had broken up with her boyfriend. There's a fine line between questioning with respect and research. I needed to be sensitive, but at the same time, not timid. I was told Jill had a tendency to drink too much and would frequently pass out. Her niece, Sylvia, knew this, so that evening didn't seem different. Sylvia was ready to go to bed, so she tried to awaken Aunt Jill. Her aunt wouldn't wake up. Aunt Jill wasn't passed out; Aunt Jill was dead.

Sylvia had a 4-year-old daughter sleeping in the apartment, but Sylvia was so guilt ridden that she hadn't realized Aunt Jill was dead, she called a relative to pick up the young girl. The police and I moved Jill's body from the sofa, to the floor, and into a body bag.

I found myself praying again, "Please don't let the little girl wake up as we're moving this dead body."

A male relative entered the apartment to take the 4 year old to his home. The little girl remained sound asleep as he carried her out of the apartment. She was clueless. That was a good thing. Other relatives arrived to comfort Sylvia. I expressed my sympathy, as Sylvia continued crying hysterically. Through tears she mumbled, "Thanks."

The week of our Ephrata Fair arrived. I routinely take vacation that week, so I can volunteer with ambulance. I had signed up as deputy coroner that Monday, thinking, "I still have the whole week to enjoy, and what are my chances of having a difficult call on that Monday?"

Monday at 7:45 a.m. my phone rang. It was our county dispatcher calling, "We know you don't go on until 8 a.m., but this is in your backyard, and it's almost 8 a.m." I hesitantly answered, "Not a problem, I'll take the call."

She told me it was a crash in front of Esbenshade's Nursery, the place I go to for relaxation and comfort. The place I go to buy my annual geraniums. A place I love going to. That morning I dreaded driving to Esbenshade's.

As I got out of my Jeep, I looked at the beautiful geraniums in Esbenshade's parking lot. I looked at the smashed car and saw the dead man. I thought, "Sometimes there's just too much sadness interwoven with what should be happiness."

His car crossed the centerline, and "ate" as we say, a mobile home being pulled by a tractor in the opposite lane of traffic. The impact was so violent that pink insulation from underneath the mobile home was tangled in the wreckage of the car.

Police said it appeared that the driver of the truck, hauling half of a modular home, tried to avoid the collision by driving off the road, to the right, but the car hit the trailer on the left side. When you're on scene, you don't know where this person was going, where he was coming from, what thoughts were going through his mind in the last seconds of his life. You just do your job. It's a somber task much easier said than done.

A news reporter came upon the accident by chance. She shared some sobering thoughts; "Fatal accidents are a sort of meat-and-potatoes reporting task, made ordinary by their regularity." This accident occurred on an absolutely gorgeous, blue-sky Monday.

Standing in front of the deceased's car, she expressed the same thoughts I had, "What was that last moment of life like? Did you feel your spirit rising from your body? Did you know where you were going? Did you feel a sadness, a surprise, a joy, at the passing?"

I thought about the knock on someone's front door, or a visit at his or her workplace. The survivor will see the police officer with the solemn face, and think, "Oh." And then, "Oh God!"

I stood there looking at the wreckage that just gave up a son, or brother, or wife; the guy who drove his family crazy, and delighted them; the guy who hung his bathrobe on the hook that morning, never to return home. His family was not there, but we were. We paid tribute to him. While we didn't know him, we felt we did.

That evening I was sent to another horrific, tragic motor vehicle accident. A 22-year-old male was returning home, after he and a group of friends had gone to a hospital to visit his wife and infant daughter, who was born that day. They were following each other on a dark stretch of a two-lane road. Bruce lost control, crossed the centerline, went airborne, and his car was wedged sideways, in between two large trees, approximately four to five feet off the ground. When I first saw the car, I couldn't stop myself from saying out loud, "Holy crap! That is unreal!" It was a sight I'll never forget.

Bruce's body was mangled in the vehicle. The towing company arrived to discover the truck they brought couldn't remove the car from that height. So we waited. While coroner calls don't demand the speed in responding as ambulance calls do, I try to get there as quickly as I can. But it's often a lengthy process of working and waiting. It was dark when I arrived, and seemed even darker when I left, which was eight hours later.

The towing company returned with a larger truck. Bruce had been wearing a seat belt, which was holding his body inside the car. It was a horrific sight to watch the tow truck operators remove the vehicle from between the two trees. Bruce's body limbs began to fall out from open, crushed parts of the car. His left arm fell out of an opening, followed by his left leg; both dangling in the air. Everyone stood quiet and still, as we watched, and held our breath that his entire body wouldn't fall out of the car in mid air.

Just then my cell phone startled me. A police officer up the road was calling. "The guy's dad is up here, and he wants to walk down to see the car. What do you think?" Sometimes I give things a lot of thought before I answer. This time I didn't need much time, "No! Absolutely not!" I had quickly thought to myself, "If this was my child, would I want to see him dangling out of a car wedged between two trees? No." Fortunately, the police agreed and kept the father and others away. While I understood the father wanting to see the crash, I also realized the father would have to live with those images the rest of his life. I will never forget the images, and I didn't know the young man.

The towing company finally extricated the car, and it was lowered to the ground. It was another sight I'll never forget.

Bruce was wearing a red pullover shirt, with a white undershirt that had a "Recreation Commission League Champs" insignia on the front, jeans and a brown leather belt. In the left front pocket of his shirt was a pack of Marlboro Lights, a cigarette lighter and $21.00 in currency. On his wrist was the security bracelet, issued to visitors at the hospital where his daughter had just been born. I completed the death certificate and toe tag; gathered my information; and helped load him into a body bag. Then I headed home.

Thoughts kept going through my mind. I couldn't stop thinking about the anguish of all of the people involved. Bruce's friends, who had shared in his pride of becoming a father, then witnessed the horrific accident. His father, who had just experienced the joy of becoming a grandfather, and hours later the joy turning to anguish over the loss of his son. The baby girl, who would grow up knowing her father died on the day she was born. Bruce's wife, and mother of their baby. Did she know by this time that Bruce was dead? I wanted to express my sympathy to someone, but there was no one to express it to.

Several days later, two announcements were in the paper, the birth of the daughter and the obituary of her father. I read he was a computer specialist; he was a member of his high school volleyball team, which won the state championship in 2001. He was a car enthusiast and enjoyed martial arts, soccer, playing pool, and hanging out with his friends.

When I had returned home after the call I thought, "Ok, the whole week of the Ephrata Fair is still ahead of me. I can't change the beginning of my 'vacation' week, but I can try to make the most of the remaining days."

My thoughts turned to the Akron Lions Club's grilled cheeseburgers; Tom's batter dipped, fried vegetables; Wednesday night's parade, which typically draws nearly 50,000 people; and the challenges among our ambulance crews at the game stands. So much fun awaited me.

I had been training Amanda as a deputy coroner. She'd been doing well, and now was on her own. I was proud of her. I'll never forget the first call she shadowed me on. She arrived, looking as sharp as a needle. She was on the ball. She knew when to hold back, and when to be assertive. She'd do just fine.

It was Wednesday afternoon. Our Ephrata parade was to begin within several hours. My cell phone rang. It was Amanda. "I've just been dispatched to a bad crash on Route 23. All I was told was that it's a car full of young people. Can you please go with me?"

I immediately said, "Yes, I'll meet you there and stay as long as you need me."

I walked up to another horrific sight. It was one of those calls where your first, crippling response is, "holy crap!" The car was so smashed that I couldn't even tell where a body was—or if there even was a body still inside the car.

Amanda came over and said, "There's a female in the rear passenger seat who is dead, and three others have been taken to hospitals in critical condition." We removed her body from the car. Unlike the many other accidents that I've seen, this girl didn't have any obvious physical symptoms of trauma, although it was obvious her neck had snapped, and she was dead. We searched her clothes for identification.

We found a receipt from a Sheetz convenience store, which showed a purchase of one soda and one lottery ticket had been made on that day. We found the lottery ticket. It was an instant winner lottery ticket—she'd never had the chance to cash it in. We also found a debit card in her pant pocket. That was it— there was no purse—nothing but the winning lottery ticket, a debit card and a receipt.

As we were removing her body from the car, four cell phones began to ring, all at the same time. Each phone had a unique ring, which jangled discordantly with the others. It was a disturbance I couldn't tolerate.

"May we please turn those off?" I asked the police officer. He looked at me strangely. "No!" he answered.

The cell phones kept ringing, each with an annoying, different ring tone. I wanted more than anything to stomp on those phones until they stopped ringing.

I helped Amanda as much as I could. When I felt comfortable that she was handling the situation, I headed back to Ephrata—just in time to hop in the ambulance for the parade. As festive as the parade was, it was one night that I didn't feel festive. Once again, I was compelled to put on my happy face in order to smile and wave to everyone. Despite the fact that I had just helped pull a dead girl out of a car on the side of the road, I had to pretend that everything was fine. That's what people want—so that's what we give them.

Later we learned that the dead girl was 18 years old, and a graduate of Lancaster County Academy, where she was one of the commencement speakers at her graduation. As one of two students to deliver a speech at the academy's graduation ceremony in June, she spoke of second chances and overcoming obstacles. In one copy of her speech, she wrote:

"We are all here for different reasons. Some of us made choices that we would not change, but they brought us together on this day. Some did drugs, some got pregnant, some hated their schools, some did not care, and some had problems at home. Yet we all share that common bond that we came back to set our lives straight. Even if only for a short time."

Her final sentence drove me to tears.

She was a student at Harrisburg Area Community College, majoring in business administration and was employed by Sheetz, Inc. She also volunteered at the Susquehanna Association of the Blind. She loved music, reading, drawing and writing.

In April of the following year, the driver of the vehicle saw, for the first time, photos of the wreckage he left behind that day in September, after he had smoked marijuana and got behind the wheel of a car. During his hearing, the 18 year old shook his head as he looked at the pictures, and he began to cry.

He was only two days shy of his 18th birthday when he crashed the car into a tree, killing the 18-year-old female and paralyzing the two other male passengers. Both passengers were still recovering at a Philadelphia hospital, and it was thought that they might never walk again. The driver was committed to a Perry County youth development center, for a minimum of six months, and ordered to pay restitution of $3,212,163. He also was ordered to perform 200 hours of community service. The price of bad choices.

During the hearing, the deceased girl's mother showed the driver her daughter's graduation picture.

"I am and will always be her mom," she said, tears filling her voice. "The most heart-wrenching part of that statement is that although I will always be her mom, she is no longer here to be my daughter. How do I come to terms with that? She wasn't just my daughter—she was my best friend."

"This is not about vengeance," she calmly continued, "I know your intention was not to destroy the lives of your friends. I do believe in accountability, though. I have not asked for restitution because I know that it won't take my pain away. Money would do nothing but serve as a constant reminder of the day she was taken away from me."

One of the paralyzed passengers gave a statement that was read to the judge. The accident had occurred on his 18th birthday.

"I feel like my life has been torn apart because I will never walk again," the statement read. "It is difficult being a teenager knowing you will have to use a wheelchair for the rest of your life."

By the end of the hearing, the driver's remorse was evident.

"If I'd have known what would have happened that day, I never would have gotten in that car," he moaned through tears.

"I wish I could bring her back. She was my best friend. I wish I could fix everything, but I can't. I can't."

The judge was dismayed to learn the driver had continued to use marijuana after the accident. The driver said none of the passengers were aware that he was under the influence while driving the car. The driver was tried as a juvenile and charged with homicide by vehicle, driving under the influence of a controlled substance, and other related counts, after police determined he had been driving 76 mph in a 35-mph zone.

September proved to be a fatal month. While our Ephrata Fair was its usual success, there were many fatalities that month.

A 24-year-old York woman was killed on a beautiful September afternoon, in a two-vehicle crash. The woman was driving west on Route 30 when her sedan ran into a parked tractor-trailer. The driver of the tractor-trailer was legally parked on the right shoulder of the highway when she struck the back of the trailer. The car was wedged underneath the rear of the trailer.

Amanda and I responded together. Traffic was backed up for miles as we approached the scene. She drove on the right shoulder, as I walked in front of her vehicle, to be certain no cars pulled off to the side as she was driving. We finally reached the scene. It was another "holy crap" call. It was impossible to see a car was under the trailer. Looking at the back of the trailer, all I saw was the wording, "Air Ride Equipped." The bar that goes along the back of the trailer, which is on trailers to prevent cars from driving underneath them, was not visible. It had been pushed under the trailer upon impact.

The deceased had multiple traumatic injuries, and most likely never knew what hit her, or, what she hit. Driving home, Amanda and I looked at all of the trailers with bars on the back of them. I told myself that I wanted to research how much energy is required to push a bar under the trailer, but that project is still on my "to do list."

The following week I was sent to pronounce a 41-year-old man dead. He had died in a fire in his home, along with his big, black dog. As I walked through the house, something again amazed me. Here, in this house, with minimal furnishings, was enough mouthwash to satisfy the alcoholic need for several weeks, and a computer that would put some computer geeks to shame. I keep saying it's not for me to judge. But I am constantly amazed at people's priorities.

It has to be difficult when your child dies before you. I can't even imagine it. It's one of those things you stop yourself from thinking about.

I responded to a call for a natural death of a 52-year-old female who had lived with her mother. The daughter, Betty, had numerous medical problems, and I suspected her mother knew the end was near, but that doesn't make it any easier. As I sat at the kitchen table with the mother, she shared stories with me. Stories of teaching Betty how to cook. Stories of them playing cards together and of her letting Betty win.

I listened, and I sensed the deep companionship that had developed through their years of living together, after the death of the mother's husband.

She calmly asked me, "Will you please stay and have dinner with me? I just finished making one of Betty's favorite dishes, ham and potato soup." How could I say no? I ate with her, and listened to more stories, until family members arrived. I again expressed my sympathy; she gave me a hug and walked me to the door. She thanked me for spending time with her. As she was about to close the door, she quietly said, "I'm really going to miss her."

I left there thinking how many genuinely good people there are in this world. Unfortunately, newspapers sell more when filled with bad news. Fortunately, I've seen much goodness in people, and often at the least expected times.

Many natural deaths followed that one. I was sent to Terre Hill for a dead, 72-year-old female. I found the house without any problem. It was a plain, red brick house that blended right in with the rest of the houses on the street, which sat tight against each other. I walked up the steps and was met by a very cordial group of people. They directed me to the dead body of Maria.

After completing my investigation, they asked if I would join them on their patio while we waited for the undertakers.

As we walked through the home, I couldn't help noticing how meticulous the entire home was. It seemed so out of character for the neighborhood. It was decorated to my liking. As we entered the patio area, I was again pleasantly shocked. The patio was totally secluded from the neighbors, and adorned with beautiful shrubbery and flowers. I commented on how lovely the home and patio were. The family said they had lived there for many years, and Maria had taken great pride in fostering a place of refuge from the outside world. She had achieved her goal. I sensed the entire family had contributed to achieving Maria's goal. They were a caring, sensitive family, and they were at peace with her death.

The undertakers arrived. I didn't want to leave. I wanted to stay in the refuge of their secluded and peaceful patio. I didn't want anymore drama in my life. "Can't I just stay here?" I thought. I knew I couldn't, and I knew the days ahead would bring more sadness, but it was refreshing to be in a tranquil setting with people that accepted death as a part of life.

I felt blessed to be able to share this brief time with them. It was humbling to be with them as they reminisced of fond memories. Driving home, every song on my radio was beautiful. Even the news was tolerable.

A few days later I was blessed again, not by my feelings, but by the family members of a deceased, elderly man. Amanda and I responded to the call. Again, it was in a meticulously decorated home. Catholic shrines were everywhere. We had to move Bibles and rosaries to find a place to put our purses and notebooks. Palm branches from Palm Sunday adorned each room. Candles were burning. As we explained our procedure to the family, they began saying, "Bless you." Their sincerity was touching, but by the time we left, I had lost count of the number of times we'd been blessed by them.

Amanda was now on her own. She called me early one morning to see if I would go with her to the scene of a fire fatality. The weather was frigidly cold, and it was sleeting. I put on my long johns and layers of clothing before she picked me up. I literally dragged myself to her car, and pulled myself, along with my layers of clothing, into her car.

We hadn't gotten too far when we realized that her windshield would not stop freezing. So every mile or so, she pulled over, and I squirted some anti-freeze liquid onto the windshield, and then she drove another mile. We were almost out of anti-freeze, and we still had quite a distance to go. We came upon a convenience store that was open. Amanda went in to buy more anti-freeze, and I said I'd wait outside and smoke a cigarette. That was a joke. It was too cold to even light a cigarette.

She bought a large bottle of anti-freeze, and we continued our routine of drive one mile, pull over, squirt; drive one mile, pull over, squirt; until we finally got near the burned building. We pulled into a flower shop parking lot. I looked at the flowers and thought how lovely the flowers looked, and how miserable I felt. Then I saw the lighted sign with the time and temperature, 9 degrees F. No wonder we were cold!

Sometimes you're so cold or so hot that you have to pull from resources you don't know you have until you need them.

Nine row homes were destroyed in the fire. The dead man was credited with possibly saving the lives of several people. I must admit that I sat in the car quite a bit of the time while Amanda was out doing her work. I was so cold I thought I'd never be warm again. Even when I returned to the comfort of my warm home, I thought I'd never be warm again or feel human again. But somehow you do.

Sometimes you never make it to the scene before you turn around, and go back to the comfort of your home. One evening a dispatcher called me, saying my services were needed in a neighboring municipality. I was only a mile or two from home when a police officer on scene phoned me, "I don't think you need to come out, this man had been diagnosed with terminal cancer. He was being treated at our local cancer center."

I pulled off to the side of the road; placed a call to the cancer center, and a doctor confirmed that the deceased had terminal cancer. He would sign the death certificate. I notified county that I was not needed on the call and returned home.

It had been a long, 24 hours, and I needed some sleep. Before dawn arrived, my phone rang, and I thought, "I just don't know if I can go on another call." But it was the cancer center calling. They had come into work and found a note saying, "Bernie won't be in for his scheduled treatment today; he died last evening."

The woman wanted to know if this was true. My first thought was to scream into the phone, "No, they just left that note to see your response!" But I pulled from an inner resource and said, "Yes, I'm sorry, he passed away last evening." The woman continued, "This can't be, he was doing so well. We liked him so much." What could I say? "I'm sorry." That's all I could say.

Until now, my coroner calls had all been for adults. They had all been calls I was able to leave and return to my normal world. Then came a call in Ephrata Township. It was for a 7-week-old baby. No, it couldn't be, not a 7-week-old baby, dead, in my backyard. I had the dispatcher call Dr. Jim Beittel, who was our pediatric deputy coroner, and have him call me. I gave him directions to the house. I knew exactly where it was. He said I should go to the home and he'd meet me there. It was an early, April morning.

As I pulled into the driveway, I wondered how I would handle this call. I told myself over and over, as I gathered my items, that it would be okay, "This, too, shall pass." It's a saying I recite during difficult times.

A relative answered the door, and I immediately sensed the devastation. I saw the dead baby boy in his infant seat. He seemed to be sleeping. He was so cute.

I asked where I could put my things. The family was very gracious, and told me I could use the entire kitchen table. I felt like screaming, "I don't need that much room!" I placed my items on the kitchen table and went to check for a pulse. There wasn't any. It was obvious he had been dead for several hours. I noted the time of death. Then I stumbled to the table where my book and forms were.

Now what? "Ok, I'll write down the time of death," I thought. Not like I'd forget it, but it gave me something to do while praying for Dr. Beittell to arrive. No sooner had I finished that, than I heard a knock on the door. Dr. Beittel was here. He looked at the infant and came over to me, "Have you pronounced the infant?" Yes. Just his entry into the home brought a sense of calmness and peace. I asked him what the procedure was. He explained that I would complete my report and he would do an additional report. Together we would examine the infant.

In his kind and gentle way, he explained to the family that we needed to undress the baby and examine him. He suggested they might want to go into another room while we were doing this. They immediately objected, "We only had such a small amount of time with him already; we want to be with him as much as possible."

Taking the baby out of the infant seat, undressing and examining him, as the family watched, was one of the most difficult things I had ever done. After we were certain there were no signs of trauma on the infant, I put his clothes back on him. Dressing a dead infant is emotionally draining beyond words.

Dr. Beittel went to his vehicle to get a pediatric body bag. I was expecting a traditional body bag, only smaller, but it was more like a black doctor's bag or a black suitcase. He opened the top of it, as I stood motionless. He quietly nudged me to pick up the infant and place him in the bag. Again I prayed not to drop the infant, as my entire body was shaking. I thought about all of the times I was proud of myself for not having noodle legs. Now my entire body was a giant noodle. I dug deep inside for strength that I sometimes doubt I've brought with me. I picked up the dead infant, and gently placed him in the bag.

We turned our attention to the mother. She said the infant had been colicky, and just didn't seem right the entire evening. She had tried everything to soothe him, but nothing worked. As the rest of the family slept, she remained in the main room, rocking him, trying to get him to sleep. The parents had decided they would call the doctor in the morning, if he wasn't any better. She said that at one point she slept, thinking he had finally fallen asleep. A few hours later she woke up and thought he was still sleeping, so she continued rocking him and she fell back asleep. When daybreak came, she went to put him in his infant seat and at that point noticed he was unresponsive. The child had died a natural death, a natural death at 7 weeks old. It just didn't seem right.

I remained calm and professional. I thanked Dr. Beittel for assisting me, and I began driving home. I turned the radio on. Every song annoyed me. I kept hearing the family's pleas to let them have him a little longer. Visions of re-dressing him kept going through my mind. The news on the radio annoyed me. But the silence was worse.

I pulled into my driveway, turned off my Jeep, and began crying. Feelings of guilt spread through me. Whom was I crying more for, the family and what they had just gone through, or me and what I had just gone through? I couldn't sit in my Jeep all day and drown in pity. I had to take a shower and go to work. I had to put on the happy face. You need to go on, like it's a normal day, knowing that for another family, things will never be normal again. Knowing that it will be quite some time before you feel normal again.

Dr. Beittel died suddenly on July 25, 2006, while he and his wife were visiting their son and family in California. On every pediatric call since then, my first thought was, "I wish Dr. Beittel was here."

He had served in the Air Force Reserve Medical Corps and returned to Lancaster to open a pediatric medical practice, where his daughter today continues the practice. He worked tirelessly for the safety and health of children. Dr. Beittel also had a life long love of music. His involvement with the Lancaster Opera Company spanned 30 years, where he performed and served on the board and as president. His last performance was as Kasper, in "Amahl and the Night Visitors," where his eldest son Paul, then age 14, was a soloist.

Amanda and I attended a "Celebration of Life of Dr. Beittel" at the Fulton Opera House, as did many of the other deputies. His children and grandchildren participated in the celebration. There was laughter and there were tears. It was the epitome of services, so deserving of the life he had led.

Several weeks later, Amanda called me. I could sense the urgency in her voice, "I've just been dispatched for a dead 2-month-old baby. Will you please go with me?" This was her first infant death. As I answered, "Yes, of course I will go with you," I was thinking, "Oh, how I wish Dr. Beittel was here."

We didn't have any trouble finding the residence. There were a lot of police cars in front of the home. We mustered our strength and exited her car. We were met by a police officer. He told us that the mother of the dead infant had just recently returned to work. A friend, who ran a day care center in her home, was caring for the baby. The sitter had gone to the playpen to get the baby ready, as his mother would soon be picking him up. The sitter realized that he was not breathing, and dialed 911. We were directed to the basement.

We walked past what I thought was a doll on a table. We got to the playpen and there was no baby in the playpen. An officer told us that we had walked by the infant. We backtracked and found the dead infant on the table.

There aren't words to describe the heartbreak that consumes you when you see a baby, lying dead, on a table. Two-month-old Bryan was pronounced dead by Amanda.

The officers told us the parents were outside and wanted to see their dead baby. After consulting with Dr. Kirchner, we agreed that the parents could see him, but they couldn't touch him. Grief and desperation might cause them to create bruises or trauma that were not there when he was found dead. The officers said they would bring the parents downstairs. I began having visions of them doing drastic measures to hold Bryan. I was nervous.

The parents were brought down and permitted to look at their dead son, lying on the table, still looking like a doll. To my surprise, neither of them attempted to hold the infant. But both became hysterical. Sobbing, screaming and hysteria began. The police officers were compassionate. They literally carried the parents up the steps and outside, where other family members had now gathered.

We carefully packaged the body for transport to the morgue. I went outside and spoke with the family. After expressing my sympathy, I told the relatives, "These parents are going to need your support." I sensed a great deal of support would be given by the family.

The following day, in Dr. Kirchner's blog, he wrote:

"The worst. A baby. By a combination of circumstances one of the female deputies received the call. She called another female deputy to go with her since it was her first baby death. We miss Jim B. (Beittel) so much. A baby death devastates the family, grandparents. Also, emotional trauma to the police officers investigating and our deputies. And all of the morgue crew, including me. No matter how long you have been doing it, the entire event is emotionally draining. A lot of kids and grandkids get an extra hug that they don't understand."

The infant's obituary included a picture. It read, "Bryan brought so much love into the hearts of all who knew him and will forever be lovingly missed by his family." When I read the obituary, I thought, "This sounds like someone who was 82 years old; this shouldn't be the obituary of a 2-month-old child."

Then you have natural, peaceful deaths. While these bring some immediate distress, they bring closure and peace. The family often knows the time is soon, as in a call to Columbia, for an 87-year-old female. Her family had seen her the prior evening. On this day, they had stopped again, to find her still in the same outfit she had been wearing the night before, and lying unresponsive on her bed. There were boxes of Christmas decorations scattered throughout the house, as if she planned to decorate for Christmas the next day. While the family was sad, they found peace and solace knowing that she hadn't suffered, and had died doing something she always loved, getting ready to decorate for Christmas.

Five days before Christmas, I was sent to Caernarvon Township for a homicide. The boyfriend of a 34-year-old woman was reportedly distraught that she had moved out, and taken their 9-year-old daughter with her. Every morning she would stop by his house on her way to drop off their daughter at the bus stop. On this day, the mother never left the home. It was two days before her 35th birthday.

He shot her in the back of the head with a Glock handgun. The daughter witnessed it, ran to the bus stop and screamed, "My daddy just shot my mommy, someone call 911!"

The investigation was lengthy and tedious. As the investigation proceeded we learned the father had been taken to jail. His one phone call from jail was to a police officer at the house. He wanted to exercise his "parental rights!" He wanted custody of his daughter. He wanted to decide where his daughter would spend the night. I sadly thought, "This is the same little girl who I just saw crying, because she's scared that Santa won't know where she's at, and he just killed her mother in front of her. Now he wants to exercise his parental rights? What about the rights of his daughter to live a normal life?"

Her Christmas and many days to follow would never be normal. I was disgusted. The whole picture was wrong. But I had no right to voice my opinion, so I remained silent. That was a very difficult thing to do.

We had established a command post in a home next to the incident. The owners of the home were kind and generous. We were supplied with as many Christmas cookies and milk as we wanted, and they left us use their bathroom, all while remaining quiet and respectful of the work we were doing.

Fourteen hours later I was sent to a residence close to my home. Companions had been watching television, and she decided to go to bed. Todd stayed up. When she woke in the morning, she noticed Todd was not in bed, and found him on the sofa they were sitting on the night before. Todd had strong, prescription pain pills for a back injury, and he had taken too many.

As I respectfully stood back, to allow them to spend a few moments with Todd's dead body, I looked around, trying to find something else to focus on. Although it was four days before Christmas, it wasn't the holiday decorations I noticed. It was all of the American pride symbols, and the beautifully decorated room they were in. This was a couple truly proud to be Americans. All of the flags, and "I Love The USA" decorations, were confined to this room. I wondered, "Was this 'his' room? If so, Todd died in his room of pride and joy."

Often people aren't lucky enough to be discovered so soon after their death. Fifty-year-old Bruce lived alone, had a few days off for Christmas, and hadn't returned to work on his scheduled day. His co-workers became concerned. One of them drove to his house. He noticed Bruce's truck was there, and the first door he tried was unlocked. The co-worker went inside, and searched until he found Bruce, dead on the toilet. Bruce was a big morbidly obese man. It appeared he sat on the toilet, and took his last dump and last breath.

We realized we were going to have some difficulty moving him from the bathroom onto the funeral home's litter. What we didn't realize, was that when we finally positioned ourselves, and mustered enough energy to lift him off of the toilet, the toilet would come along with him! It was another laugh or cry situation. But you always remain professional.

One year ended with a peaceful call. An elderly couple had completed taking down all of their holiday decorations. She stated she was tired and just not feeling herself, so she was going to slip into her pajamas and lie down on their bed. This was in the early afternoon. Her doting husband of many years, put the decorations in storage, prepared dinner, and went into the bedroom to see if she was up to eating. He found her dead. The husband was happy they had shared one last, wonderful holiday, with all of their family.

They had lived a good life, and he was thankful for their time together. He was grateful she hadn't suffered. As I assisted the undertakers in removal of her body, the husband asked me, "Is there anything I should be doing?" I said, "No, not at this time, but thank you for offering." He went to the table and began clearing away her dishes. There was a genuine sense of peace exuding from him. I wished I could bottle it and pass it along to the rest of the world.

It reminded me of how my grandmother handled the passing of my grandfather. They had gone to bed one evening and she woke before him in the morning. She got up and went about her usual, busy work. Later in the morning she looked in, and thought he was still sleeping. By noon, when he still wasn't awake, she became concerned. She called their family doctor, and he told her he'd stop by, as he was just leaving for lunch. When he arrived, he told my grandmother it appeared her husband had been dead for many hours, having died peacefully in his sleep. My grandmother never shed a tear, not that I saw anyway.

They were two people totally devoted to each other. They had a good life together. They believed that death is a natural part of life. It's a trait I don't believe many people have. I'm not certain I am that strong. But they don't look at it as being strong. To them, it's a stage of life, and acceptance of death goes with it.

Then there are calls that sadden me to my core. But along with feeling sad, I find myself guilt ridden with a tinge of anger. So many calls involve the abuse of drugs, both legal and illegal. How does a person get themselves in these situations, and why do they continue to abuse these substances?

I'll be the first to admit there were times in my life when I walked along the edge. I've never tried illegal drugs. I was too afraid of what would happen to me. I like to be in control. But give me a beer and a cigarette, and I'm happy. I know these are bad habits. I justify them by thinking, "We all need a vice." No, we don't. We choose our vices. I'm fortunate that the times in my life when I walked along the edge, I jumped off and landed on the good side. Too many people don't land on the good side.

Rick was a 31-year-old male, who was known to enjoy illegal drugs, and lived in a dumpy apartment. In the middle of January, police were contacted by Rick's landlord, and asked to stop by and have Rick turn down his television. The landlord had received complaints from neighbors that the television was blaring, day and night, for the past several weeks. The police arrived and heard the television blaring. They smelled an all too familiar smell, the smell of schmutz.

They knocked on the door, but no one answered. They opened the unlocked door to find Rick dead. The last mail that had been brought in was dated December 22. The first thing I thought was, "Here's a young guy who laid there dead for weeks.

Laid there dead, while we celebrated the Christmas holidays. No one came to see him. No one knew he was dead. No one cared about his life, other than his loud television."

Then I learned he had family that had disowned him. He had a family portrait, in a frame, with glass on the front. He had used the picture to lay out his drugs and paraphernalia on the glass. Looking at the family portrait, with the drugs on top of the glass, I was saddened. I thought, "Which priority was on top?" The one that killed him.

The smell Rick's body produced was unbearable. The police and I took turns going outside for a breath of fresh air while awaiting the funeral directors. During my first trip outside I smoked a cigarette, and counted my blessings that cigarettes were the worst things I ever smoked.

The funeral directors arrived, wearing their self-contained breathing apparatus and huge white suits that looked like space suits. They had booties over their shoes. They were not going to expose themselves to anything that may be in the apartment, or on Rick. I have never used Vicks or a mask on any call. I'm not saying that out of pride, I'm just stating a fact. There were a few times I felt I might vomit, but I never have. There are people who use Vicks, rubbed under their noses, to help mask the smell. It's a smell I can't describe. Imagine the smell of rotting meat and multiply it by one thousand. It's a smell you never forget.

At this stage of death, a body is extremely bloated. While this was a young, white male, he appeared to be a black man. He had been a thin person, but now was bloated to the size of a morbidly obese person, covered in blisters. This is when schmutz becomes scary. Schmutz is our non-medical term for the disgusting stuff that comes out of your body after you die, and begin to decompose.

You know that one touch to the body will cause it to pop, and schmutz will be squirted. To us, people at this stage are known as "poppers." On popper calls, I wear double gloves and my safety goggles. I tie my hair back. I tuck in everything I can. It's like boiling spaghetti sauce, you know if you're not careful, it's going to end up everywhere, including on you.

We cautiously began moving the body. The popping started. Schmutz squirted everywhere. Any jewelry the deceased was wearing pops off, and becomes a flying object. You duck and dodge as necessary. It's not a fun experience. The smell gets worse as the body pops. You think it can't get worse, but it does. Sometimes we'll stop and step outside to breathe some fresh air.

As we lifted the body from the bed, all of the materials on the bed came along. Rick had his feet still on the floor. It appeared he was heading to bed, and fell face down onto the bed. We lifted his feet and the carpet was literally torn from the floorboard, attached to his feet. The smell of urine and bowels, which are eliminated immediately following death, are not even noticed, they blend in with the smell of schmutz.

"Schmutz" has a very technical explanation. In living humans, our cells use enzymes to cleave molecules, breaking them down into things they can use. These cells keep our enzymes in balance, to prevent them from breaking down the cell's own walls. At death, the enzymes operate unchecked and begin eating through the cell structure, allowing inside fluids to leak out.

The liquid from the cells gets between the layers of skin and loosens them. As the process progresses, sheets of skin peel off of the body. This liquid makes its way through the body. As it does this, it comes in contact with the body's bacteria. The bacterium in our stomach breaks the proteins down into amino acids. When we die, they stop feeding on what we've eaten, and begin feeding on us.

Dead people lack workable stomach muscles, so gas builds up, and the stomach bloats. This bloating is also noticeable in other bacterial hot spots, such as the mouth and genitalia. The tongue protrudes. Bloating continues, until something gives, usually it's the intestines.

Flies lay their eggs on the body's open points, primarily on the eyes, mouth and genitalia. Maggots form. Maggots look like squirming grains of rice. Maggots eat the subcutaneous fat. They love fat. Maggots are gross. The skin is now bluish and transparent.

The body begins to decay, each stage having its own, unique odor.

A "light meal" will remain in the stomach for approximately two hours; a "medium meal" for about four hours, while a "large meal" will remain for up to six hours. All of these facts are vital when an autopsy is performed. None of them seem important when you are on scene with the odor.

Schmutz is nasty. When we are told, "she's pretty far along," they aren't referring to a pregnant lady. They are referring to the stage of death she is at. "Pretty far along" is not a user-friendly stage.

I think going to motor vehicle accidents can be just as nasty as schmutz calls. I was sent to Manor Township early one morning. I pulled up and saw a Jeep, sitting upright, slightly off to the side of the road. I noticed a huge, blue tarp covering the top of the Jeep. As I approached the vehicle, the police told me that they were not certain who had been driving. There were two male occupants; one was dead, and the other was at a local hospital. The surviving man claimed the dead man was driving. The dead man couldn't speak for himself.

I went to the Jeep and cautiously pulled back the tarp. There was no body there! I frantically asked, "Where's the dead man?" They forgot to tell me he was underneath the Jeep. He had been ejected and dragged several yards. I looked underneath the Jeep, and there he was.

He had multiple traumatic injuries; numerous broken bones; exposed body organs; some were scattered along the path the Jeep had taken before coming to a stop. There was so much blood and gore.

It was determined that the 45-year-old dead man was the passenger. The driver was charged, and found guilty of homicide by vehicle while driving under the influence, and failure to drive on the right side of the road. The driver was 26 years old. His blood-alcohol level was .273; our state's legal limit is .008. Our pathologist testified that the amount of alcohol the driver consumed before driving was enough to kill someone. It did.

One Valentine's Day it was sleeting and cold. I've always felt Valentine's Day is overrated. It is a day for card companies and flower shops to make money. I believe Valentine's Day puts too much pressure on relationships that are already strained. It's a nice day for children to give out little valentine cards, or for couples who have rock solid marriages to support the fine dining establishments. But the truth is, a lot of unhappy people hide behind postcard portraits.

This Valentine's Day proved to be deadly for a 24-year-old father and his four-month-old son. They were less than a quarter of a mile from home, when their car was struck by a van that crossed the centerline, and struck them head-on. The wife walked to the scene to see why all the sirens had seemed to stop near her home.

She learned her husband and baby had been killed.

The images of the card, "To Mommy On Our 1st Valentine's Day"; the infant items strewn everywhere; the faces on the firefighters, as they were told we're ready to begin extrication; the anguish and despair of the wife and mother; are images I'll never forget.

I walked past the group of firefighters, to take another look at their suggested means of extrications. One of the younger firefighters looked at me and said, "You couldn't pay me enough money to do your job." I had no reply. I kept walking, with my head down, to avoid the sleet, and having him see my tears swelling.

The extrications were difficult. The car had ended up in a field, off the side of the road. The ground was icy, but slushy.

Body limbs had been amputated upon impact. The fire chief asked me, "How are we going to do this, with these arms and legs amputated?" I calmly answered, "You carry duct tape, don't you?"

I left hours later, and took myself off duty. I was too emotionally and physically drained. I went home and did my reports. It's hard to put your emotions aside and concentrate. Three hours later it was time to shower and go to my full time job. So I put on the forced, happy face, and went to work. But I was crying inside.

Several days later both obituaries were in the paper. I read the father was a graduate of Millersville University, where he earned a Bachelor's of Science degree in Business Management. He enjoyed his work as an analyst. He enjoyed life and everything around him, especially his family. He was fascinated with white tigers. His deceased son loved the attention of people talking with him and holding him. He would giggle freely when others would tickle him. A few of his favorite things to do were spending time swinging, taking bubble baths, and lying on his father's chest. After reading the obituaries, I was crying on the outside.

People think a birthday is a time for celebration. Personally, I've always thought of my birthday as just another day, with another year added to your age. It's just a number. It's all a matter of attitude. My attitude is that I couldn't care less about the number of years that I've lived. It's about what I've done, or not done, during those years.

Perhaps some of my attitude is due to the fact that I have two brothers and no sisters. All three of us were born on May 30th. We're not triplets or twins. We were each born several years apart, but all on May 30th. Each birth was a natural delivery, and after the birth of my youngest brother, our newspaper published an article, with a picture of our mother, holding my brother, John, and the odds of this happening. It was astonishing.

But it also meant that on May 30, we had to celebrate all three birthdays. As a child, that didn't seem fair. I felt robbed of my birthday. But now, I look forward to getting together with my brothers on our birthday.

One year I was on call on May 30th. It had been a quiet day for me. Around 11:30 that evening, I was called to respond to Lancaster City. They had no additional information, which was unusual. I arrived to find a massive number of police. I was shown where to park, and directed to the rear of a pharmacy. One of my forms requires listing all drugs, prescription and non-prescription, that are found in the property. As I looked around the room, I thought, "There's not enough paper to write down all of these drugs!"

After pronouncing the man dead, I went back outside to collect information. I learned the deceased was the brother of the mayor of Lancaster City. The mayor had stopped by to discuss arrangements for an upcoming bike race, and found his brother dead in the back office of the pharmacy. As we were waiting for the undertakers, I noticed the mayor standing by a fence, which surrounded the rear of the property. It was a nice, wooden fence, low enough that you could see over it. I went over and expressed my sympathy to the mayor.

We began talking about the weather, the small talk you make when you don't know what else to say. There was a beautiful dog inside the fence, so during pauses of silence, I began talking to the dog. I mentioned that it was my birthday.

Suddenly the mayor said, "Really, it's her birthday today, too! May 31st!"

"No," I respectfully answered. "My birthday is May 30th." Then I realized that it was now May 31st. It was no longer my birthday, but it was the dog's birthday. I wished the dog a happy birthday and told the dog about my two brothers and I sharing our birthday, on May 30th. After I rambled a good ten minutes, the mayor turned towards me and said, "She's deaf, she's not heard a word you've said."

I stopped talking, and I left him express more of his grief. His brother had died of sudden, unexpected cardiac arrest. Driving home, I felt foolish for talking about my birthday. When you realize small talk is going nowhere, you stop talking, listen and observe. Sometimes words unspoken are best.

Some people think clothing is overrated. Personally, I like wearing clothing, unless I'm in the shower. I can't count the number of calls I've responded to where the deceased is stark naked. Most of them seem to be obese people. Is that because they get warm quicker than non-obese people? I haven't figured it out. I do know it is uncomfortable to walk into a room, filled with police officers, and a huge, dead body is lying naked on the floor. I try to fixate on pictures on the walls, books on the table, almost anything but the huge, naked body.

It was a hot and humid day in July. I was sent to a municipality in the opposite end of the county. Fortunately, Amanda was able to go with me. It was on the Lincoln Highway, which seems to go forever through our county. I kept slowing down, and Amanda kept saying, "No, you're not even close, keep going."

We finally saw police cars outside a tavern. I pulled in and parked. As we exited my Jeep, we met a man, who seemed to me to be the most handsome state police officer in Pennsylvania. He briefed me on the deceased.

Wally routinely went down to the tavern below the apartment he rented. Due to a change in staff at the tavern, no one noticed Wally had not been in for several days. A tenant of an adjoining apartment, smelled a foul odor in the building, and went to see if Wally would help him find the smell. After knocking on Wally's door, and Wally didn't answer, he opened the door and realized the smell was coming from Wally's apartment. He stepped inside the apartment and saw Wally lying dead on the sofa.

Wally's health had been declining over the past months. He had lost a significant amount of weight. He would never tell the bartenders what his health problems were, but they knew something was wrong with him. The owners of the tavern instructed the staff to give food in takeout containers, to Wally, telling him they were leftovers that would end up being thrown away. Wally took the containers to his apartment. I think Wally knew his days were numbered. But Wally accepted the food and took it with him, after having his two or three daily beers.

Wally had a stockpile of uneaten food. I wasn't certain which was causing the worst smell, the rotting food, dead Wally, or a combination of the two, with the extreme heat and humidity. One large container of untouched food was near Wally's head. It appeared he placed it on the sofa, laid down, and died.

I still picture the room, as if it happened yesterday. Wally was wearing a bright red, sleeveless tee shirt, and navy sweat pants with white stripes on the sides. He had a watch on his left arm that was too large for his arm. The empty cigarette boxes, the cigarette butts, the squalid conditions Wally lived in.

But what struck me the most were the boxes of untouched food. I believe in the theory, "Do a random act of kindness today." These people did this, day after day. They didn't have to do it. They chose to do it. If there were more people like them, the world would be a lot better place. I was fortunate to remain alive long enough to meet the owners before our departure. I expressed my sympathy and genuine gratitude to them for all they had done trying to help Wally.

When I say I was fortunate to remain alive to meet the owners of the tavern, I mean it literally. The apartments were on the second floor and had no air conditioning. I had all of my information, and I needed to contact Dr. Kirchner with my findings. I asked the handsome police officer three questions, "Where can I get something cold and non-alcoholic to drink? Where can I use a bathroom? Where can I go that's out of the sun to prepare the toe tag and death certificate?"

His answers came rapidly and to my delight, "Inside the tavern they have a cooler where they sell bottled water. They have a bathroom you may use. Out behind the tavern is a picnic table that's in the shade and you can use it as a desk." I went inside the tavern, purchased a bottle of water, and used the bathroom. I was surprised how nice it was. I thought, "If I'm ever down this way again, I'll stop in and see what it's like from a different viewpoint."

I went to find the picnic table. It was directly behind the tavern, and only several feet from railroad tracks. I neatly arranged my notes and water on the table. It seemed so peaceful. It was time to call Dr. Kirchner. I decided to stroll in the middle of the railroad tracks while speaking with him. I was kicking stones and relaxing. It was a refreshing relief from inside the apartment. Our conversation finished and I was returning to the picnic table. Suddenly, I was nearly swept away by what appeared to be a huge, fast moving train!

I ran to the front. "Oh, my goodness," I tried explaining, "I was just nearly killed by something that looked like a train!"

The handsome police officer looked at me like I was from another planet. "Yes, that was the Amtrak train that travels through here several times a day."

"Why aren't crossing signs or warnings there?" I frantically asked. He calmly explained that there aren't any crossings there. "But I was on the tracks, talking on my cell phone, I had no idea a real train goes along these tracks!"

"Oh, yes," he answered, "and it goes about 90 miles per hour!"

I thought I'd been sweating before, but now I was really sweating. Thank goodness Dr. Kirchner hadn't asked anymore questions, or they would have had another death to deal with.

Several weeks later I was sent to an area of railroad tracks near the Lancaster Stockyards. I hung up the phone and thought, "Oh, no, railroad tracks again!" It was dark and Amtrak workers had noticed a body lying in a ravine. To get to the body, I had to walk over railroad tracks. I begged a policeman, "Please walk with me across the tracks." He looked at me strangely, but granted my request without asking any questions.

There were no signs that the dead man had been struck by a train. His body was decomposed. The death was not suspicious and we suspected his cause of death was a drug overdose—possibly from a lethal heroin-fentanyl mixture. Over the past two weeks a heroin-fentanyl cocktail already had killed one person and caused over a dozen overdoses in Lancaster. Quiet Lancaster is not exempt from its share of abuses.

Deaths during the Christmas season seem more taxing on everyone involved. On a Saturday in December, I was called to respond for a male who was found dead. His friends told me John was to meet them at 10 a.m. to get a Christmas tree. When he didn't show up, and didn't answer his phone, they went to find out where he was. They found John lying dead in his bed. His death was unexpected, and everyone was devastated. Driving home Christmas songs played on every radio station. As much as I love Christmas songs, they can be saddening.

Twelve days before Christmas an elderly lady had been complaining to her husband of flu-like symptoms. He dutifully took her to the doctor, who gave her an anti-spasmodic medicine. They returned home and she took her medicine.

Later, she told her husband she wasn't feeling well again, and was going to the bathroom. Her husband said, "I'll make you something light to eat, maybe that will make you feel better."

When he was finished preparing the meal, she hadn't come out of the bathroom. He went to check on her, and found her slumped on the toilet, dead.

He commented to me, "I guess the doctor didn't give her the right medicine".

Everyone responds differently. "They," and I have yet to figure out who "they" are, say to never judge others' actions, because you don't know how you would react in any given situation.

January and its cold days and nights arrived. I was to respond for a man found dead following a fire in his home, which was less than two miles from my home. I received the call around 3:00 a.m. I knew it was extremely cold and sleeting outside. I knew I would be outside a lot. I took the information from the dispatcher and thought, "What should I wear? Is it a young person? Is it someone I know?" So many thoughts go through your head as you're writing down the information, and worse thoughts as you're driving to the scene.

I found the road and saw the firetrucks lined up along a steep driveway to the residence. I realized I'd have to park at the bottom of the sloping driveway, and walk up to the home. I cautiously slid to the house, which was a total loss. I was told that a neighbor spotted the house on fire, and it was fully engulfed when the firetrucks arrived. The neighbors told the firefighters that it was owned and occupied by a single male.

The man was found dead, in bed, as firefighters did an overhaul of the property. After the body was removed, a fire marshal and I began looking for any means of identification on the charred body. Suddenly he said, "Damn it!"

We thought we were almost finished with our investigation, when a handgun was found underneath one burned arm. This threw a twist into our investigation, and meant many more hours of investigating.

As I slid down the driveway, to do my reports in the warmth of my Jeep, a barrage of reporters with cameras approached me. Where did they come from? I realized tears were running from my eyes due to the cold weather. I wanted everyone to go away. They wanted to know everything and anything.

I told them, "I was called out to pronounce a person dead. It was a very taxing night for the firefighters. They are not only dealing with finding a dead body, but also the frigid weather. They had to drag fire hoses many yards, up the ice-covered lane, to access the house. You should be interviewing the firefighters, not me. They are volunteers, being out all night, and most have to go to work in the morning."

Then came one of my infamous calls. It was a call to Little Britain Township. It was dark and I thought I was doing well with my directions. I was confidently driving when I saw a huge sign, "Welcome to Maryland!"

I had driven too far. I turned around and found the house, which was at the county and state line. When I filled out my mileage form, I deducted the mile I had accidentally driven out of my way. My mileage still ended up being 110 miles. The call ended with the family doctor signing the death certificate, as the deceased had been diagnosed with terminal cancer. I hoped I wouldn't have any calls in Little Britain Township again.

Amanda was still training with me when I received a call for a crash on the Pennsylvania Turnpike. I was dreading going on the turnpike. Amanda and I went together to avoid the turnpike having to absorb the cost of two vehicles being on the turnpike without paying a toll.

We found a two-axle, empty, straight truck, which had been in the west bound passing lane, lost control, crossed over the right lane of traffic, and went down an embankment. The truck then struck a tree, spinning the vehicle 90 degrees. Then another large tree stopped it. Neither man was wearing a seat belt, and both were ejected from the truck. They had flown the surviving occupant to a nearby hospital and were uncertain which one was the driver.

I began gathering my information. I asked what make the truck was, as it was now just pieces strewn everywhere. One officer told me, "It's a "Mit." He realized I was clueless. "A Mitsubishi," he clarified. I have learned more about trucks and guns then I ever wanted to know. Who knew Mitsubishi made trucks? I didn't, but I do now.

We walked around the bottom of the embankment and helped gather the strewn items. We found a Bible. I found myself staring at the Bible, wondering what their last words were, where had they been, where were they going. I continued collecting personal items and pieces of the windshield, which contained hair, for the purpose of reconstructing the accident and determining which one was the driver.

We learned the dead man was a former pastor and director at a teen haven, was married, and had a son and daughter. He was an avid weight lifter and Pittsburgh Steelers fan. His wife stated he had a strict workout regimen he followed. He never smoked or drank. He used to say, "No pain, no gain." I doubted that he felt any pain that day.

It's not often I have to respond for a person in their late 80s, who is dead. One evening, our county dispatcher told me my services were needed at a funeral home in Lancaster. I asked her, "Are you certain you have called the right person? A coroner is being requested to a funeral home?" She said, "Yes, that is correct, and that's the same thing I thought when I took the call."

If I had to pick a "nice" coroner call, that would be the one. The owner of the funeral home, who had no past medical history, was found dead by an employee. The lady was seated at her desk, in the midst of signing checks, and had died. She died doing what she loved. Her and her late husband had established the business in 1945, in Conestoga, and later expanded to Lancaster. They were both licensed funeral directors and, at the time of her death, she was the supervisor of the Lancaster location. Her family and co-workers treated me like family. They were gracious, kind and caring. It was obvious they were like one, big family, and they treated everyone with the utmost respect.

They were all seated in the office, with the dead lady still in the desk chair. We remained in that room, and they offered me a chair as I was gathering my information. What could have been an awkward situation, being in a room with a dead lady sitting in the desk chair, was anything but awkward. It was comfortable. These people are trained to remove bodies, and later they removed her body with genuine respect, coupled with sadness. The police officer with me told me that this funeral home had handled the service for his late father. He showed me the style of casket that his late father was buried in. It was a calm and humbling experience.

My calls seemed to go from one extreme to the other. Garth, a 50-year-old father, had recently been released from a VA hospital, where he had been treated for alcohol dependence; cocaine abuse; marijuana abuse; bipolar disorder; post-traumatic stress disorder; GERD; and tobacco abuse. His treatment plan included sobriety and abstinence throughout his 12-step meetings; obtaining a sponsor, and attending weekly aftercare group programs.

His VA discharge paper stated, "Vet will get a home group. Vet will share at the meetings. Vet will offer any help at the meetings. Vet will develop healthy lifestyle habits. Vet will exercise. Vet will get a hobby. Vet will get a phone. Vet will get a job." That's a pretty tall order.

Garth went to live with his son. The son saw his father sitting on the sofa around 2:00 a.m. the previous night. The following afternoon he saw his father again, still sitting in the same position. The Vet did not follow the plan.

A week later another son found his mother dead. His 50-year-old mother was taken by ambulance, to a local hospital, for a drug overdose. She signed against medical advice and left. She returned home around 11:30 p.m., and went to sleep on the sofa. Her son, who was aware of her addiction problems, slept on a chair in the living room, to keep an eye on her. They both dozed off. In the morning he tried to wake her but she wouldn't wake up. His mother was dead.

As I was entering the home, one police officer said, "We have to leave, but watch out for the son. He had a tendency to act strangely. We've had a lot of dealings with him in the past." The police then rapidly left. I was scared.

I entered the home and saw a body, lying on the floor, covered by a sheet. I went to check for a pulse.

I pulled the sheet back and saw something strange on her eyes. I asked the son, "Do you know what is on her eyes?"

He calmly explained, "I placed a quarter on each eye to pay her debts, so she can enter through the gates of heaven."

Driving home I wondered if she didn't owe more. I wondered how much I would owe. Should I leave two quarters on my counter, so no one has to pay my debts?

Farming accidents are calls we all dread. They're usually so gruesome. I was sent to a call that was originally dispatched as a "farm rescue," but ended up being a farm fatality.

Another son had found his father dead. His 47-year-old father had been unloading large bales of hay from an upper storage area on a farm, where they both worked as hired laborers. The son left the barn around 2:00 p.m.

Several hours later the son returned. He went to the back of the barn and saw parts of his father protruding from bales of hay. He dialed 911, then began trying to remove the heavy bales of hay. The average hay bale weighed 600 to 700 pounds. His attempts were unsuccessful.

When I arrived, all of the family members and neighbors were gathered at the barn. His family spoke of his passion for farming; of 27 years of marriage; of his devotion to his family. What should I say, "I'm sorry for your loss?" I wished there were something more I could do or say to ease their pain.

Sometimes you don't have to say anything because there is no one to extend your sympathy to. It was a call in Lancaster City and I needed to climb three flights on the fire escape, and crawl through a broken window, to get to the dead female. It was in an apartment building. Local drug dealers were familiar with it.

This apartment was unoccupied. Inside was a 37-year-old female, lying dead on the floor, surrounded by drug paraphernalia. The owner was going to show the apartment to a prospective tenant, found her lying dead, on the floor; dialed 911, and left; with the door locking behind him. The only entrance was the fire escape, until the owner returned later with a key.

I stared at the dead female, her clothes and jewelry. She was wearing designer clothes and jewelry; brand names that I never even look at the price tags. I thought, "I probably don't want to know how she was able to dress like that."

That evening I was sent to Lancaster City for another woman wearing designer brand clothes. Grace had moved from New York to Lancaster, with her two young children, and their two dogs.

She was a 48-year-old recovering alcoholic, obsessed with her appearance. She had a companion, Jack, who told me Grace felt she was a social outcast in New York, so she packed her things and brought her children to Lancaster County, in hopes of being accepted by our county. Jack saw her sleeping in the living room when he went to bed about 10:00 p.m. Around 3 a.m. he noticed she had not come to bed, went downstairs, and found her dead.

I found numerous prescription bottles, all empty, near her body. Two large dogs, two crying children, and distraught Jack circled me continuously as I attempted to collect information.

My head was pounding. I phoned the children's father in New York. "Are you comfortable having your children stay with Jack until you get here?" I asked him, after expressing my sympathy. "Yes," he sobbed, "I'm leaving immediately, and find the closest funeral home to have her body removed." I phoned the closest one and asked how soon they could be there. They assured me they would be there within a few minutes. Those "few minutes" turned into 45 long minutes.

I drove home with my head still pounding. I told myself, "I shouldn't be having the headache. What about those innocent, little children, and how this will haunt them for years? What about the dogs? Will their father let them take the dogs along?" My headache finally subsided but my sadness remained.

"John Doe." Whoever came up with that name for the un-known? A male body was found dead, floating in a creek of shallow water. There was no identification on him. There was no vehicle belonging to him. No fishing rods—nothing. Just a dead body, floating in a small creek. The water temperature was 50 degrees F. The local fire department assisted us in removing his body from the creek. I wrote, "John Doe" on his toe tag.

I spent several hours at the scene and went home to do my reports. I usually don't turn television on until I'm ready to sit and watch a Lifetime movie, but that day, I turned it on when I got home.

To my surprise, the evening news aired their top story, "Man found dead in creek!" I watched as the news reported anything and everything. Interviews with the neighbors, who stated that the area is normally a calm neighborhood, but today it was chaotic. To anyone watching the news, it appeared this was a murder scene. We had determined there was no evidence of foul play, and the death of this 47-year-old man was tragic, but to be the top news story that evening perplexed me.

Then another call with schmutz, in Lancaster City, for a 31-year-old male who was trying to kick his drug habit. He hadn't been seen for several days, and again the "foul odor" led to the room of dead Leon. It was nasty.

Leon's schmutz had dripped through his bed, onto the floor, through the floorboard, and was leaking through the ceiling below his apartment. Letters and mail had been piling up outside his apartment door. I quickly went through hand-written letters and stopped when I saw, "Tina, I can no longer see you. I am infected with AIDS and have hep. and I don't want you to get these things, so I'm leaving you."

I decided to put on my heavy-duty boots, gloves, protective eyeglasses, everything I had to prevent Leon's schmutz from getting on me. None of it did, but driving home I couldn't stand the smell I had brought with me.

I put my windows down. The smell seemed to be consuming me. I just wanted to get home and make the smell go away. Even with the windows down, it wouldn't go away. I rushed into my house, stripped off my clothes, and threw them in my bathtub that I had filled with hydrogen peroxide and water. I left them soak overnight. After washing them the following day the odor was gone from my clothes, but it took days before it was gone from my nose and thoughts.

For a long time I was on call on Mondays. It seemed that people would die over the weekend, and weren't found until Monday morning. An 84-year-old woman had gone to get her hair done on a Saturday morning. When she was finished, she walked through the shop, and towards the back door. The employees thought she had left.

On Monday morning an employee arrived to open the shop, went down to the basement for supplies, and found the woman lying dead on the floor. It appeared she had made a mess in her underpants, and was embarrassed to use the business bathroom. So she went down to the basement to change into clean underwear, and died of sudden, cardiac arrest. I stood looking at her, and wondered, "Are you looking at us now? Are you embarrassed?" I hoped she wasn't.

I began thinking about how people always say, "Wear clean underwear in case you're in an accident."

If someone is killed or injured in an accident, trust me, we're not noticing if they're clean. One of the first things to happen when a person dies is the loss of bodily fluids, by the discharge of your bowels. So who would know anyway?

A call for a homicide is a "hurry up and wait" call. Police were sent to East Lampeter Township, after receiving a report of a hit-and-run crash in a cul-de-sac. After running the license of the abandoned vehicle, they went to the address, where it was registered to a 48-year-old female.

When they entered the apartment, they found the owner of the car, lying dead on the floor, with so much blood everywhere. Her boyfriend sat, emotionless, in the room splattered with blood, and filled with an odor of smoke.

He calmly explained what happened, "I was mad at her and just wanted her to die. I stabbed her over and over, but she wouldn't die. Then I beat her up, really badly. I stabbed her some more, and then I was sure she was dead." He continued, "I decided to burn down the apartment building so no one would know I had killed her. I turned on the oven, and poured olive oil on her body. I tried and tried to set her on fire, but it didn't work, so I took her car to drive away."

Police alleged he had hit her with a large vase and slammed her head against the floor, before stabbing her in the chest 11 times, with five different weapons, including two serrated steak knives, two straight-blade knives and a pair of scissors. It appeared she had struggled for her life before she died, with blood splatters found in the kitchen, master bedroom, and on the living room walls.

As he was pulling out of her parking spot, he crashed into an unoccupied car, and his dead girlfriend's car was too damaged for him to drive. He said, "Everything was going wrong, I couldn't do anything right, so I just came back to her apartment."

He seemed more consumed with all of the "gone wrongs" attached to his attempts, than the murder of his girlfriend.

A year later, he was convicted of first-degree murder, which carried a mandatory sentence of life in prison, without the possibility of parole.

Thirty-four-year-old Angel lived with another male, in a nice apartment, in a corner building in Lancaster City. Angel's roommate found him lying dead on his bed. His roommate contacted Angel's mother, who in turn contacted seemingly half of the residents of Lancaster City.

When I turned on to the street, I had trouble navigating through the crowds of people. I became agitated, begging people to move to the side so I could get to the apartment. It was a hot, humid day, and I wasn't in the mood to deal with the crowds or the comments about my coroner uniform.

The roommate was extremely distraught, as were all the people gathered outside the door, on the sidewalks, and in the street. One look at the crowd made you realize Angel knew a lot of people.

Inside the apartment, I could hear a woman screaming, "Angel, Angel, let me see my Angel." The police officer said, "That's Angel's mother, she wants to come in and see him." I told him it was his decision. He immediately said, "No way!"

The yelling got louder. A chaplain was brought to the scene. Additional officers were dispatched for crowd control. As all of this was happening, the roommate told us he should have known Angel had taken too many drugs. We tried to talk him out of his feelings of guilt, but it didn't work. The undertakers brought their litter inside, and we packaged Angel to be transported to the morgue.

The officer went outside to let them know we were bringing his body out, and he asked the other officers to restrain the crowd. He returned inside and said, "I've changed my mind. I'm going to let Angel's mother look at him through the front door, before we take him out."

I went outside to help keep others back from the door as she viewed him. I was standing directly behind her as she looked into the apartment, saw her dead son, and collapsed on the sidewalk.

I quickly changed hats and put on my EMT hat. I asked others to help place her in a flat position on the sidewalk, as I attempted to find a pulse and respirations. I couldn't find either. I yelled to an officer, "Get your AED," and I ripped open her blouse. I checked again for a pulse, this time finding a weak one, then a few seconds later it became stronger. An ambulance had been called for Angel's mother. By the time they arrived she was conscious.

The officers and I looked at each other, and read each others' minds, "Whew!"

After loading Angel into the hearse, I realized I was drenched in sweat, and I was thirsty. I noticed a soda machine on the corner. I told an officer, "I am going across the street to get a soda, do you guys want anything?" He answered, "No thanks. Oh, and the sodas are only a quarter."

I thought, "Wow, that's a bargain." I put my quarter in the machine, and out came a Diet Pepsi. So one thing was going right that afternoon. I opened the Pepsi and thought it seemed warm, but I chalked it off to me being so hot. As I drank the Pepsi and started to cool off, I realized the Pepsi actually was warm. I went back to the officer, "Hey, my soda is warm!" He gave me a priceless look as he replied, "Why do you think they're only a quarter?"

Reading Angel's obituary saddened me, "He was a caregiver at a local home. He attended Millersville University. Angel was active in his church. He enjoyed shopping, singing, and spending time with his family. He loved roller-skating. He was a fun-loving person with a contagious smile and will be sorely missed by all who knew him."

Unfortunately, I never got to see his contagious smile.

Anyone who believes that extreme stress can't kill you is fooling himself or herself. I went to a call for a 54-year-old male, who had been in perfect health. While speaking with his wife, I learned that he had received a phone call from police in another state, telling him that his son had been arrested for alleged child sexual predator charges. The father was in disbelief. He told his wife he was having some chest pains, and she begged to call an ambulance.

He insisted that if he lay down, and tried to relax, the physical pain would go away. He went to their bed and died of sudden, cardiac arrest.

I left their home, knowing that his son would be filled with guilt. Driving home I thought to myself, "How would I react upon receiving news like that?" To him, his son was the perfect son. Life was good. Then suddenly their lives are broken. There's no Super Glue to mend the shattered pieces.

Then there are "skeletal remains." Fortunately, we don't have a lot of those calls. I had one on a hot, humid day. Fifty-year-old Keith was found dead by a man who was on his way to go fishing in a nearby quarry, when he noticed items perched on a concrete wall. He went to see what the items were, and stumbled upon the remains of a body.

Keith had taken a bottle of Old Crow whiskey, a book, his fanny pack, and jacket to the top of a nine-foot wall. He folded his jacket, made a comfortable seat, and read his book, while drinking Old Crow.

I stared at all of the bones lying in the dirt, all of the bugs circling the skull, and thought, "This is really gross. I don't want to do this. This is so sad." But then I thought about Keith's last moments on earth. He had been sitting on the wall, drinking Old Crow, and reading a book, when he lost his balance and fell off the wall. There are worse ways to die.

I learned more about Keith. He never drove a car. He didn't have a job. A friend had seen him walking, wearing his fanny pack, along a heavily traveled road, about three weeks prior to the fisherman finding him. That was the last time anyone saw Keith alive. Again my heart ached in sadness. What happens to these people who just wander through life? His family said that he would routinely disappear, often for weeks at a time.

When I went to move Keith's body into the body bag, I moved him bone by bone. It didn't feel like I was moving a human body. It was surreal. His sneakers stayed in the same spot. I picked up the sneakers and placed them in the body bag. His clothing remained in the same spot. I placed his clothing into the body bag. The bugs were now attacking me.

Bugs were everywhere. The deeper I dug to get the bones out of the dirt, the more bones and bugs surfaced. Bugs were flying in my face and hair. I kept thinking, "This is nasty. This is wrong. I tied my hair back and I have goggles on! How are the bugs finding their way into my face and hair? Why am I here doing this?" As I drove home, the only comfort I could find was that at least I didn't take a nasty odor home with me that day.

I was now training another deputy coroner, Alexis. She rode with me to a call. During the drive, I reviewed with her our policies and procedures, "It is extremely important to remain professional at all times. No matter how gross or funny something is, you need to remain calm and collected. Laughing is not an option." The call was to a row home in downtown Lancaster.

We went inside and met a woman who calmly told us, "He's up in the bedroom on the third floor. You may go if you want, but I'm not going back up. It's too many steps for me to keep walking up."

It was a stifling, hot day. The house had no air conditioning, not even fans.

We climbed the steps to the third floor, where I pronounced Rick dead. He had died a natural death. It was so hot in his room that we could barely breath. We hurried back down. Rick's wife said she had not seen him for two, maybe, three days; she really wasn't certain. Looking at their home, it was apparent that these people lived day by day, never throwing anything away or cleaning.

They saw each other in passing through their home. That was their marriage and it worked for them. Rick slept on the third floor, and she slept on the second floor. She rarely went to the third floor.

That day, she realized she hadn't seen Rick in several days, so she ventured up to the third floor, and found him sleeping so soundly, she couldn't wake him. She couldn't wake him because he was dead.

She rambled on about her life, she was a Christian and Rick wasn't. I sensed some peace when she said, "Even though we had nothing in common anymore, we had a good life together." Then she turned to me, and asked, "So, do I just leave Rick up there on the bed?"

My immediate thought turned to a comment made when we were examining Rick. A police officer jokingly said, "Bet if we leave one of our latex gloves on this mattress, come back five years later, it will still be in the exact same spot!" I wasn't willing to bet.

My thoughts turned back to her question. My silent screams asked her, "What do you think you'll do with Rick? Just leave him up there, along with the other stuff?" It was all I could do to keep a straight face and explain, "No, men from a funeral home will be here soon and take Rick away. They will talk with you about what to do with Rick's body." I think she understood.

We left and headed to buy a cold soda. Now we could laugh and vent, "No, you don't just leave Rick up there with everything else!" But we also discussed the sadness, and wondered what would happen to her. The sadness in how so many people live, but we agreed that there is some comfort in knowing they don't realize how they live.

When my phone rings after midnight, it's a pretty certain bet that the call is for an automobile accident. So many violent crashes leave images that will stay in my mind forever. One of those sights was a single vehicle accident in East Earl Township. A 40-year-old male driver, and sole occupant of a vehicle, was speeding, lost control, crossed the centerline, drove through the front yard of a home, and crashed head on into a huge tree. He was ejected from the vehicle, and died on impact, from massive traumatic injuries.

I stood back and looked at the tire marks in the front yard. I looked at the house, which was dark. I wondered, "Were people inside the house and had they looked outside when they heard the crash? Had they seen his mangled, amputated, bloody body lying in the yard? Were they peeping out now from behind the curtains?"

I stared at the deceased, and the gray muscle shirt he was wearing, which was now shredded and saturated in blood. It was a hot, August night. I became consumed with his traumatic injuries, his severed limbs, his exposed organs, and I wondered what he looked like moments before the crash. I knew I had to fixate on something else.

I looked to my right. Beyond the farmland I could see a lighted cross. It must have been on top of a church. It was huge and beautiful. I took a few pictures of it, but the cross didn't show up on my pictures. But it was there. I saw it. It was the only comforting sight I saw that night.

I returned home, did my reports, and with the image of the lighted cross in my mind, I fell asleep. Then my phone rang. I was to respond to a local hospital for a five-month-old infant, who was pronounced dead on arrival at the hospital. I put on my uniform and headed to the hospital. Our new pediatric deputy was on vacation, so I was flying solo.

I had been told I was to examine the infant, interview the parents, and transport the infant to the morgue. That was a tall order. I called Nick, "Can you please, please help me?"

He agreed and he said he would meet me at the hospital. I arrived at the hospital and couldn't find a parking space. I was agitated. I finally saw an open space in a handicapped spot. Never did I think I'd park in a handicapped space, but that day I did.

I prayed for forgiveness as I pulled into the handicap parking space, and as I was doing so, I recalled the day I prayed for forgiveness for using a tombstone as my desk. I trust I was forgiven.

I was directed to one of the emergency rooms. The infant was lying naked, dead, on a table in the room, with an oral airway still in his tiny mouth.

I was told an ambulance crew had responded to the home for a call of an unconscious infant, arrived to realize the infant was dead, but immediately began CPR, and continued until they arrived at the hospital, where Jacob was pronounced dead. The family was devastated. His parents, and four siblings, were ready to head for their vacation that morning. I was examining the infant when Nick arrived.

Nick asked me, "Are you okay?"

I answered, "Yes, I think so, but we need something to transport the infant to the morgue." I told him there was a bin inside the entrance, which was there if someone wanted to drop off a newborn baby, with no questions asked. I think it's a good program, but that day it seemed ironic that the only thing I could find to transport the dead baby was a "drop off bin." Nick said he'd check it out, while the police officer and I remained in the room, as I completed my examination of Jacob.

Nick returned, telling us the secretary at the front entrance said, "The basket can't leave the hospital! What if someone wants to drop off a baby, and the basket isn't there?"

I wanted to scream, "Give us a break! What are the chances that someone will want to drop off an unwanted newborn within in the next hour?"

I tried to tell myself, she's just doing her job. I looked at the police officer and asked her if she could use her authority and get us the basket. It wasn't even really a basket; it was like the bins that newborns are put in. The little plastic containers where they put the cute pink or blue name tags on after delivery.

The officer left the room for a few minutes, came back and said, "Nick, go get the bin and bring it in here." She continued, "You have a maximum one hour use of the basket, it must be returned to the facility within one hour." I felt the receptionist would be watching the clock and waiting for the return of the basket.

Again I felt like screaming, "What if this was your grandson . . . wouldn't you want him removed in a professional manner?"

Nick brought the bin into the room. We wrapped the infant with several hospital blankets, and did everything we could to prevent anyone from realizing Nick was leaving the hospital with a dead baby, especially in the "drop off basket."

I accompanied him to his car. He asked me to open the front passenger door. I questioned him if that's where he wanted the bin to be placed. He said, "Yes," without any hesitancy. We put the bin on the front passenger seat, and he secured it with the seat belt. I thanked him, and begged him to drive carefully.

As he drove off with dead Jacob in his car, I started wondering, "What if you're transporting a dead person and you're involved in an accident?" I stopped myself from thinking about it.

Nick called me later to let me know that he had made it to the morgue without incident. I felt the urge to remind him that he needed to immediately return the bin to the hospital, but I refrained from doing so.

Too much time for my comfort had passed by the time I interviewed the parents. The police had already interrogated them several times before I would speak with them. When I walked in the room, it was obvious they were tired of waiting for me. I felt that I should apologize for my delay. But what would I say? "The receptionist wouldn't let us use the bin to transport Jacob to the morgue?" I had no words to explain the time that they spent waiting. I told them what I so often say, "I can't say I understand how you feel, because I don't. But I can say that I'm truly sorry for what you are going through."

The parents told me they had packed everything they needed for their vacation the night before. They had packed Jacob's blanket, so they left Jacob sleep with them. The got up early that morning, with everyone excited to leave for the shore. After the other children were dressed and ready to go, they went in to get Jacob, and found him unresponsive. His mother dialed 911, and through the guidance of a 911 operator, his mother did CPR on the infant until the medics arrived.

I had to ask the routine questions. I dreaded asking the routine questions, because they were not routine questions for these parents. "How many pregnancies have you had, including abortions, stillborns, and living? Have any of your children died after birth? Is there any family history of medical problems? Did the infant display any signs of distress in the days prior to this morning?"

It's like delving into a person's personal and private life, but these are facts that are required to be documented. I finished my required questioning, and the mother asked, "May we go back and see Jacob?" I tactfully told her that his body had been removed and taken to the morgue, where an autopsy would be done to determine the cause of death. I had explained the entire procedure earlier, but I'm certain it didn't sink in.

I still wanted to scream at the receptionist for making a huge production of borrowing the bin for an hour. I asked myself, "Why people can't be a little more compassionate? Why can't they be a little more caring?" The bin was returned within an hour. No babies were dropped off during the time the bin was gone.

I again expressed my sympathy and told them, "I am so sorry for your loss and your having to wait for me to speak with you."

As I was leaving the room, the mother called me back, and asked, "Do you think he suffered?" All I could tell her, at that point, was my gut instinct, "No, I don't think he suffered. I think he died in his sleep." I sensed some comfort in his parents. It was something they had wondered for the past several hours, but hadn't felt comfortable asking. I felt humbled to be asked that question, and a great relief to learn that Jacob had died from SIDS (Sudden Infant Death Syndrome). He had not suffered.

Coroner calls for children are devastating. One summer produced a rash of farm-related child deaths. There were three deaths in seven days. These deaths were taxing on all of those responding, and certainly more so on the families involved.

A 1-year-old boy was killed when a minivan backed over him.

A 16-month-old girl drowned in a water bucket used by animals on their family farm. She wandered into the barn, and fell face down into a 5-gallon bucket of water, which was only three inches deep.

A 2-year-old girl was hit by a pickup truck that was entering their farm, and the driver didn't see her playing in the driveway. All of the deaths were ruled accidental.

Then the "Letters to the Editor" started. Most of them said the same thing, "I'm writing in response to the articles regarding the Amish children recently killed in farm accidents. Excuse me, but while these are obviously accident, they certainly could have been prevented. Why are diaper-wearing children playing in driveways or around water without adults watching them? We're not talking about 4- or 5-year-olds, but toddlers. Children are needlessly getting injured and killed all the time. While accidents unfortunately happen, ignoring small children is just asking for it. Now that is for sure."

The police held to their decision, knowing the details of the three tragic accidents, they believed they were not preventable, nor was anybody culpable. I never could decide my personal opinion on these three incidents, although one thing was certain, they were all sad and devastating to everyone involved.

Amanda had a call to an Amish farm involving a dead 8-year-old boy. She called me and said, "All I know is that it was a farming accident, a child is dead, and some sort of equipment caused the accident. Can you go with me?"

It was one of the most devastating scenes I have ever witnessed.

The father told us that he had returned to their family farm that afternoon, after paying respects to the widow of a neighbor. He ate dinner with his family, went to the barnyard area, where he pulled a tractor from the shed, to power a grain grinder/mixer. Two of his sons were present. He started the tractor. He became aware that a window was broken out of the device, and it needed repaired before it could operate successfully.

He began the repair, which required him to grid a new sheet of glass for the rubber frame. When nearly completed, a portion of the glass slipped in too far, and he asked his 8-year-old son, Daniel, to enter the device to apply counter pressure from inside. They had done this type of repair in the past, but never when the tractor was idling.

The father descended from the ladder, after finishing the repair, put the hydraulics in gear, opened the side of the grain bin, and put the auger for the grinder/mixer in gear. The grain began to enter the silo from the top, a little more rapidly than it usually does, necessitating the addition of liquid to the mix.

He climbed the ladder to add liquid from the top, saw the top of the container open, which it would not usually be, looked in, and saw Daniel's straw hat floating on top of the grain. He had an "instant revelation" that he had forgotten Daniel was in the mixer. He scampered down the ladder, hurriedly shut off the motor, climbed back up the ladder, looked into the chamber, and saw Daniel's foot sticking out of the grain. He knew Daniel was dead.

Daniel had a twin brother, David. In addition to his parents, six sisters and three brothers survived him. David was the only family member to approach us and ask to see his brother. "But we're twins," David quietly moaned. We had to say no. It was one of the most gruesome tasks I've ever had to do, removing Daniel's body from the mixer, and trying to piecemeal him, anatomically correct, in a body bag. There was no way we were going to let his twin brother see the body at that point. I've read a twin suffers pain the same as their twin suffers. I believe that.

A few days later I was sent to a beautiful home, for the death of a 34-year-old male. Ray had spent the night sleeping on the sofa in the downstairs of their bi-level home, while his wife, Rose, slept upstairs, with their three-month-old triplets. She went to wake Ray in the morning, and found him dead. I went into the kitchen to discuss the autopsy and funeral arrangements with Rose, and to ask if she had any questions.

The kitchen was immaculate, but looked like a factory production line of baby bottles, formula, and bibs. Baby things were everywhere. Relatives had arrived and were helping care for the babies. I asked her if we could go and sit down somewhere, without the distraction of the babies.

We went into the living room and discussed the details. Occasionally an adult, holding a baby, would pop in the room, with a question regarding care of one of the babies. Rose told me her husband was the chef at the Cove Restaurant. She told me of Ray's love of cooking, swimming, working on cars, and the Philadelphia Flyers. After we finished our conversation, I asked if I could see the baby room.

Rose took me into the room. Two of the babies were calm and quiet. The other one was crying. I wondered, "Was he crying because he knew what had happened? No, he was only three months old."

Some of the adults were calm and quiet, others were crying. Were they crying because they knew what had happened? Yes. The Bible teaches that we're never given more than we can handle. As I looked at the widow, the babies, and their support group, I knew they would somehow be able to handle what had been thrust in their already full laps.

Chapter 7

Successful and Unsuccessful Suicides

On ambulance calls we typically see the unsuccessful attempted suicides. On coroner calls I see the successful attempted suicide calls. They are all sad. The range of ages is beyond my comprehension.

By far more successful suicides are seen in the male species, than the female species. I've often wondered why that is. Are we stronger? Or are we weaker? Do females realize when we have a problem that is beyond our means of dealing with, and seek help?

Sometimes I find myself thinking, "What if someone jumps off of a tall building to commit suicide, and they change their mind after they have jumped. Do they have enough time to really think that much of a thought?" Then I stop myself from thinking about it anymore.

No matter what, suicides are some of the most devastating calls I respond to. The family always asks, "WHY?" The family is left guilt ridden. Could they have done more?

Then I begin wondering if the deceased is watching from either up or down, and seeing the anguish they have left behind. Then I stop thinking about that, too.

I had a coroner call on a beautiful day in October, to an area hidden underneath a railroad overpass, and covered by overgrown brush. The police told me that this area was frequently used by drug dealers, and kids skipping school. The police routinely patrolled the path, to search for kids who had skipped school.

On this day they came across the dead body of a 20-year-old man who they were familiar with. The word on the street was that he was planning on buying enough drugs to kill himself. He succeeded. He left a note in his pocket, telling his family he was sorry for everything he had done, and begging them to not cut off the long braid in his hair. He was twenty years old, isn't that way too young to be sorry for what you've done with your life? Isn't there still enough time to still do something positive with your life?

That same day I was sent to a field not too far from my home. I never knew that this field was there. Another 20-year-old male was found dead. This man was in his truck. A receipt was found in his pocket, from a purchase he had made at a local store the night before. The receipt was for bullets for the 22-gauge rifle he had used, and a pack of cigarettes. Some things, for some reason, you just never forget. I can't tell you what clothes he was wearing, but I vividly remember the country CD that was playing in his truck.

Guns seem to be the most popular method used in successful suicides. When I do allow my mind to think about this, I wonder why that is. I think I'd be afraid I wouldn't do the job correctly, and I'd end up in a nursing home for life, or in the mental ward in a hospital. Then I stop myself from thinking anymore about it.

Fifty-four-year-old Richard was being treated for depression, and lived with his girlfriend. He told her he was going out back to smoke a cigarette. She heard a loud bang, and thought a car had hit her home. She ran outside, intending to find a car into the house, but instead found Richard, lying dead on the porch. He had used a Remington 308 Winchester rifle to shoot himself in the head. I don't know one gun from another, but I do know this rifle did the job. I can't begin to describe the volume of blood that one shot created. There was a huge puddle directly under him, as well as a lot of splattering all around his body. As usual, the police warned me not to touch the gun; it could still be "alive."

Then I went inside, to deal with the distraught family. Richard had been going to counseling for his depression. But they don't give out manuals to family and friends on, "How to react following the suicide by a loved one." There is no right or wrong way to react.

Richard's girlfriend immediately began taking steps to remove everything connected with her now dead boyfriend. A contractor was called to come out and remove the blood soaked concrete patio. She called a towing company to come out and tow his truck away. She began packing up all of his belongings. As long as the police were okay with this, so was I. She scurried around the beautiful, immaculate home. I expressed my sympathy to her, as she was throwing away his carton of cigarettes. Her family arrived. As soon as the body was removed, I again expressed my sympathy to everyone, and I quickly left.

I was heading back home when I received a call for another suicide, in an area I was very familiar with. But I only saw the street sign where I wanted to turn, just as I drove past it. I still made fairly good time getting to the scene. I saw the ambulance and medic units that I am very familiar with, parked in the driveway. As I was getting out of my Jeep, one medic that I know personally walked towards me. I immediately apologized for the delay in my arrival, and explained that I had just left the scene of another call. Then I asked him, "What do I have? The dispatcher didn't give me any details."

My heart sank when the medic responded, "My father-in-law is dead." What do you say? I'm sorry? That just isn't enough, but I couldn't find words to express my sympathy.

He told me that his mother-in-law had been shopping, returned home, and was unable to locate her husband. She phoned their daughter to come over to help find him. The daughter decided to check in the garage, and found her father unresponsive. She immediately dialed 911, and did CPR until the medics arrived. She knew her husband was on the medic truck that day, and that he would be responding. Her husband recognized the address, and feared the worst. It was the worst.

There are no words to express the sadness that overwhelmed me as I pronounced him dead. There are no words to express the sadness I experienced as I watched his body being put on the funeral home's litter. I chose not to help them on this call. While the deceased had some personal issues, no one expected this. My hands shook as I rapidly completed the death certificate. My hands shook as I put the toe tag on him. No family should have to go through this. It just was wrong.

I asked the other medic if arrangements had been made for the son-in-law to be relieved from running calls. Yes, they had taken care of that. I finished my work, expressed my sympathy again, and left the scene. I think another piece of my heart was left behind as I drove away.

I kept running the scenario in my head. Daughter finds father. Daughter dials 911, knowing her husband is going to respond. Daughter performs CPR, until the medics arrived. Her father, and his father-in-law, was dead. Her mother just lost her husband. I asked myself, "Why?" Why does this caring, loving family have to suffer through this? But I've learned too many times that there often is no answer to "why?" Some things are just not meant for us to know, or understand, "why." The next day I went to purchase a sympathy card. Each card I read seemed inappropriate. Every card I read brought tears to my eyes. I couldn't find a card that expressed the depth of sadness in my soul. I finally just settled on one, and mailed it.

About a month later, I saw the medic while I was on an ambulance call. He immediately thanked me for the card. I was shocked that he remembered I had sent a card. Again, I said I'm so very sorry for their loss. What else is there to say? These are "good people," and to see them suffer as they did was beyond any words I could offer.

It was a late evening in November. I was on a coroner call for a motor vehicle accident. A young, male driver of a Jeep had lost control of his vehicle, overcompensated, and the Jeep flipped on its side, ejecting the driver. He was dragged by the Jeep, which then ran into a bridge embankment, known as, "Smithville Tunnel." I had never heard of the Smithville Tunnel, but it wasn't the last time I drove through the Smithville Tunnel. Each time I thought about that call.

I remembered how we were unable to immediately determine the driver. The car registration differed from his license. We found two names everywhere, but couldn't determine which one was his. We unofficially decided he was the "Anthony." He didn't look like a "Howard." He looked like a "Tony." Soon after making our unofficial guesses, the police informed us they had contacted his family. He was Howard.

I read about Howard in his obituary. He resided with his parents, sister, and two dogs, Brutis and Bella. He worked hard in the home building field. He enjoyed river rafting, playing poker and having fun with his many friends and family.

A year later his family placed a memorial in our local paper. It included Howard's date of birth, date of death, a picture of him smiling. He was a good-looking kid.

They also had written a sentiment, "Today is a year since you left us, the Lord said it was time to go. Our hearts were filled with sadness. Howie, we miss you so. I know there comes a time in life when we must say good-bye. We love you and miss you and we'll always remember why. With Love."

As I read that memorial, one year later, I was instantly, in my mind, back at the scene. I remembered Howard's yellow tee shirt and jeans. I remembered the massive trauma "Howie" had experienced. Knowing Howie died instantly brought some relief, but knowing the family will continue to suffer brought heartache.

The firefighters had set up lighting, and as we waited for the undertakers to arrive, the guys were listening to the Pittsburgh Steelers game on their radios. Being a Steelers fan, I would occasionally pop my head in their truck, and get an update on the score. It was now after 11:00 p.m. During one of my dreaded score checks, one guy said to me, "You better get ready, you're going to get another call."

I asked him if he was joking about the game. He said his wife just called him, and our local news reported a double homicide in Lancaster City. I closed the door after hearing double grim news, my Steelers had lost, and I was probably going to be headed to another call.

I finally called county to inform them that I was leaving the scene of the accident, and I asked if they had any calls pending for me. I was put on hold. The dispatcher returned to tell me, "Your services are not needed at this time." Okay, what does that mean? So I headed back to the warmth of my home. I stepped inside the door and took my boots off. It's always nice to come home, especially when it's cold outside. I began changing my clothes, and thinking about what I could eat, while doing my reports. My cell phone rang. My services were needed in Lancaster City! I had just driven through Lancaster City!

If I had known I was going to be sent back to Lancaster City, I would have stopped somewhere, gotten something warm to eat, used a bathroom, and warmed up a little.

I headed back to Lancaster City. A 30-year-old man had been distraught over his girlfriend leaving him, taking their 7-

and 5-year-old children with her, as she fled Puerto Rico, and moved to Lancaster.

Two days before he attacked her, he was released from police custody after being arrested for violating a protection from abuse order. He was released on $1,000.00 unsecured bail.

For the next two days, he followed her, and stalked her until that evening, when he saw her drive away from her current residence, without their children. He forced her car off the side of the road, went up to her window, and shot her. She was smart enough to slump over the steering wheel, and played dead.

Convinced she was dead, he walked back towards his vehicle, and turned the gun on himself. He had used a .357-caliber pistol. I was beginning to learn pistols and revolvers from rifles. One shot to his head killed him. She then drove herself to the nearest hospital, and was treated for a non life-threatening gunshot wound. I wondered how I would have reacted. I gave her a lot of credit for probably saving her own life, and being able to remain a living mother to their children.

Some suicides are extremely well planned and successful. A 44-year-old male took a long rope, wrapped it around a second floor porch post, and knotted it several times. Then he threw the rope over the outside porch, went down through his house, took a chair outside, and stood on the chair, with the rope. After wrapping the rope around his neck and knotting it, he kicked the chair out from underneath him. This happened sometime during the night.

When he did not report to work the following morning a co-worker went to his home and saw his truck still in the driveway. The co-worker flagged down a police officer to assist him in looking for the man. They entered through the rear alley, and saw the deceased dangling from the rope, hanging in the air. It was obvious he was dead. When I arrived, he was still in the exact same spot. It's a sight I'll never forget. He was wearing a hooded sweatshirt, and had put the hood up before he wrapped the rope around his neck. He was wearing sweat pants and shoes. All you could see was a little bit of his face, peeking out through the front opening of the sweatshirt hood. It was an eerie sight.

His co-worker stated he had been depressed recently over a sour relationship with his girlfriend, but they never thought the depression was that bad. Sometimes the signs just are not there. Sometimes the signs are there, and family and friends can only do so much to help.

Those who are left to find the suicide victims, become victims themselves. They are guilt ridden, angry and sad. It's something they should not have to experience. Most times there is nothing more they could have done. Try telling that to someone who just finds a friend or loved one dead from a successful suicide. Understandably, it's difficult, and most times it takes a long time for them to accept that fact.

A man was casually driving on a back road, admiring the beautiful, open farmland. Suddenly, he sees what appears to be a body, lying in a field. After dialing 911, he gets out of his car to check it out. He finds 70-year-old Charles, lying dead from a gunshot wound to his head. The driver was devastated.

We learned Charles lived nearby, with a companion. That morning he told her he was going for a walk. She didn't know he had taken his Charter Arms revolver with him. She never knew he owned any guns. For a reason unknown to everyone who knew Charles, he walked into the field and killed himself.

Most of the suicide calls I have been on are men. One beautiful spring day I was sent to the scene of a successful female suicide. A 75-year-old lady who lived alone had given a house key to a neighbor in the event there was ever an emergency. When the neighbor noticed the papers were starting to pile up outside, and Barbara didn't answer the door, she used the key to enter the home. She found Barbara seated on her bedroom floor, unresponsive, and she dialed 911.

We found numerous, empty bottles of prescription medicines, along with a nearly empty glass of water, next to her body. We found a note she had written, stating that her family would be better off without her.

What really shocked me was what we found in a wastebasket, near her dead body. Many rough drafts, torn up, of her suicide note. Each note was worded slightly different, but all said basically the same thing. I began to wonder, "How long did she spend writing these notes? Why would she put so much time into writing her suicide note? Did she think no one would ever find the notes that she obviously wasn't satisfied with?" Some things you just can't figure out.

Ironically, the following week, I had a call for another successful suicide of a 66-year-old female. She was reportedly depressed over the death of her husband, which happened three years ago. The family knew she was lonely and depressed, but they never had a clue that her depression was that bad. She spoke with her son on the phone the evening before I was called to her residence. Her son felt the depression vibrating throughout their conversation, but again, he had no clue of the depth of it. The next day he stopped by to chat with her, hoping in some way to help her erase her depression. When she didn't answer the door, he used his key, and entered the home. He found her dead body, lying next to the H&R .22 caliber she had chosen to end her life.

She had left a note that said she was very sorry for being a bad mother. Once again, my brain rattled inside my head. How can you be such a bad mother at the age of 66, that you chose to end your life? Is she able to see the grief and despair in her son's eyes? I read her obituary, which stated that she was a lifelong member of St. Joseph Catholic Church. Don't Catholics believe that committing suicide is a sin? I don't know.

Then I read that she was an avid bingo player. Perhaps if she would have gone and played bingo that evening, she'd still be alive. Perhaps if someone would have called her to go play bingo, she would have heard the sound of her yelling, "Bingo!" rather than the sound of the revolver, if you even hear the revolver fire.

Some things you just can't figure out. One month later I was sent for another successful female suicide, just as I had convinced myself it was a fluke that I had several female suicides in a short period of time.

Forty-three-year-old Cindy was depressed over her husband moving out of their home. Her mother was concerned over her depression, and would check on Cindy quite frequently. It was Sunday night of a Memorial Day weekend. Mother and daughter had chatted on the phone. Cindy told her mother she might go out for a little that evening. Her mother was encouraged by that statement, hoping her daughter's depression was subsiding. Later that evening, Cindy's mother began trying to reach her by telephone. After numerous unsuccessful attempts and the clock approaching midnight, the mother called her son to go over and check on his sister. He had a key to the house and he found the house locked, but his sister didn't answer the door.

After unlocking the door, and searching the house, unable to find her, he noticed a strange odor coming from the garage. He opened the inside door leading to the garage, and saw his sister humped over the steering wheel of her car. The car their father had just bought for her on Friday, after her husband had taken their only car when he moved out. He immediately opened the car door, garage door and windows, for ventilation, and dialed 911.

The police, ambulance and firefighters arrived, but it was too late. As I looked at her, I thought about my own habits when I am getting out of my Jeep. She looked exactly like I pictured I look, as I am about to get out of my vehicle.

Her car was turned off. Her seatbelt was undone, although still slightly hanging over her left shoulder. The car keys were in her left hand, and her purse strap was in her right hand.

My personal opinion was that she ingested the pills from the empty prescription bottles, found on the front seat of the car, left the car running, with all intentions of committing suicide, and then changed her mind. But if she had changed her mind, why hadn't she done so earlier? Another successful suicide, which possibly could have ended as an unsuccessful suicide, but didn't.

There was one successful suicide that I'll never forget. Not like I'll forget any of the others, but this one was so sad. There aren't adequate words to describe the many emotions that went through my mind that day, and many days to follow.

Sometimes I think I sort of understand the suicides that are committed on the spur of the moment. But the planned ones never cease to make me wonder why they didn't see the pain and sorrow they would leave behind. I guess when you've reached that point of crossing the line, you just don't look back or ahead.

I had started training Nick as a deputy coroner.

At first, I had doubts about Nick making it as a deputy coroner. The first call he arrived at to shadow me, he was wearing shorts and flip-flops. This is not acceptable. I told him to start carrying a change of clothes in his vehicle.

The following call, which was about 12 hours later, he again arrived wearing shorts. While it was extremely hot and humid, shorts are just not acceptable. One of the police officers asked me, "Would your trainee be arriving in shorts and 'clogs'?"

I moaned, "Yes, that would be him." After the call I reviewed again, with Nick, the reasoning for not wearing shorts. Foremost, it is disrespectful, and secondly, you can go from one call in a nice home, to another call at a crash, where you're down on your hands and knees, examining a body that is lying in blood.

Following that call, Nick always arrived dressed appropriately. Nick passed all of my tests to determine if he would make it. Trust me, my drillings are hard. If I say someone is ready to go solo, they have to be capable. Nick has become a valued friend, in addition to a competent deputy coroner. Although I still need to tease him about needing to use the Vicks when going on a call that involves schmutz. But I am forever indebted to him for his constant, unwavering, friendship and support.

So Nick arrived in his shorts and clogs. By this time I have seen, and pronounced, a 49-year-old male, dead from a hanging. His daughter had gone to his home, which was a beautiful home in a secluded area, to visit with her father. Her father was nowhere to be found.

When she entered his bedroom, she saw a note, which read, "Mike, seems like everything is screwed up around here, and to top it off, today I noticed the water heater is leaking! If everything goes as planned, you will have to sell the house to pay the bills. Give whatever is left to June and Robert. Let them get what they want first, if anything, and you, too! No viewing, no funeral, no embalming! I want to be cremated. Spread my ashes up at Young's farm, where we had the cabin, if you can. No one else needs to know. I trust you Mike, June, Robert and Mom. Nobody else. Tell George Brown that the judges for the fair need to be called. That's about all."

Her father had signed the note, and had written the date and time on it.

She frantically searched for him, and found him hanging from the rafter, in a detached garage. He had used rope from a bobsled in the storage area above the garage. He had knotted it several times, from the bobsled, to the rafter and then around his neck. Then he jumped from the second floor of the garage.

His family was devastated. It was emotionally draining to try consoling the family.

I couldn't help looking around, and noticing all of the nice items that were there. I thought, "Why not just sell everything and move into an apartment, if you couldn't afford to maintain this huge property? What if the hot water heater had not been leaking, would you still be alive?" I wished I could have chatted with this man the day before.

Nick and I gathered the information needed for my report, and then we each went our separate ways. Driving home, I kept thinking about how many times in life we all get to that line. I tend to call it a fence. I feel that most of us sit on the fence, at least once in our lifetime. It's just a matter of which side of the fence we fall off. He fell off the wrong side.

Two days later, I read his obituary in the paper. There was a service planned! There would be a viewing! I reeled as I read the obituary, and remembered all that he had written in his final note.

The successful suicides continued. One call was for a 43-year-old male, who died from a single gunshot wound to his head. It was the year 2006. I was dispatched to a cemetery. Yes, to a cemetery. I was directed to a tombstone, where the deceased was lying, face down, in front of a tombstone. His weapon of choice was a Colt Cobra 38 special handgun.

The police informed me he had never gotten over the death of his mother, whose tombstone was at the head of the deceased. Expecting the year of her death to be recent, I looked at the tombstone, and saw she had passed away in the early 1990s. So many things just don't make sense.

How can one still be so distraught, after so many years, that you shoot yourself, in the head, at your mother's gravesite? I happen to know the man, which made it even more difficult. Who knew he had such deep-seated problems? Who knew he was on the fence?

His head landed within inches of his mother's tombstone. I looked at the position of his body, and I wondered if he had measured, and calculated, exactly where his head would land, after he shot himself.

I prayed for forgiveness, before placing my book and purse on another tombstone. I needed something to use as a desk, and that was the only thing I could find.

Then, I turned from staring at his body, to fixate on another object. I stared at the tombstone. There were two dates, a birth and a death, on her tombstone, with a dash in between. I thought to myself, "There are two dates on most tombstones, and a dash in between the dates. Shouldn't it be what you've done during the 'dash' that counts?" I hoped that my dash would be worth something.

Later that day, I felt the need to stop by his place of employment, to express my sympathy. They were all shocked and devastated. I was at a loss for words, other than, "I'm so truly very sorry." I left the business, hoping they knew of my sincerity.

Once again, the hand of desperation took another victim. Fifty-eight-year-old Paul lived with his companion, in a beautiful, immaculate home. Paul had been going to counseling over the past several months, following the death of his mother. The counseling didn't work.

One afternoon, while his companion was at work, Paul took a vacuum cleaner hose, and attached it to the exhaust pipe of his car, which was inside their garage. He secured it to the pipe with duct tape, and the hose was inserted in the car, through one of the car windows. The car was still running when the companion returned home from work that evening. The anguish and sadness on the face of his companion was haunting.

Some people say that suicide is a coward's way out of a mess. I don't believe that. I believe that the person has an illness that needs treated, and the treatments, (counseling and/or medication) are not always effective. I think most people get to their line, and it's a matter of crossing the line, or turning back. Paul crossed the line.

The young people we treat on ambulance calls, that have attempted suicide, are extremely sad. I've learned that there are a lot of different ways that people attempt suicide.

"Cutting," is a term I was not familiar with, until our first call for an attempted suicide by a young girl. She had cuts all over her body. Some were severe and others weren't. We learned she had been cutting herself for years.

She said, "It feels good to feel the pain." That statement stretched my level of belief. How can it feel good to suffer self-inflicted pain? I'll never know. She had done a good job of hiding her cutting from her family and friends until this day, when a close friend saw blood, squirting from her arm. Her friend dialed 911. She tired to explain it, "I didn't know my cuts were that bad, but I just couldn't stop cutting."

Several hours later we were dispatched for another attempted suicide. This call was for a 40-year-old woman, who had attempted to kill herself. We arrived to find her walking around in her apartment, complaining how everything in her life that had gone wrong. Dressed in skimpy, silk pink pajamas, she explained to us that she had taken her nail file and tried to slice her wrist, but it didn't work. Nothing was going right for her. She couldn't even kill herself, and do it right.

As I was trying to get her to put some clothes on, my partner found a pair of boots, and set them on her coffee table for her to wear. She looked him straight in the eyes and said, "Oh, great! My luck is already bad and now you put shoes on a table! Don't you know that's really bad luck?"

Not long after that incident, we were dispatched for another attempted suicide. This one was totally different. A 55-year-old employee at a nursing home, put a gun to his head, and pulled the trigger. He should have been dead by the time we arrived. With half of his head blown away, he was still alive, and fighting. The more he fought, the more his blood splattered. Where he got the strength to continue fighting us, as we continued trying to save his life, baffled all of us.

We finally had gotten enough drugs in him to sedate him, had the bleeding relatively under control, and carried him down the steps to our litter. It seemed like forever until we got him to the hospital. He died several weeks later, after being removed from life support. We never found out what had made him cross his line.

Amanda was dispatched for a suicide, off of Pumping Station Road. She told me she had directions, but I said I'd meet her there, as I knew exactly where "Pumping Station Road" was. I pass by it every time I go to my brother's house, or to my parents' cabin. I thought, "This is a piece of cake for directionally challenged me, I'll probably get there long before Amanda does." I was wrong. I turned right, onto Pumping Station Road, and drove back the lane, expecting to see police cars around every curve, in the heavily wooded area. I drove until there was nowhere else to drive. So I turned around, thinking perhaps I missed the cars. Perhaps they had been pulled off to the side somewhere.

So I drove back out, this time much slower. Still not seeing any police any cars, or any cars! Okay, I'm confused. I returned to the main road and called Amanda. I then learned that Pumping Station Road also runs to the left of the road. That was news to me!

I finally found the area, as everyone was finishing, and packing their equipment. A 46-year-old male had put a .357 revolver under his chin and ended his life. When you read the obituaries, these same people all seemed like happy people, living normal lives. This dead man was employed as a cabinetmaker. He was an avid hunter, which probably explains how he was familiar with the other section of the road. He was an avid sports fan, and especially loved the Boston Red Sox. Reading his obituary made me wonder about my own obituary. Will mine mention that I loved the Baltimore Orioles and the Pittsburgh Steelers?

Too often the cries for help cannot be answered. Thirty-one-year-old Rick had a past history of depression. His family had done everything they could to try to help him. He attended counseling on a routine basis. He took medications to lift his spirits. Nothing seemed to work. Numerous times he had threatened to kill himself, but had never attempted to do so, not that anyone was aware of. He lived alone, in a modest home, with his dog.

One cold winter morning, Rick dialed 911, and said, "There's a medical emergency at this address." Before the dispatcher could obtain anymore information, she heard what sounded like a gunshot in the background, and he no longer was on the line. The police and an ambulance responded. The police broke in the door, as they had no idea what had transpired. In doing so, the dog escaped. They searched the house, until they found Rick's body, dead in a corner. A cell phone and a Smith & Wesson .357 revolver, were on the floor next to him. He had dialed 911, and then shot himself. He bled to death before the police arrived.

I tried to figure out why someone would call 911, and then kill themself. Then I figured it out. He wanted the police to find him; he didn't want his family to find him. I gave him some credit for that. After his body was removed, the funeral directors returned to the room, and helped me clean the floor. There was so much blood. But by now my concern had shifted to the dog. I asked the officer, "Is anyone looking for the dog? Should I go look for the dog?" He assured me that the neighbors all knew the dog and the dog would be found, and taken care of. I trusted them.

When I read his obituary I read the usual, "Died unexpectedly at his home." So often I have wondered what people think when they read that. Do they think the person had an illness, but was not expected to die? Mental illness is a disease, so I suppose it's appropriate.

Then I read that Rick's love, throughout life, was the outdoors. He enjoyed hunting, boating, camping, fixing cars, and was a National Hot Rod Association member. What surprised me the most was reading his survivors. Relatives were named and then there it was, "His faithful companion, 'Jake,' a black Labrador Retriever," was sorely missing Rick." I wondered what was so terribly wrong in his life, that he killed himself. But I'll never know. I can only find some ounce of comfort in believing that it is truly a disease, and a disease that cannot always be cured.

Then you have the attempted suicides, where the person is trying to get attention from others.

Our ambulance was at the scene of a totally bizarre attempted suicide. Jerry had told his girlfriend, Patsy, that he was going to kill himself by overdosing on medications. After he ingested all of the drugs he could find, Patsy called 911.

As we were entering their home, we heard Patsy screaming, "I can do a better job of killing myself than you can!" She took out a knife, and began cutting herself. Then Jerry started vomiting.

As we're calling for another ambulance, he stops vomiting and says, "Oh, yea, well, watch this!" and smashed his hand through the glass door. Seeing this caused Patsy to begin vomiting. Okay, now we've got Patsy puking, and Jerry bleeding profusely. Yuck!

I settled him down, had the bleeding under control, and I bandaged his hand. I was proud of the nice packaging job I had done, considering the circumstances I was working in. He was covered in vomit, but I was able to ignore it. I had just finished wrapping his hand, when Patsy came storming over to him, and ripped off my nice packaging! "Let him bleed to death!" she screamed.

I tried my hardest to explain, "Well, you see how it is, we really can't just let you two here, battling it out to see which one of you can kill yourself first." Another ambulance finally arrived, and the two were separated. It was not our last encounter with them, but as far as I know, they are both still living. Some people spend most of their lives walking down the path of self-destruction.

A 30-year-old male, Tom, had a late-night argument with his live-in girlfriend. She told him she had a new boyfriend, and her and their three children would be moving out. After they went to sleep, he took a large nail, and screwed it into the wooden ceiling beam in their kitchen. Then he took a dog leash, and secured the one end to the nail, and wrapped the other end around his neck.

Tom did this while standing on their kitchen table. He left his toolbox on the table, along with one of those little plastic picture viewers you buy at an amusement park. I looked inside the viewer. There was a picture of his three children. Did he take a last look at them before he kicked the table out from under him? Did he give any thought to them coming down to the kitchen in the morning and finding him hanging from the ceiling?

Tom was wearing a new, Philadelphia Eagles tee shirt. One young child questioned me, "We just got him that shirt for Father's Day, didn't he like it?" Sometimes you just can't find the right words to answer the difficult questions.

As I looked around the house, I noticed all of the Philadelphia Eagles and Philadelphia Phillies caps, mugs, all sorts of sports items for the Philadelphia teams. As I looked at him, I thought about the Phillies, being just games away from going to the World Series, and now he wouldn't be here to see them play. He wouldn't be here to see his children play. He wasn't here to see the depth of suffering they were all experiencing. It just seems so selfish, but he had crossed that fine line.

For some reason unknown to me, hangings and domestic quarrels just seem to go together.

Hanging yourself seems selfish, crude and gruesome. You know someone is going to find you dangling from a rope, or in this case, a heavy-duty extension cord. A 44-year-old male had been distraught because his former girlfriend had called it quits. She told him he could no longer live there, so he moved back into his parents' home.

He had been in the process of remodeling the basement of her home, so he went to her home one morning, telling her he was just going to work in the basement until lunch, and then he'd leave. Lunchtime came and she noticed his vehicle was still in her driveway. She went to the basement, to find him dangling from a heavy water pipe running through the basement ceiling. The police arrived, cut him free, and made an unsuccessful attempt to resuscitate him.

He'd been dead for several hours. He had told her on several prior breakups, that he would kill himself if she didn't take him back. This time he kept his word.

He told her he was going to work on the remodeling of the basement. She trusted and believed him. Then she is the one that finds him dangling from the ceiling. It just seemed so wrong. Again, I looked at everything but his body, as we waited for the undertakers.

I walked into the basement room that he had been finishing. I looked at the walls that he had finished, decorated with outdoor scenery. I looked at the artificial log-burning fireplace in the one corner. I looked at the sofa with the soft, animal printed throw lying on it, the candles, and the nice television sitting in the other corner.

I became immersed in picturing myself, lying comfortably on the sofa, covered with the throw, watching a Lifetime movie, the candles lit, the artificial fireplace glowing, a beer on the coffee table, and I thought, "Life doesn't get much better than this." So somehow, in my mind, I could rationalize why he just gave up on life, after knowing he was no longer welcome in this room.

But then I have to come back to reality. To deal with his guilt-ridden friend and the family members who had arrived. It's so difficult to separate yourself.

So many of the calls I have responded to left the big question, "Was it an accidental overdose or an intentional overdose?" I'll never know. I don't know the thoughts that were going through the person's head as they took more and more illegal drugs. Was their life that bad that they hoped to not wake up again, or did they just want to get higher and higher. It's always so difficult for the survivors, because you just don't know. Some of these appear to be intentional suicides, but unless there's a note or they've expressed this intent to someone, you just don't know and you never will. That's a tough pill for everyone to swallow.

The holidays always seem to be filled with successful and unsuccessful suicide attempts. One Christmas we were dispatched to an apartment for an attempted suicide. Inside we found a man sitting calmly on his sofa. He told us that none of his children had even called to wish him a Merry Christmas. It was obvious that he was very lonely.

He continued telling us that he wanted to die because he was so depressed, but he didn't know how to kill himself. By this time I was emotionally drained. I left my partner do the talking, "We can take you to the hospital, and they can work with you to help you overcome your depression. There will be lots of other people there. You can have a nice meal."

My partner's doing a great job of convincing the man that the hospital would be an ideal choice for him right now. While he continued, I gazed around the apartment. There was very little furniture in the apartment. It didn't seem like a "home." But there was a huge, flat screen television, which filled one whole wall in the living room. I'm amazed at people's priorities. He finally agreed that the hospital sounded like a nice place to spend the rest of his Christmas day

Too many people find it easier to curse the darkness than to light a candle.

Chapter 8

October 2nd, 2006

I knew that this would be the most difficult chapter to write. I'm not saying the other chapters were easy. In my mind, every single call I've responded to has taken its toll on me. However, none took their toll on me as Monday, October 2nd, 2006, did. I was considered a "seasoned deputy coroner" in our county by that date. I had shattered the notion that coroners must be men. But that day shattered this seasoned coroner.

I don't remember too much from that morning. I was at work, doing my normal Monday work. I went to the bathroom, and my cell phone rang. I didn't give it much thought, not even the, "Oh, no, another coroner call."

It was Nick calling. He asked me, "Do you know what's going on in Bart Township?"

I said, "Excuse me, but I'm at work, I have no idea what is going on in Bart Township." That was the end of the conversation. At that moment in my life, Nick was still sitting on the edge, as to my acceptance of him as a deputy coroner.

Why was he calling me and disturbing me? I was a tad agitated. I finished in the bathroom, and thought, "Oh, what the heck, let's see what the CAD is showing, if anything, in Bart Township."

I pulled it up on my computer, and saw what seemed to be a zillion ambulances, medics, helicopters, and fire police on scene. Okay, so something was going on in Bart Township, but it wasn't my concern. I continued my work. I guess I just never gave any thought as to the amount of units that were dispatched. I had my other work to do.

I mentioned to my co-worker that there were a lot of emergency vehicles, including helicopters, in Bart Township. She said, "I'll bet your phone will soon ring."

My cell phone soon rang. It was a county dispatcher saying I was to respond to Bart Township. She told me, "You're to respond to Bart Township for a 'hostage situation in a school.' She told me I'm going to need assistance. I told her I knew whom I wanted to call to assist me, and I would make the call. She calmly said, "Janice, you're going to need more assistance than one person." I said, "Give me a minute or two, I'll figure it out, and let you know."

I went back to the bathroom and changed into my uniform. I headed out, with the dispatcher's directions lying on the front seat of my Jeep.

There are so many things that I remember vividly, and so many things that I don't remember at all.

Amanda had told me the day before that she couldn't go on any calls with me on Monday, until after 4:00 p.m. Her husband is a schoolteacher; they have a baby, and she didn't have a babysitter lined up. When she told me that I thought, "No big deal, I'll call you for any calls I get after 4:00."

Amanda was the first person I called at 11:40 a.m. that day. At first she thought I was joking, but then she could sense the seriousness in my voice, and she knew that I needed her. She told me she would find a babysitter, I gave her the directions county had given me, and she said she would meet me at the scene.

I called Kevin, at Ephrata Ambulance, and told him I might be late for our executive board meeting that night. I also asked him if he would print out the CAD site, so I could later see the companies that were on scene. Kevin printed them out, and they compile pages two and three of my scrapbook dedicated to that day.

From the pages Kevin printed out, the initial call was dispatched at 10:48 a.m.

I was told to take 272 South, and then pick up 222 South, bearing left where there is a split in the road. I was told I would pass Willow Street and Refton. Then I was to turn left on White Oak Road, in New Providence, and then make a right on Mine Road. The directions sounded simple enough.

Those directions are on the front page of my scrapbook.

I called my father, and told him where I was going, and what I was responding to. He said he had just heard on the news that there was not a school involved. Okay, I was confused. I just needed to get to the scene. My job is to get there in a timely manner, and that was all I was thinking at that point. My father told me it sounded like I was heading in the right direction.

Then I called my "rock of salvation," Angie. I've often called her for directions, or just to vent, before arriving on a scene. I would never have made it a lot of times, without her voice on the other end of the phone. I'm not talking only about directions, but just friendship and reassurance that I could handle any call I was dispatched to.

I told Angie where I was headed, and that I had just spoken with my father, who said he heard about this hostage situation on the news. I said, "Maybe there will be something about this on the local news tonight, would you throw a tape in to record the news, just in case it is on the news?" She was as clueless as I was, but she said she would put a tape in their television, just in case it was on the local news.

That was taken care of. Now all I had to do was find the location. I continued following the directions I had been given. I'm driving down this road that seemed to be leading nowhere. I began thinking I was lost, that I made a wrong turn somewhere. I decided to drive another five minutes, and then call county to let them know that, once again, I'm lost. I've gotten lost responding to so many calls that I actually take thank you gifts to the dispatchers in appreciation of their helping me out with directions. But you have to remember that I cover our entire county, which is 945 square miles in size and has sixty independent municipalities.

Within my self-imposed five-minute time span, I saw helicopters flying overhead of me. Now I felt confident that I was on the right road, but now I started getting nervous. Why are there still helicopters flying overhead?

I will never forget driving over the crest of the hill that leads down to the schoolhouse. My first thought was, "Why are there so many police cars there?" My second thought was, "Where should I park?" One of the fire police officers directed me to an open spot behind a police car, but still quite a distance from where all of the activity appeared to be going on. The fire policeman told me that I should park back from the scene, as they were still airlifting children from the scene. They are airlifting children from the scene?

Now I was really confused and scared. I parked my Jeep as directed, and looked down the incline. I could see what appeared to be a one-room Amish schoolhouse on the left.

I saw a white sheet that was way too familiar to me, lying on the ground in front of the schoolhouse. I knew immediately that there had to be a dead person underneath the white sheet.

Amanda had phoned me, saying that she had found a sitter, and was only about ten minutes behind me. I looked at the massive number of police officers and emergency personnel in the schoolyard, and that's when it hit me. This was going to be a trying day. Since the services as a coroner are not immediate, I took the opportunity to stand outside of my Jeep, and smoke a cigarette. Then I saw Amanda's car pulling in behind the line of emergency vehicles.

I waited for her to walk to my Jeep. She asked me what we have, and I said, "I really don't know, other than some hostage situation, which appeared to have happened in the Amish schoolhouse." We decided to smoke another cigarette before walking down the road. As we smoked and talked, we both mentioned the white sheet lying outside in the schoolyard, near the entrance to the school. We both knew what it symbolized. In a desperate attempt to console both of us, I told her I had smoked half my pack of cigarettes, just driving to the scene, and she admitted having done the exact same thing. But somehow it just didn't seem to matter.

Amanda and I walked down towards the school. As we approached the scene, we were asked to "sign in." Not too many coroner calls require you to "sign in." You have to print your name, the department you are with, then put your signature beside that information, then a police officer initials it, along with the time you are entering the scene. So we "signed in." That is a privilege, but also a sign that forewarns you that you are about to enter a site you probably would wish you weren't at.

There is so much I don't remember, and so much I wish I didn't remember.

Our new pediatric coroner, Carroll Rottmund, had been called to respond to the scene. Carroll phoned me and said, "I'm at work at the hospital. I can leave immediately, but I'll be in my scrubs."

I suggested she take time to go home, and change into her coroner's uniform, which she did.

Then a police officer approached me and said, "We have no idea how many children are dead inside the schoolhouse." Hearing that, I called our county dispatcher and requested that our secondary coroner contact me.

John Wanczyk called me, and said he would do anything that needed done. I asked him to stop by the office, and pick up lots of body bags, toe tags and death certificates, as I had no idea how many deceased people we had. At that time I still had no clue what had transpired. But I felt a slight sense of relief, knowing John was gathering supplies, and on his way. John is a person I would trust with my own life.

Amanda and I stood motionless, like two lost souls. We stared at the groups of Amish adults, sobbing quietly. We stared at the police officers, some still in their bullet proof vests; others in shirts drenched in bright, red blood. I noticed the baseball bats lying on the ground. The whole scene looked like a battlefield. There were medical supplies covering the entire schoolyard. It looked like someone took an ambulance, turned it upside down, and opened all of the compartments.

They weren't ready for our services, so what should we do? I couldn't keep looking at all of the scattered debris.

Amanda mentioned that she needed to use a restroom. Now we're out in an area that doesn't have a Turkey Hill on every corner. A block in Bart Township, is the same as a mile in other municipalities. We looked around to see if there was a spot that we could designate as the outdoor, female bathroom, but we couldn't find any place. We've both used the outdoors as a bathroom before, so it wasn't anything new to us, but there just wasn't any place to serve as our "female bathroom."

No sooner had we agreed that there was no place suitable, then a truck pulled into the open field behind us. The truck was towing port-a-potties! We rushed over and greeted the man driving the truck, and told him how thankful we were to see him and his cargo. He asked us to give him five minutes to set up and then we could use the bathrooms.

That was only the beginning of the heaven-sent people who would be with us that day, and into the evening. The port-a-potties also served as a great hiding place for the many of us who smoked. If we went behind them, we were obscure from any media. It proved to be a great sense of relief in more ways than one.

So John's on his way, as was Carroll. By this time Dr. Kirchner and Dr. Good had arrived on scene. Dr. Good had called me earlier, asking for directions. I told him that I'm the last person on earth to ask for directions, and gave my phone to an officer, who gave him directions.

Shortly thereafter, Eric, also a deputy coroner, approached me. He was there with his fire company, but was willing to assist me if needed. I know Eric and I trusted him completely. I asked him if he'd be willing to be the photographer. I told him I had my camera, and if he could figure out how to use it, and remain committed to the scene for the duration, the job was his. He agreed and I never doubted his ability.

I now felt I had the best group of people to assist me. I made the decision to have Amanda take notes, as I examined the bodies. I knew she would do an excellent job. She drew pictures, depicting the body positions, areas of wounds and detailed documentation.

Eric was the official photographer. John would assist in any way needed, and Carroll would observe and take notes if needed. I ran my plan by Dr. Kirchner and Dr. Good. They both felt the plan sounded good, and had no problems with it.

Not long after we had finalized our plan, I was told to respond to the trooper in command. He informed me that media were arriving, and even news helicopters were flying in the police mandated, "No flying zone."

I thought, "They're just doing their job, trying to get the best story and the best pictures. So what if they have to pay a $500.00 fine? They'll get some good pictures that will override the penalty." Why do I always try to put myself in the other person's shoes?

The officer requested that the young girl, who was covered with the sheet in front of the school, be pronounced, examined, and removed from the front yard. He wanted this done before anymore media arrived. I assembled my crew.

I spoke with the Bart Fire Company incident command officer to see who he felt would be capable of holding tarps up, to prevent the media from seeing, or photographing, the scene. I sensed this would be a gruesome task, and I wanted to be certain that the people assisting us stood the best chance of handling whatever we would see.

Several firefighters were sent over to assist us. They created a tent, with their tarps, for us to work under. I climbed underneath the tent. I pulled the white sheet back, and saw a beautiful little angel. Her body was ridden with bullet wounds and covered in blood. I pronounced her dead.

As I began my examination of the 7-year-old girl, I began feeling that I just couldn't do this. She had the face of an angel. Her eyelashes were so vividly dark and long. Why was she lying dead in the front yard of her school? School is a place you should feel safe going to. School is a place your parents expect you to return home from safely after the end of the school day. This was so wrong.

The weather that day was beautiful. It was an absolutely gorgeous fall day. The leaves were magnificent. It was a picture perfect day, except that I was in the midst of a situation that I kept hoping was a nightmare, and I would soon wake up.

Pronouncing her dead, and examining her body, was one of the hardest things I've ever had to do in my life.

Suddenly it dawned on me; these are most likely all Amish children, who all dress alike. I needed to find a way to distinguish them. She can't be just, "Jane Doe A." But I had no other choice. My heart ached and my eyes became watery. I continued my examination of Naomi Rose Ebersol, as I later learned her identity.

I dictated to Amanda, every single wound on her body, detailed descriptions of every article of clothing still remaining on her body, down to her Strawberry Shortcakes underwear. She might be "Jane Doe A" on the toe tag, but I was going to give her more dignity than that.

Amanda continued drawing pictures, of the position of her body, and the wounds to the front of her body. Eric was taking photos with my camera. Then came the horrific task of rolling her over to exam her posterior side. Bullet wounds were on her spine and back. I began dictating the locations and the number of wounds to Amanda. Underneath the tent, that I was so grateful the firemen had put together for us, I started having trouble breathing.

I couldn't count anymore. My head was spinning. I had to get out from under the tent. I just couldn't look at this little, innocent girl's dead body anymore. Sometime, while underneath that "tent," Naomi became my little angel. She will forever remain my little angel. Her face looked so trusting. She seemed at peace. But my heart and soul were shredded to pieces.

I stepped out from under the tarps and said, "I'm finished." I prepared her toe tag, as we waited for an ambulance to load her body into, for identification by family members. She was "Jane Doe A." I pronounced her dead at 3:10 p.m.

Again, I experienced this enormous feeling that this is just so wrong. This beautiful little angel shouldn't be a "Jane Doe," but she was. At that point I questioned myself whether I could continue pronouncing people dead at that scene. But I knew I had to.

"Jane Doe A" was loaded into an ambulance, and we had a few moments of breathing time. Much needed breathing time. We all went behind the portable bathrooms and smoked several cigarettes. Then a lady approached me and said, "Oh, Janice! Are you okay?"

I knew I should know her, but I couldn't figure out who she was. Then she told me. She was Deb, the person who had taken me under her wings when I joined Ephrata Ambulance. A person I think the world of. I asked her what she was doing there. She told me she was there with the county counseling team that had been dispatched to the scene. We hugged and cried.

She asked me, "Is there anything anyone needs?" I said, "Yes, one police officer needs Ibuprofen, not aspirin, for his knee, and I have a list of brands of cigarettes we need." I thought, "I know she's not here to run and do our shopping, but she asked what we needed, and I told her."

She calmly said to make a list, and someone would go and get what we needed. I questioned her. "Someone will go get us cigarettes?" She said, "Absolutely," in a very firm voice. So I finished making our list and collected money. I gave the list and money to her, and within a short time our items were delivered to us. Now I'm not condoning smoking, but this was one day you didn't want to decide to quit. Deb was there all day and into the evening. She was the one who was there to comfort me, when I finally broke down. I'm forever indebted to her.

So now we're back to the waiting. The waiting and smoking cigarettes. I tired to find the room I've constructed in my brain where I put the horrific images that I never want to see again. I knew the room was getting full, but there should still be enough room for some more graphic images. But I couldn't find the door. I couldn't even find the room. I finally gave up searching for it, and decided to wait until later, and then put all of the images from that day in the room, and lock the door. I was convinced I could find my self-constructed room at a later time.

The Salvation Army trailer arrived and their volunteers began preparing food. They had hot and cold food, as well as drinks. By now we were looking for any diversion from the dreaded anticipation of entering the schoolhouse. So we headed to the Salvation Army trailer. I learned these people who were preparing and handing out food, at no charge, were all volunteers. I recalled all of the times I had walked past the bell ringer, during the holiday season, and didn't think twice about not putting any money in their collection bins. I vowed then and there to never walk past another Salvation Army bell ringer, without putting at least some change, or hopefully some dollars, in the container.

They had some kind of soup, but there was no way I could eat soup that day. I think they had hot dogs, too, and I rarely turn down a hot dog, but I just couldn't eat anything. However, the cold beverages were a heaven sent. The people working the stand were so friendly, and I continued feeling guilty for walking past their bell ringers. But it didn't stop me from taking many cold sodas that day. I knew I'd repay them for the sodas I had taken. They were still passing out refreshments when I left the scene, which was close to midnight.

We watched and listened to the quiet sobs and comments. "It was hell." "She kept begging me to help her." "She was so small." "Why couldn't I have saved her?" "Who was the girl I treated, and which hospital is she at now?"

State troopers stood, in a daze-like trance, with blood-soaked shirts. Groups of Amish adults leaned on the wooden fence surrounding the schoolhouse, sobbing quietly. Heads were buried in hands. People were praying. Children were sitting on the ground, motionless.

For a few minutes, it seemed like I wasn't there. My body was there, but my mind and soul were up in the air, floating around, watching everything going on, and listening to the quiet sounds. For as many people as were on scene, it was eerily quiet. I believe this was because everyone was in a state of shock, and doing their respective jobs. The magnitude of the tragedy didn't register with me that day. I was there to do a job. A job that I would have given anything not to have been assigned to.

Still not knowing how many deceased were inside the schoolhouse, Amanda and I sat down on the front porch of the school, and started preparing additional toe tags, "Jane Doe B"; "John Doe A"; on and on. There was blood on the porch outside of the schoolhouse. We needed a place to sit, and we needed to be together. We found boxes that had been brought in by the police that had contained booties and items they needed. I ripped apart the boxes and made mats for us to sit on.

I will never forget Amanda and I sitting on the porch scrunched together, filling out the toe tags, and one of our deputies taking a picture of us. At the time it didn't mean anything to me. Later, it was the one and only picture that I wanted. I discovered it was somehow deleted, when the police took my camera to download pictures and try to identify the girls.

So many times I have wished that I would have that photo, but I don't. I don't know why I want it so badly, perhaps because at that moment, we didn't know what we were about to walk into, and we were leaning on each other for support. Perhaps it's something that only I understand.

I looked around the outside of the school. Baseball bats were lying in the yard. Several scooters and bikes were lying in the yard. I remember seeing the outhouses. One with a sign on it, "GIRLS," and one with, "BOYS." Staring at the metal gate in front of the school, I wondered what purpose it served. I stared at the double seesaw and swing set and the small baseball diamond, which had wear spots in the grass for bases and home plate.

Huge gray draft horses grazed in the field out back. There was a school bell in the cupola, and a whitewashed board fence around the perimeter. If I could have removed all of the ambulances, blood, and police officers, it was like a picture perfect postcard scene. The kind you see in tourist shops.

But then I saw the groups of Amish, looking anguished, speaking quietly to each other, and burying their faces in their hands, with tears streaming down their faces. While their belief is to forgive like Christ did, not a man-made forgiveness, they believe that Jesus takes care of us, even when bad things like this happen. While they believe these children are in Heaven, they still weep and mourn, just like everyone else, but then they turn to Christ.

So we continued waiting. Then we were told that we're to go inside the schoolhouse to pronounce those in the schoolhouse dead. By now we had been waiting for what seemed like an eternity.

We now learned that the police felt confident there was only one girl inside the schoolhouse, along with the perpetrator, who we were told, had shot and killed himself. We were told to "double boot," which means to put on a minimum of two pairs of disposable booties over our shoes. That's your first clue that there's a lot of blood at the scene you are about to enter. I triple booted. We had everything in order to enter the schoolhouse.

As prepared as I thought I was to enter the schoolroom, I was wrong in my thinking that I had everything under control. I had everyone under control. There's a big difference. You try your hardest to convince yourself that everything is under control. As long as everyone is under control, and you have confidence in him or her, it will work out. But I truly believe you're never prepared to see anything like we saw that day. The images will stay with me forever. Weeks later, I gave up trying to put all of the images into my room. My self-constructed room wasn't large enough.

Lancaster County has approximately 150 Old Order Amish schools. Each one contains one room, 30 feet wide by 34 feet long. The room hosts between 25 and 38 desks for pupils in grades 1–8. One unmarried, female teacher, and several young aides preside. Every school is exactly the same. But no one will ever think of any of them the same again.

We timidly entered the schoolhouse. We saw blood, broken glass, desks in array. We saw a female, towards the chalkboard in the front of the room, lying dead in a massive pool of blood. We saw a man, lying on the floor on the left side of the room, also in a pool of blood.

The horrific sight inside this one-room, Amish schoolhouse seemed surreal. I did my usual glancing at the dead, then my usual looking at anything but the dead. There was so much blood. There were so many desks with cute pictures that appeared to be in the midst of being colored, with globs of blood strewn on them. Then there were other coloring pictures that were untouched by blood.

There was nothing to do but look at everything, at that point. We had been told we could enter the schoolroom, but once we entered, we discovered the police investigation had not been completed. So there we were, standing in the corner of the room.

I saw a poster on the right wall, with the rainbow, and the words, "Honor Thy Mother and Father" on it. Underneath it were pictures of John Deere tractors, along with the parents' names, and then the children's name, or names, in the cases of brothers and or sisters. I saw Naomi's family's names. I fought back my tears. I could not allow myself to cry.

Directly in front of the one female body was the chalkboard. Underneath it hung a poster on "Money," and showed pictures of different coins, and their values. The floor was white with blue or gray squares here and there. I searched for a square that didn't have blood on it. My mind was starting to lose itself, and I had to find something to do. I couldn't find any clean squares.

Amanda and I cautiously inched a little closer to the right wall. On the wall was a progress report. It appeared that the teacher filled in their progress in different subjects each week. The better they were doing, the higher they were on the chart. I frantically searched to find Naomi's progress chart. She had been doing splendidly well.

I realized I was becoming totally consumed with Naomi and her death, and I knew I couldn't allow this to happen. I still had a lot of work to do. I turned away from the chart and looked towards the entrance. There were all of their Igloo style lunch pails, lined up along the bottom of the wall. On top of them were the boys' straw hats, hanging neatly on wooden pegs on the wall. It again seemed like a nightmare.

None of these, none that I could see, had any blood on them, yet I couldn't walk one foot without being engulfed by the blood on the floor. I remember seeing what appeared to be a hundred or more of the little yellow numbered police tents that they set up on crime scenes. They were everywhere.

There were desks piled on top of each other, near the front door. There was a side door next to the teacher's desk. There were fresh flowers, untouched, on the teacher's desk. Near the front entrance was a milk crate, containing materials that seemed to be out of place in this schoolroom.

Plastic zip ties lay scattered throughout the room. Then I saw a piece of wood, possibly 4 x 4, with ten eyebolts screwed into the wood, each eyebolt approximately ten inches apart. That's when I realized what this killer's intentions were. I was mortified. The plastic zip ties are often used to hold cable or wires together. In this case they had been used as wrist and ankle restraints. These were young, innocent children. All children are children of God, but these children were so trusting. I had trouble convincing myself of what I was seeing. I wanted to have this all go away and let the day start over. But I couldn't.

So again we stood and waited. Now where should I look? By now I was having trouble standing in one spot. I thought about sitting down, but there was nowhere to sit that wasn't covered in blood, and that would have been unprofessional. So we stood and stared.

These children have no concept of violence. They don't understand guns. They don't watch TV. Until that moment, Amish schools had been viewed as the safest of retreats from the world. I figured out years ago, that I was going to see things that nobody was meant to see. I was going to be part of the worst moments, and the best moments, of people's lives. But this scene was absolutely the most horrific thing I'd ever seen. This wasn't part of what I had signed up for. Why me?

I was now informed that I was to pronounce the female inside the school dead, and to do what was necessary to have her body removed. I pronounced "Jane Doe B" dead at 5:55 p.m. There were two bullet wounds to the rear of her head. One exit wound was noted on the right front of her head. I placed her toe tag on her left hand. The rule of thumb is that a toe tag is to be placed on the toe. I guess that's why they're called "toe tags."

I always try my hardest to place the toe tag on the toe, but in this case, the deceased was fully clothed, and I didn't want to disturb any of her clothing, so I opted for her left hand. Just getting to her body, amidst the sea of blood was a task. A task I'll carry with me the rest of my life.

My head was swirling and my heart was aching. She's much more than a "Jane Doe B!"

We learned she was Anna Mae Stoltzfus, 12 years old. Much later I looked at Amanda's drawings, which depicted Anna lying in a supine position, with her legs crossed at the ankles. My first thought was, "What was she doing when she was shot, that her legs were crossed?" and my second thought was that Amanda had done the expected excellent job of documentation.

By now I was emotionally and physically drained. One person was telling me, "Don't you dare touch her face!" while my heart was questioning that if I were her family, would I want to identify her with her face covered in blood? No.

I had no doubt in my mind. If I lost my job over it, so be it. But I just couldn't do that to any family. I asking for the next due recovery ambulance, and was informed that it was New Holland. New Holland? They are in my backyard, what were they doing so far away from their home coverage area?

New Holland's ambulance crew was flawless. Crews just don't get much better than their crew. The debate went back and forth, clean her up or not. I finally said to the New Holland crew chief, "Get a lot of 4 by 4s ready, along with some sterile water, and the minute we get her into your rig, you start cleaning up her face."

She replied, "Oh, that's not what we heard. We heard we were not to touch her face." I begged, "Please, just do it. I'll take full responsibility."

I gave them my word that I would take responsibility, and I was willing to accept any consequences that might follow my decision. They agreed to get the materials ready to clean her face.

Anna was not a petite girl. She was lying on the floor in this one-room schoolhouse, surrounded by blood. I accepted the inevitable. We can't get to her body, and package her for removal from the school, without our clothes becoming drenched with blood.

I glanced at the shooter, and the thought ran through my mind as quickly as it left, "Why did you do this?"

We continued towards her body with a body bag. Now we're not walking like normal people walk. It's more like an extremely cautious tiptoe. It was scary, and I couldn't figure out why I was scared.

The shooter was lying on the floor on the opposite side of the room, dead. But he was too close. There were too many guns everywhere. There was too much blood everywhere. My head continued spinning. I stopped for a moment and looked at the teacher's desk. There were pretty, fresh flowers on her desk.

I wanted to go outside and smoke a cigarette, but I knew I couldn't. As we were log rolling her body, to move her into the body bag, the police said that the shooter's body was now to be pronounced, examined, and removed.

I tried talking to myself, "Okay, remain calm. We're in the middle of moving a body, engulfed in a sea of blood, into a body bag, and I had personally committed to myself that her face would be cleaned up before any family members, or the teacher would see her. Now what?"

I couldn't be in two places at one time, and I would not leave Anna in the hands of anyone else, despite my complete faith in the others, it had now become personal.

I'm a believer that angels walk with us, and someone above carries us when we can't walk anymore. At that very moment, John suggested that he could pronounce the shooter dead. He suggested that he and Eric take care of having that body removed. I felt a sense of relief and gratefulness to John for his quick thinking.

I stayed with Anna.

New Holland had backed their ambulance to the entrance of the schoolhouse. We carried her out, and they had their litter ready for us to put her body on. I quickly said again, "She's going to have her face cleaned up, this is not an option. This is going to happen." We got her inside their rig and they had bottles of sterile water, towels, everything was ready. We cleaned her face up as best as we could.

Despite all of the blood, her face looked peaceful, with a mouth of braces. I was satisfied. Anna's mother was still at the schoolhouse; but her father was on his way to a hospital where another of their children, also a victim from the shootings, had been taken.

Her mother was brought inside the ambulance. "Yes, that's her," she said through tears, before being helped out of the ambulance. Anna was now to be transported to the hospital for a full body x-ray. After her mother had left the ambulance, the others went to find an undertaker to transport Anna to the hospital.

I was left alone in the ambulance with Anna.

It hit me like a bolt of lightning. I was sitting in the back of an ambulance, with a dead, innocent Amish girl. My eyes had just seen a sight that no human should have to witness. Thoughts swarmed through my mind, "What about all of the other students? What about their families? What is going on here? Does anyone know I'm in here?"

That's when I lost it. I knew it was all right for me to cry now. I was alone in an ambulance, in the dark, with a dead girl. I cried and cried. I didn't think I would ever be able to stop crying. I was oblivious to everything else. I vaguely remember a female coming inside the ambulance and seeing me crying—sobbing uncontrollably.

Then Deb stepped inside the ambulance and told me it's okay to cry. Let it all out. She told me that this was normal. "No, this wasn't normal!" I wanted to scream back to her. But Deb could sell freezers to Eskimos. She helped me compose myself, and before too long the funeral home's vehicle pulled up, and we moved Anna's body into their vehicle.

By now the body of the shooter, Charles Roberts, had been pronounced dead, was removed from the school, and was being taken to our county morgue.

Slowly people began leaving the scene. Amanda had been instructed to follow one of the bodies to the morgue. I don't remember which one it was. All I knew was that she was gone.

Every person on scene that day did his or her very best, considering what had been presented to us.

I don't remember a whole lot after that. I don't remember most of my drive home. I still can't believe I found my way home. Every song on the radio annoyed me. I thought about my belief that music sweeps away the cobwebs in our minds. I thought, "I have more than cobwebs, my whole brain needs cleaned. My soul needed cleansed." I was angry at my radio, because the songs weren't cleaning my brain or soul, so I inserted the first tape I found into my tape player. "Somewhere Over The Rainbow" started playing. I started crying, again. I ejected the tape in anger. Somehow I made it home.

I pulled into my driveway, dragged myself inside, and turned on my computer. I still had my reports to do. I told myself, "I can do this."

I began doing my report on Naomi, and lost it again. I called Angie. She immediately said she could come right over. I told her, "No, I need to do my reports. Please, just talk to me, and try to settle me down, so I can finish my reports." I told her, "I can't even spell the words, black socks."

I don't remember what she said to me, but it calmed me down. I did my reports and downloaded my pictures. I didn't even realize then that the picture of Amanda and I wasn't there. As I looked at the pictures, I started sobbing, uncontrollably. It has to be a nightmare. I looked at one photo, of the pretty picture being colored, with a gun lying on the floor, right next to the desk. This was just so wrong! Somehow I completed my reports.

I guess I went to bed after that. It must have been around 1:00 a.m. I don't remember. I don't remember getting up during the night, so I might have slept. But then, I don't remember the following day, Tuesday, at all. I have absolutely no recollection of Tuesday. It's like that day didn't exist in my life.

Later bits and pieces began emerging that helped me find some of my life from that Tuesday. My picture was on the front page of the Wednesday, October 4th, edition of *The Washington Post*. I was sitting on the steps at the altar of Georgetown United Methodist Church. When I saw that picture, I remembered that I had driven back to Bart Township on Tuesday. I don't know why. I don't remember what time of day it was, but I do remember I needed to go back.

Oftentimes on ambulance or coroner calls, we'll go back to the scene, later, just to see the area again. When you're on the scene of a motor vehicle accident, with a car into a pole, and you've got a life to save, you don't look at the things around you. But later you go back and look at the site again. I don't know why, but some of us do it and some of us don't. I do.

Sometimes, at fatal crash scenes, there are memorials erected at the site. Other times, it's hard to even find the tree or pole where the accident occurred. But it's something I do, and I remember wanting to drive back to Bart Township. Not to look at the schoolhouse, not to look at anything in particular, just to go back to the area.

I remembered seeing a church, with a sign out front that proclaimed, "Open For Prayer." Prayer, that would be good, and it's open. There were very few cars, if any, in the parking lot. I parked and found my way to the entrance. I cautiously walked inside. There was no one there. Okay, now what? Pray. That would be good. As I headed towards a pew, I noticed flowers, cards and pieces of paper on the altar. I walked up to the altar and began reading the notes. Notes to the families. Notes saying the families were being held in prayers. Bunches of flowers. Single flowers. What had I brought to leave for the families? Nothing. That realization sent me back into despair, and I sat on the altar steps, and once again fell apart.

I felt so selfish, so rude, such an intrusion. How could I come in here, and not bring something to express my sympathy to the families? Oh, sure, I had my thoughts and prayers in my head, but these other people had gone a step beyond that, they brought flowers and cards. I had brought nothing with me!

All of the emotions that I had kept bottled up inside me during the past 24 hours exploded. I cried and cried. I thought I would never stop crying.

Then I realized I had paper in my purse, and I could write a note and leave it on the altar. I collected my composure and began thinking about what I would write. Then I noticed a lady with a camera, standing in the middle of the pews. She approached me and introduced herself. Her name was Katherine. She told me she had taken some pictures of me, before I realized she was there, and she asked me if I minded. If I minded? I mumbled, "No, I didn't mind." I couldn't have cared less about anything at that point, other than finding something to leave for the families.

I told her I stopped in to pray, because the sign outside said it was open for prayer, and then I realized that others had brought flowers and cards, and I had not brought anything. She was so nice to me. She sat down with me and we talked. I asked her if she would check what I would write before I left it there, she agreed.

Together we sat in a pew, and I came up with something that she agreed was appropriate. I walked up to the altar and placed my note on the altar. I started crying, again. Katherine asked me if I was a family member or a relative. I told her no, I was only one of the coroners on scene, but I needed to come back to the area. I told her that somehow I ended up here, at this church, and I was hoping to find some peace before I left.

Katherine sat with me and we talked about how cruel the world can be one day, and how beautiful it can be the next day. We talked and talked. I don't remember most of the conversation, but I do know that she helped bring peace to my heart. She gave me her business card, and I put it in my purse without looking at it. She told me I could call or email her anytime, and I sensed she truly meant it. So many people say that, but you know they really don't want to hear your sorrows or your issues, they have their own to deal with.

I prayed. I don't know what Katherine did while I was praying. I was ready to leave, and I felt I was doing better now. I just wanted to find my way back home. I stood up, and there was Katherine. She walked with me to my Jeep, and asked if I was certain I was okay to drive home. I said yes and I meant yes. I was filled with more peace than before I left home. I thanked her for her time spent with me, and I returned home.

I'm not certain if the phone calls began on Tuesday or Wednesday. All I know is that once they started, they never stopped. Reporters were calling, all wanting to be my best friend—throwing names out at me like I would know who they are. I don't watch any news, except occasionally our local news. I didn't care who they were, just leave me alone! Someone from CNN called and asked if they could come to my home and do an interview. I was frantic and appalled. How dare they invade my private life? I finally asked one of them, "How did you get my phone number?" He said, "It's in the phone book." Oh, yes, it is.

I felt like I was living inside a snowglobe, constantly being turned upside down and shaken around. I took my phone off of the hook.

Now it was Wednesday morning. I had said I'd take Tuesday off, and I would return to work on Wednesday. On Wednesday morning, I realized that wasn't going to happen. So I put my phone back on the hook, and thought, "Maybe today everyone will stop bothering me." But they wouldn't stop calling me.

I answered the first one or two calls with the "no comment" phrase. Then a really clever lady called and said she wasn't looking for any interviews, she just was genuinely interested in knowing how I would spend the day. Would I go about my routine things, what would I do? I thought she seemed nice and sincere, and that she must be a caring person to wonder how I would handle that day, which was now Wednesday.

I told her that I had a doctor appointment for my flu shot and then I was going to the Lititz Fire Company for some business I had to finish with them, and I felt comfortable going to both places. So I would go to those two places, and the rest of the day would just be played by ear. She thanked me for my time, and seemed so genuinely sincere in her wish for me to find peace.

My guard was up as I left home to go for my flu shot. I was paranoid that reporters were following me. I began thinking, "I can't live like this, this is crazy. Just leave me alone!"

I went for my flu shot and my doctor asked me how I'm doing. I said, "I'm okay." Then he said, "Are you sure you are okay? You're not going to do something stupid, are you?"

At the time, I had no idea what he meant by "something stupid." I told him, "No, I won't do anything stupid, and yes, I am okay." Months later I realized what his statement implied.

I got my flu shot and headed towards Lititz. I stopped at a convenience store along the way. I now wanted to look at the newspapers. I get the morning paper, and on Tuesday and Wednesday, I had not even opened them. They were lying on a pile in my living room. But now I was starting to feel sort of human, and I wanted to see what was in the newspapers. That's when I saw *The Washington Post*, with my picture on the front page, with, "Photo by Katherine Frey" underneath the picture. I put two and two together. Katherine from the church was Katherine from *The Washington Post*.

I looked at the front pages of some of the other papers, and they all had the same, huge headlines. It was then that it hit me, as to the magnitude of this tragedy. I stood staring at the papers, getting ready to buy one of *The Washington Post* papers.

A young man, who was standing next to me, looked at me, and said, "Isn't that just horrible what happened?" I answered, "Yes, it was." He continued to tell me that his wife's brother's ex-sister-in-law's brother's boss was in the wedding of Charles Roberts. You have to realize that in Lancaster County, that kind of relationship description is very common. I expressed my sympathy to him and his extended families, and purchased a *Washington Post* paper. I put the paper on the front passenger seat of my Jeep and proceeded to Lititz.

Why on earth would anyone want to put that picture in any newspaper, especially on the front page of a large paper like *The Washington Post*? It took me a long time to figure that out. A close friend of mine told me that he cut out the picture, hung it in his office, and when he thinks he's having a bad day, he looks at that picture and realizes that his day isn't really that bad. So I'm the poster child for "despair?" I didn't like that idea.

Then someone told me that to her, the picture represented the agony that an average person was going through, following that Monday. So now I was the poster child for the "average person?" I liked that concept better.

I pulled into a parking space at the Lititz Fire Company. It's one of my favorite places to visit. Their chief is one of the nicest people I know. The guys who run with Lititz Fire Company are first class. They always make me feel comfortable and at home when I'm there. I walked inside, looking for Chief Ron Oettel. I saw a man inside the office, just standing there. He looked Amish. He seemed to be lost. I ignored him. Then I saw Ron. A wave of calmness swept through me.

Ron has seen a lot in his time as chief. He was on the scene of a fire in Lititz, several days before Christmas one year, in which the entire family died in the fire. I have the utmost respect for Ron. I thought back to the day I had stopped by, and Ron had his hand in a cast. He told me he had been in a fight with his computer tower, and the tower had won. He continued with his story that he had been so frustrated with his computer at home, that it was either throw the tower through the window, and have it land on his wife's flowers, or bang it with his fist. He chose to bang it with his fist, and ended up with a broken hand. I didn't believe him. He took me into his office and showed me the knuckle imprints on the computer tower, which he had removed from his home, and brought to the fire station. Okay, now I believed him. Everyone has his or her breaking point.

But that Wednesday, Ron didn't quite seem himself. He pulled me aside and told me that there were multiple media units parked in the rear of their station, and there were reporters set up, inside the back of the fire company, waiting to interview me.

He asked me if I had seen David Muir when I arrived. David Muir? Who is that? Ron described him as wearing a blue shirt, jeans, dark hair, and had a slight dark, handsome complexion. Oh, that's the guy I thought was an Amish guy that just happened to be hanging around. Ron said he's with a television station. Ron continued to explain the media just started showing up, saying they were waiting to interview me. He would do whatever I was comfortable with.

If I wanted them off of the property, he'd take care of it, and knowing how he took care of his computer issues, I knew he could take care of having them removed from the property. I asked to use the bathroom and think about this.

As I sat on the toilet, I wondered how they knew I was going to be in Lititz. Then it struck me. It had to have been the nice lady, who pretended she just wanted to know how I was going to spend my day! I had told her exactly how I was going to spend my day!

At first I was angry, then I tried to put myself in their shoes. They are reporters. They are just doing their job. I walked out of the bathroom and told Ron I would do an interview. He introduced me to David Muir and other people who I had no idea who they were. I think I only remember David Muir because he caught me so off guard. I honestly thought he was a cute Amish guy hanging around, and he turned out to be so very nice to me. I had the privilege of speaking with him on numerous occasions during the following year.

So we walked to the back of the Lititz Fire Company, and I answered questions. Then one of the reporters asked if I could go out front and answer some questions. Sure. Whatever. We went to the front of their station and I just couldn't do it. I didn't want to talk with them anymore. But I kept telling myself that they're just doing their job, and I should be more understanding and less emotional. They were all gathered in front of me, with their cameras and microphones. I mustered every bit of strength from within, but there just wasn't enough there. So I asked Ron if he would stand with the group, and I would pretend as if I was only talking with Ron. That worked. I answered their questions, but in my mind, it was only Ron and I there at that time. I left there and headed home, now even more paranoid than before.

Phones went back off their hooks.

I read my emails. One invited me to attend a counseling session at Bart Fire Company that evening. Wow! That was like a blast of fresh air. Counseling. I knew I needed some counseling. I called Amanda and told her I thought we should go. She was reluctant at first, but then said she would go. I kept thinking, "She must be a much stronger person than I am. I need counseling."

We attended the counseling, and the number of people there overwhelmed me. Some of them were talking about the counseling sessions they had attended on Monday. I was shocked and saddened. There was counseling on Monday? Why didn't someone tell me? Why didn't someone tell me that I could have gone to the Bart fire station on Monday, before I drove home, alone, in the dark? Why didn't someone tell me that I could have spoken with professional people, who can help you get through something like this, on the day it happened? Why didn't someone tell me that counselors had been at the Bart fire station around the clock since the incident? Why didn't anyone tell me that there were others aching like I was, and that they were together at the Bart fire station?

Why was I left alone?

I wondered who else was left alone. Who else was forgotten? I think so often of the caretakers, and the people left behind to pick up the pieces at gruesome sites, and too many times, they are just forgotten. Too many times people just think we're just doing our jobs.

Yes, we're just doing our jobs, but we're human. We hurt inside just as much as anyone else. Why are so many people overlooked when it comes to taking care of those who take care of others?

We broke up into groups, as there were too many people for a mass debriefing counseling session. I had been to one debriefing before, following a nasty ambulance call, so I sort of knew what to expect, as far as the rules.

Everything that is said in the room stays in that room, forever. If you have to go to the bathroom, or want to go outside and smoke a cigarette, that's okay, but one of the counselors will go with you. They needed to be certain you're ok. You may say as much, or as little, as you wish.

We started by going around the circle and introducing ourselves, and telling of our role on October 2nd. As had happened at the one that I attended years before that, so many people said, "I only helped knock down the fence, to make the path to the helicopters shorter," or, "I only was there with the fire police." I thought to myself, "Every single person in this room performed an invaluable job. Why are they saying, they only did this, or only did that?"

Then people started telling their stories. The truth was now coming out. As much as we were trying to hide behind the walls we had built, they were crumbling. A lot of people were having trouble sleeping. A lot felt they could have, or should have, done more. Many questioned their actions during the chaotic moments of making life and death decisions. Many people were very angry. Angry that this tragedy had shattered their peaceful, calm lives. People were becoming agitated with their spouses, and or, children, over things that had never bothered them before. Many felt, that even when they talked about it with someone else, no one felt the pain that they felt.

Sights of children wearing straw hats and riding bikes would send some into a panic mode. The sound of a helicopter sent one person to get professional help.

Some wanted to watch the news and read as much as possible. Others had no desire to watch the news or read the papers. Everyone felt that no one else understood how he or she felt. Nearly everyone was angry with the media. I felt guilt ridden that I had done interviews with the media. Everyone had his or her own trigger points.

Certain things that you saw would put you back at the scene. We were all dreading Mondays, especially Monday mornings. But we knew we couldn't avoid a lot of these things. We couldn't stop Mondays from following Sundays; and we couldn't stop them from sending us back, in our minds, to the scene. The mind is a great thing, but it's also a very scary thing, as it's so uncontrollable at times.

The group I was seated with was inside a bay of the fire station. There was a large, roll up type door, with windows, along the front of the room. I remember seeing a truck backing up to the door. Someone was probably delivering more food supplies, or something very innocent. But when I saw the truck, backing up towards the door, I was suddenly back at the scene, picturing the shooter's truck, backed up to the front of the schoolhouse. I couldn't concentrate on the counseling.

I wanted to stand up and scream, "Go away!"

Fortunately, it was now my turn to share things that were annoying me. I said, "That truck that is backed up in front of the door is putting me back at the scene, and I can't get it out of my head." Within minutes, someone took care of having the truck moved. We continued sharing our stories, as we continued crying.

I immediately bonded with Kelly Kirk-Wentzel and Anita Imhoff. Kelly was there as a counselor, and Anita is Supervisor of Operations at Christiana Ambulance. I had never met either of them before that evening, but they became invaluable friends to me.

Out of respect for the people who attended that counseling session, as well as the ones I attended thereafter, I will not divulge any of the specific information revealed during the sessions. I will say, that had it not been for those counseling sessions, I am not certain I would have been able to return to a relatively normal state of mind. There are some who never have. Several turned in their equipment and badges following that day, to seek more "normal" jobs. I was fortunate that I was helped by the counseling, and was able to move forward.

Hours and hours later, Amanda and I drove home. I felt so much better than I felt before the counseling. Amanda wasn't saying too much. I asked her what she was thinking.

She told me that she didn't think she wanted to go to anymore counseling sessions. She felt they depressed her more than helped her. She was saddened by how difficult a time so many people were having. She felt she would do better by not attending anymore, although she did appreciate getting to sit in on one. She never attended anymore sessions.

I lived for them. I lived because of them. Each person is so very different and there's nothing wrong with that.

We were each given a brochure outlining indications of critical incident stress. I read it when I returned home. Some of the symptoms I could easily relate to, while others I thought would never happen to me. I read through the list:

Reliving the incident. (How could I stop that?)

Poor concentration; difficulty remembering. (But there were so many things I wanted to forget.)

Difficulty making decisions.

Difficulty adding, or subtracting. (When I read that one, I thought, "No way, that will never happen to me," but several days later, I went to subtract a $40.00 cash withdrawal from my checkbook, and I couldn't do it.)

Sadness; irritability; and crying. (I did a lot of that.)

Withdrawing from others. (Sometimes I yearned for my friends, other times I wanted everyone to just leave me alone.)

Difficulty sleeping; focusing on the trivial. (The smallest things would irritate me, but the rest of the symptoms, I didn't seem to have.)

So I was encouraged that I might have a chance of getting through this, as I figured I had less than half of the symptoms listed. I didn't tempt fate by trying to count them, as I had just read the "difficulty adding and subtracting," and at that time, I thought that wasn't one of my symptoms.

Through counseling, I learned that I will never be the same, "normal" person that I was before October 2nd. I had to learn to find my "new normal." I found comfort in that. I could do that.

I could expect to think about that day, forever, but I could learn to deal with my thoughts and feelings. I accepted that it is ok to answer, "Well, I've had better days, but thanks for asking."

Kelly sent me a nice note, towards the end of the year. Parts of it included, "Hi Janice, I've thought of you often and wondered how you have been doing. Christmas is such a joyous time, but also a difficult time, as it stirs up many memories of the past year. The events of October 2 are still so fresh that there is no way that I would expect that 'everything is okay.' After a tragedy, a person will go back and forth through the cycles of grief. At some point in time, you will discover your 'new normal.' Please be patient with yourself. I wish you a peaceful and happy New Year!" While her letter arrived near the end of December, I was beginning to find my new normal. But I still had a long road ahead of me.

We have a monthly coroner training class the first Thursday of each month. It's at 6:00 p.m. and it's usually held at Lancaster General Hospital. Amanda always drives and picks me up. We always go out to eat after the meeting. So that was my only plan for Thursday, and I was so anxious to spend time and try to relax with my peers.

On Thursday morning, Dr. Kirchner called me and told me that I was to be at the Bart Fire Company that evening by 9:45. I was to be there for a live interview with him and Greta Van Susteren. Greta who? I didn't know who this "Greta" was, but this was obviously not optional. I said I would be there, but I wanted Amanda to be with me. He agreed.

I asked him what we were to wear. I'll never forget his response, "Don't fret over what you're going to wear, fret over what you're going to say."

I called Amanda, and informed her of our obligation to be at Bart fire station. She picked me up that evening, and we headed to our monthly meeting. I asked her what Dr. Kirchner meant by his comment about the fretting. She asked me, "Don't you know who Greta is?" I answered truthfully, "Nope." Amanda said, "She's a cutthroat reporter." Amanda continued to say she might ask questions that are inappropriate, or insensitive, and that was why I was advised to fret over what I would say.

We attended our monthly training session, of which I have no recollection whatsoever, then went for a bite to eat after the meeting.

We talked, listened, cried, and formed a bond that I thought would never be broken. I learned later, something I already knew; that what seems to be is not always what seems to be. Then Amanda and I had to leave to go to Bart Township for the interview.

Greta wouldn't be there, but we were to be interviewed by her, live, via satellite. It was a dreary, rainy evening. The interview went well, despite being done under a tent and in the rain. I must admit, it was extremely trying, as we didn't know what question Greta was going to ask us. We couldn't see her. We were talking into the dark, pouring rain. The entire interview took less than fifteen minutes.

Then we drove back to Ephrata, from Bart Township, in the rain. We were both drained, emotionally and physically. Being home felt so good. My answering machine was filled with messages from reporters, begging me to call them for an interview. I deleted all of the messages, and went to bed. As much as I felt the need to talk about October 2nd, that evening, there was no place like home. I went to bed and tried to sleep.

But my phone continued ringing. I didn't answer it. Then Amanda called, and as she was leaving her message, I picked up the phone. She asked if I had gotten a call from Ann Curry. I told her I might have, I wasn't certain, and I had erased all of my messages. She again proceeded to enlighten me about reporters.

She told me that Ann Curry is very well respected, and Amanda felt that of all the reporters that had left messages, Ann was the only one Amanda felt that we should at least reply to. Okay, I'll contact Dr. Kirchner.

I called him and told him that Ann Curry wanted to do an interview with us. He immediately said, "Yes. Ann can name the time and place, and we'll be there." I sensed this Ann person must be a top-notch reporter. After getting the contact information from Amanda, I called and arranged the interview.

This one was again going to be at the Bart fire station. By now I was beginning to dread driving to Bart. It was a bittersweet feeling. I loved the area. It is as peaceful and gentle as it gets. The people are so down to earth. But now I was starting to tire of the drive to Bart, to say the same thing, over and over. What more was there to say? It's all been said, over and over.

The only drives to Bart that I looked forward to were the scheduled meetings with the families involved and my counseling sessions.

Eleven girls, from seven families, had been in the school. Five innocent girls had been murdered.

By Friday, I knew each of these girls, as if they had been my own children.

Naomi Rose Ebersol, aged 7, died at the scene. Naomi was a second grader, who had five brothers. She was my angel, with a face I will never forget. Naomi played "boy" games with her brothers, and they in turn obliged her by playing dolls with her. For her seventh birthday, she had gotten a dog, and named her "Shirley." It seemed like an unusual name for a dog, but that's what made her dog special, just like she was.

Marian Stoltzfus Fisher, aged 13, was flown to, and pronounced dead on arrival, at Lancaster General Hospital. Marian loved helping her father with the farm chores in the evening. Being the oldest girl, Marian had her own bedroom. Her two sisters, Barbie, 11, and Emma, 9, shared a bedroom. The family also had one older and three younger sons.

Anna Mae Stoltzfus, aged 12, died at the scene. Anna and her sister, Sarah Ann, had six brothers. They both loved singing. Sarah loved to read. Anna enjoyed doing the laundry for her family of ten. She also enjoyed tending the cash register at the family's market stand, which sold homemade lawn and house furniture.

Lena Zook Miller, aged 7, was flown to, and died, at Penn State Milton S. Hershey Medical Center, Hershey, Pa., on October 3rd. Lena was very close to her older sister, Mary, who had also died, as a result of the shootings. They shared a bed, covered by a rose quilt given to them by a family member. Lena was the more talkative of the two sisters.

Mary Liz Miller, aged 8, was flown to, and died, at Christiana Hospital in Newark, Delaware, on October 3rd. Both Mary and her sister Lena were toting new, purple Igloo lunchboxes that Monday. The lunchboxes had been purchased in a box lot of items, at the West Nickel Mines auction. Mary loved the outdoors and was a little less talkative than Lena.

Five girls were injured but still alive.

Rosanna King, 6, was removed from life support at Hershey Medical Center, and sent home to die, at the request of her family, on October 4th. However, the family noticed some signs of recovery at home, and she was taken back to the hospital. Rosanna was considered a memory-game whiz. She loved reciting Bible verses, and helping her mother in the kitchen. She was as comfortable playing ball with her four brothers and two sisters, as she was playing with dolls. Rosanna loved to sing. Her classmates went to visit her, and sang to her, not knowing if she heard them. Today, Rosanna is confined to a reclining wheelchair, is not able to talk, and is totally dependent on her family members for personal care, mobility, and feeding by a tube.

Esther King, age 12, was one of Rosanna's sisters. Esther, like Rosanna, also loved singing. She was fond of animals, and enjoyed her "stamping." She would stamp decorations on cards, and give them to family and friends. Esther remained hospitalized at Lancaster General Hospital.

Rachel Ann Stoltzfus, age 8, remained hospitalized at Children's Hospital of Philadelphia. Rachel was a sturdy redhead, the only redhead in her family of ten. A fourth grader, she shared a bedroom with her younger, only sister. Like most of the other students, Rachel also carried an Igloo to school that day. Hers was purple, and contained one of her favorites, a ham and cheese sandwich.

Barbara (Barbie) Stoltzfus Fisher, age 10, was flown to, and stabilized at a Reading hospital, then flown to Children's Hospital of Philadelphia.

Sarah Ann Stoltzfus, age 8, was taken to Lancaster General Hospital. Sarah was another one of the girls who loved to read and sing.

The interview with Ann was set. Three chairs were set up in the rear of their bay. Some man told us the chairs were for us. We decided to let Dr. Kirchner sit in the middle seat, and Amanda and I sat next to him. No sooner had we sat down, then in walked this lady, who I now recognized. I remembered seeing her on television, and thinking very highly of her reporting. She was so beautiful.

She sat on a chair in front of us, and said we would chat a little before the actual airing began. She told us that after the filming, it could be edited, so we could be comfortable, and not worry. That worked for me.

We began talking about that Monday. We were totally engrossed in talking about that Monday. Suddenly, a pristine woman approached Ann with a squirt bottle and hairbrush, and began spraying Ann's hair, and brushing it. Ann calmly turned to her, and asked, "What are you doing?" The woman replied that she's fixing her hair. Ann told her in a calm, but effective voice, "My hair is the last thing on earth that I'm thinking about right now."

The woman quickly gathered her items and disappeared. I immediately thought, "Ann is truly a caring person." That action, displayed by Ann, won my heart. She was doing her job, but at the same time, she was very sensitive of the people involved, and to the emotions and feelings that we were carrying.

After the brief prelude to the actual filming, she asked if we were ready to begin filming, again reminding us that anything could be edited. Yes, we were ready. Amanda and I were both ready to go have a smoke, but Ann was so nice, we opted not to mention it. The filming began. I don't remember most of her questions. One question, however, will remain with me forever. Ann asked Dr. Kirchner, "Is this is the worst thing you have ever seen?" His immediate response was, "Yes!" She continued to question him, "You were the chief surgeon on the USS Forrestal, during which you witnessed the death of hundreds of soldiers, and you're saying this Monday in Bart Township was worse than that?"

His answer proved his sensitivity and rationalization. He calmly replied, "Yes, this is the worst thing I have ever seen. You have to remember that those were soldiers who were at war. Their families knew that they might not return home. These were innocent children, who had left their homes that morning, with all expectations of returning home that afternoon."

After the filming was finished, she asked if there was anything she could do for us. I sensed she truly meant it but I didn't know of anything she could do for me. Then Amanda surprised me. She told Ann that one of our senior deputies collects autographs, and Amanda had promised him she would try to get an autograph for him. Ann immediately said yes, and called one of her assistants to get some paper or photos, I'm not certain which it was, and she asked Amanda how she should sign it.

When I watched the airing on television, I saw the same caring person who I had met. She was obviously there to do her job, but you could sense the compassion she was feeling. I've never seen another reporter display the same feelings as she did. Her feelings were from her heart. It wasn't like she was doing her job. She had become engulfed in the sadness that surrounded her, and she was sensitive to fact that others were also swallowed up by the sadness that they had experienced. I am grateful that there are reporters like Ann.

I had been saving newspapers and articles as I came across them. Months later I began to go through them. I read things I might have forgotten if I hadn't saved these articles, which are also a part of my scrapbook.

Dr. Kirchner sends an email blog, every morning, to all of the deputies and a host of other people. Tuesday morning's blog included the following statements:

> *The nightmare continues. Another child died at HMC at 0430. How are we to deal with this? How are all of the hundreds from PSP, EMT, ATF, FBI, Salvation Army to deal with this tragedy?*
>
> *In my mind is forever imprinted the scene. The clear beautiful day. The carriages of the Amish. The circling news choppers. The many many volunteers. The crime scene tape. All of the coroner deputies assembled and working without flaw. The schoolyard with the covered child body. The baseball bats lying where they were dropped. The debris of the disaster scattered over the yard. The fence. The yellow tape.*
>
> *And then the schoolhouse. The posters on the wall. The greeting that said visitors brightened the pupils' days. The fragmented glass everywhere. The upheaval inside. The bodies inside. The weapons of this death. The smiley faces on many places. The evidence of the boards to seal the doors. The tie wraps on the floor. And the incredible trashing of a quiet Amish School so out of character. And overall the profound sadness of all who were there.*
>
> *For a very large group there was little background noise. I wish I were an Anabaptist, and was able to accept this as God's will and survive it.*
>
> *We will do the posts starting at 0800. We will do the children first and try to return them to their families*

as rapidly as possible. That is my promise to the Amish steering committee and the families.

The shooter seems to be an individual who broke out of a perfectly normal lifestyle to the perpetrator of a horrific fantasy. As bizarre as it was violent. I do not believe he targeted the Amish. I believe he picked this quiet little school without phones, without alarms, with open doors, without pupils with cell phones, to buy himself time to carry out his mission. No autopsy will ever find that dark place in his brain where lived this horrible scheme. We will never know and best not speculate.

These things have no answers.

I have helped myself by talking and writing. The damage to the soul is permanent. I will do anything I can to help anyone involved.

I thank everyone involved and I am extremely proud of all you deputies who did it very well.

And I thought the Leola murders were bad.

On April 9th, 2006, Jesse D. Wise, 21, was accused of killing six of his family members, inside their Leola home. It seemed that when Lancaster County received widespread news coverage, it usually isn't good.

Dr. Kirchner always puts things on the table as he sees them. While some may not agree with this philosophy, I admire it. I'd rather have someone be forthright with me, than sneak behind my back with a dagger.

His next blog that I put in my scrapbook is from Friday, October 6th. Excerpts from it include:

And it goes on.

Janice and Amanda did very well with me on FOX at 2200 with Greta. In a tent with the rain. In the churchyard surrounded by many, TV trucks. Good thing they have their own electric source, or Bart would be in brownout. I am looking shop-worn. The ladies looking great.

> *The question is easy. Then today with Ann Curry of NBC. I really looked forward to meeting her. It is funny how you flesh out the persona of a TV personality.*
>
> *The damp all so appropriate for the funeral. Funerals in bright sunshine always seem incongruous.*
>
> *Two posts for today. The homicide victim from E-town and the MVA.*
>
> *Like my driver last nite said, "Why do all arguments get settled by guns? Whatever happened to a good old fist fight?"*

I am just so overwhelmed at how much I don't remember, and how much I wish I didn't remember.

As I pulled out my stack of newspapers, while writing this book, it was the first time that I've actually read, and comprehended what I read. The *Intelligencer Journal* is our county's morning paper. They got the breaking story.

The morning paper from Tuesday contained a huge headline, "DEATH OF INNOCENTS," with a picture of an Amish man's head buried beneath his straw hat, obviously crying. The sub-headline read, "Gunman invades Amish school; kills 3 girls, self; wounds 7." Months later, the same paper was auctioned on EBay for a huge amount. Again I tried to control my anger, and accept the fact that people are just trying to make money. But again, it seemed wrong.

Pennsylvania State Police Commissioner Jeffrey B. Miller said, during a press conference Monday night, "No one deserves what happened here today." He also said that Roberts had no prior criminal history and that the killings may be linked to an event that happened years ago in Roberts' life, but did not state the nature of the event.

Pages and pages of the morning paper were filled with pictures from the scene; a picture of Roberts' home; a photo announcing the engagement of Roberts and Marie Welk; a time frame of the incident; quotes by Roberts' family and friends.

Family members had stated, "He was a good son and a good father. I just don't understand why he did it, why he killed those
kids. He was a gentle person. He was a family man."

Roberts' wife, Marie, stated, "The man who did this was not
the Charles I've been married to for almost ten years. My husband was loving, supportive, thoughtful—all the things you'd
always want, and more. He never said no to changing a diaper.
Our hearts are broken, our lives are shattered and we grieve for
the innocence and the lives that were lost today. Above all, please
pray. Pray for the families who lost children. And please pray,
too, for our family and children."

According to friends and co-workers, Roberts, normally
outgoing and friendly, had become introverted and tense in recent weeks. The dark mood changed late last week, as Roberts
turned jovial.

Miller commented, "It seems to us that he may have made
a decision to do this within the past few days, and that seemed
to have relieved some of the pressures he was exhibiting to his
co-workers. On Monday morning Roberts took his children to
the school bus. He returned home and wrote notes to his family, before driving about a mile to the school. Roberts carried
into the school a 9 mm Springfield semi-automatic pistol, a
Browning Ruger bolt-action .30-06 rifle, about 600 rounds of
ammunition, cans of black powder, smokeless gunpowder for
reloading, a stun gun, two knives, and a box containing a ham-
mer, hacksaw, pliers, wire, screws, bolts, earplugs, plastic ties,
toilet paper, tape and a change of clothing. He used a 2x6 and
2x4 boards with eyebolts and flex ties to barricade the school
doors. Roberts fired three rounds from the 12-guage shotgun
and 13 rounds from the semi-automatic handgun. It is clear
to us that he did a great deal of planning, just from the list of
materials I just laid out. It appears as though he intended to
prepare for a lengthy siege. He came prepared. It wasn't a spur
of the moment thing. It appears he did a lot of time in plan-

ning and intended to harm these kids and intended to harm himself."

People who turned on news stations all over the world Monday and Tuesday saw Miller's face and heard his words. For about 48 hours following the shootings, Col. Miller shouldered the burden of describing to the world what happened inside the one-room Amish schoolhouse. In the tragic time, he brought an air of calmness to the world. Col. Miller told of a checklist, in a wirebound notebook, found in the cab of Roberts' truck, with his list of supplies he was gathering for his standoff. Witnesses stated they saw Roberts buy a soda outside of the West Nickel Mines Auction center on Monday morning and stand outside, sipping the soda and watching the children at recess in the schoolyard.

I often wish that I had thought to turn on my television during that week. I just never thought about it. Many people told me that the news covered the story for days, around the clock. I wish I could have been at home, watching it unfold on my television, rather than at the scene.

The nation learned that Roberts had never gotten over the death of his premature daughter, Elise Victoria, who was born on November 14, 1997, and died approximately twenty minutes after her birth. We learned Roberts and his wife had three healthy children following the death of Elise. A girl, Abigail was born in 1999; a son Bryce in 2001 and a second son, Carson was born in 2005. Roberts took the death of Elise extremely hard, according to family and friends. A heart-shaped marble gravestone, etched with a lamb with Elise's information on it, was shown over and over on television, and in the papers.

Roberts left suicide notes to each of his children and one to his wife. Parts of the note to Marie included: "I don't know how you put up with me all those years. I am not worthy of you, you are the perfect wife you deserve so much better. We had so many good memories together as well as the tragedy with Elise.

It changed my life forever I haven't been the same since . . . I am filled with so much hate, hate towards myself . . . hate towards God and unimaginable emptiness. It seems like every time we do something fun I think about how Elise wasn't here to share it with us, and I go right back to anger."

The notes to his children told them he loved them and they were good children.

Our county hospitals train for "mass casualty" incidents. That Monday, they were called upon to put that training into action. Each hospital treated and stabilized the girls as they arrived, and then transferred them to hospitals that specialize in childcare.

Dr. Michael Reihart, Lancaster General's emergency room incident commander, maintained his composure. "This was an extremely frustrating, scary event. Any time a child is injured it is very, very difficult for everyone involved. But in all of my years of experience, I have never seen such teamwork. A 'code green' was declared around 11:00 a.m., which meant that everyone in the hospital was put on notice that 'mass casualties' were expected. All of the girls brought to our facility sustained gunshots to the brain, thorax and extremities. They were all very serious."

While LGH is Lancaster County's designated trauma center, it does not have pediatric specialty care, so Reihart knew they would have to stabilize, and have them flown to another hospital. He recalled hearing repeated announcements; "A child with head injuries" was on the way to the hospital. He thought, "Is this a mistake? Is there just one child and they keep repeating it? How can all these children have the same type of injury?" His staff focused on what they could do and the lives they could save.

When you take a trauma alert patient to Lancaster General, you are expected to remove all of their clothing before arrival, so the trauma team can act quickly in treating them. I've taken many ambulance patients to the trauma room. When our ambulance pulls up to the emergency entrance, we are met by a host of staff, offering their assistance. I have never left the hospital without thinking how truly blessed our county is to have the resources provided by the LGH trauma center.

It is like a well-rehearsed musical. Everyone knows exactly what to do. There is no hesitation. They are prepared for traumas. X-ray technicians, respiratory specialists, cardiologists, the list of skilled doctors, goes on and on, awaiting your patient's arrival. A pastor is there to take family contact information.

I spoke with a trauma nurse, who was a part of the team that day. She told me she remembered suddenly seeing black shoes and black socks on one patient, and she asked, "Are these Amish children?" "Yes," she was told. "Yes, all Amish children."

Reihart later said that in his 25 years of working in emergency medicine, "I've never seen anything like this . . . it was surreal, the horror of it all. It was the biggest disaster scene in Lancaster County. It wasn't a car accident or a gang shooting, it was children, and Amish children, the most innocent of all . . . it rattles your foundation."

Back in Bart Township, the State police had offered to drive, or fly, the Amish families to be with their children. All declined to fly, and made arrangements to be driven by friends. Police had driven the Stoltzfus family to Christiana Hospital in Delaware, where they believed Anna Mae was being treated.

When they saw the girl lying in the hospital bed, they knew it was not their daughter. A team of Amish elders traveled to LGH, in an effort to gather information about the girls. But the children, except for Marian Fisher, who was dead on arrival at LGH, had been transferred.

Meanwhile, the Millers had yet to learn where Lena and Mary Liz were. They felt one of their daughters was lying dead inside the school. Troopers rushed them to Christiana Hospital, to see if either of their daughters was there. When they arrived, they saw the Stoltzfuses in the parking lot.

The Stoltzfuses had just learned it was their daughter, who had been lying dead, in the schoolhouse.

Inside the hospital, the Millers learned that Mary Liz was on life support. The doctors spoke honestly. She was in grave condition and brain dead. Knowing that, they requested she be removed from life support. Then, about 10 p.m. they were told that their other daughter, Lena, was at Hershey Medical Center, also in grave condition.

A little after midnight, Mary Liz was disconnected from life support. Her parents had held her, and kissed her goodbye. Then they left to be with Lena, who would also soon be taken off of life support. It was close to 2 a.m. when Lena was disconnected from life support, and died almost immediately thereafter, as she lay cradled in her parents' arms. She was the fifth girl to be pronounced dead.

I cannot imagine the feelings that must have been felt by the Millers. Holding your one daughter, and watching her die, knowing another daughter is in a different hospital. Knowing that you must go, and hold a second daughter, and also watch her die.

I kept telling myself that we're never given more than we can handle. But why was this innocent family subjected to travel to the depths of despair and confront the face of death in two of their daughters? All within hours of each other. I couldn't find any answer.

Tuesday's *New Era*, our evening paper, held the headline, "HORROR IN SCHOOLHOUSE." The sub-headline read, "5 Amish girls killed, 5 critically wounded in shocking massacre; killer planned to molest young victims as he had 20 years before."

The 32-year-old milk-truck driver was still distraught, over the death of his premature infant daughter, nine years ago. He had loaded himself with weapons and supplies to molest and to kill: bullets, guns, lubricating jelly, eyebolts and tape. There was, however, no evidence that any of the victims were sexually assaulted. I believe that his intention was to be there for a long time. I believe he intended to sexually assault his victims. I believe, if there is any salvation in this whole bizarre, twisted event, it would be that Roberts didn't get to follow through with his plans. That's the only salvation that I can find.

Roberts meticulously planned his attack on the school, gathering supplies with a checklist, and methodically gathering the children, before ending their lives.

His wife, Marie, discovered something was terribly wrong when she returned home and called her husband, after finding the series of suicide notes. The notes detailed Roberts' grief over his daughter's death nine years ago. Again, the paper was filled with pictures.

A picture of the home where the Roberts family lived; the truck believed to be the one that he used to pick up milk before he went to the school Monday morning. Roberts was a truck driver who visited the farms and picked up milk. The Amish families were familiar with him, and they worked side by side. A picture of emergency vehicles lining White Oak Road at the site of the Amish school. I could see the rear of my red Jeep in the picture, and then I realized I was parked much closer to the scene than I had thought.

Wednesday's paper again had huge headlines, "Slayer of Amish girls tortured by his past." It also announced that two more victims had died; and five remained hospitalized. Roberts' statement that he molested young family members, years ago, was never substantiated.

The timeline of the day's events had now unfolded. At 3:00 a.m. Charles Carl Roberts IV, age 32, a milk tanker-truck driver, returned to his Georgetown Road home in Bart Township after delivering milk from area farms to a processing plant.

8:45 a.m. Roberts walked two of his children to a nearby bus stop. He returned home, and after his wife left, wrote the suicide notes.

10:00 a.m. Roberts drove a borrowed pickup truck to West Nickel Mines School, about a mile away. Roberts backed the truck up to the school and entered the school holding a clevis, a U-shaped metal fitting with holes in the ends. He asked if anyone had seen something like it along the road. Teacher Emma Mae Zook, 20, had just brought the 26 schoolchildren in from morning recess. She was teaching German and spelling. Emma's mother, Barbie, was in the school visiting, as were other members of the Zook family. Emma's sister-in-law, 23-year-old Sarah was there with her 2-year-old daughter and newborn son. Her sister, Lydia Mae, was eight months pregnant.

 Roberts went back to the truck, and then returned to the classroom holding a gun. When the older Zook saw the gun, she looked at her daughter, and they darted outside the school. Roberts told a young boy to go after the two women and bring them back or he would shoot everyone. When the little boy left, 9-year-old student Emma Fisher escaped with him, leaving her two older sisters in the schoolhouse. Marian, 13, died, and Barbie was seriously injured. It was a split-second decision that probably saved her life. He released the 15 male students, a pregnant woman, and three women with infant children.

Roberts lined all 10 remaining girls—students age 6 to 13—in front of the blackboard, tied their feet together, tied them to each other, and barricaded the doors.

10:36 a.m. The teacher reached a nearby home and called 911.

10:45 a.m. State police arrived at the school. They tried talking to Roberts, using public-address speakers, but Roberts didn't respond.

Shortly before 11:00 a.m. Roberts' wife returned home and found the suicide notes. She tried to reach him on his cell phone.

11:00 a.m. Roberts used his cell phone to call his wife. He told her that he left notes for her, and the children, and that the police are at the school and he will not be coming home.

Moments later, Roberts called 911, and said, "I will start shooting if the police don't leave in two seconds." Police traced the 911 call to Roberts' cell phone. They tried to call back, but couldn't get through.

Roberts began rapidly shooting the girls, in the backs of their heads, firing about a dozen rounds from the pistol, and three rounds from his 12-gauge shotgun. He also shot once at the police, missing. Police, without returning fire, attempted to storm the school. Discovering the doors were blocked, they entered through the windows.

They found Roberts, and one girl, both dead. A second girl died in the arms of a state trooper, as he carried her out of the school. A third girl died on the way to LGH. Overnight, a girl who had been taken to Christiana Hospital, and one taken to Hershey Medical Center, also died; bringing the number of fatally-wounded girls to five.

As the county and nation mourned the tragedy, the families of the murdered children began preparing funerals.

The funerals are held in the homes of the deceased. They gathered benches from neighboring farms, cleaned house, prepared food, and comforted one another.

Everyone is dressed in black, and the immediate family will continue to wear black, exclusively, for a year. Long before the hour set aside for a funeral, scores of horse-drawn buggies pulled into each farm. The funeral goers filed inside the home, filling most first-floor rooms, and spilling outside to the porches.

The deceased lies in a coffin, in a separate room, with relatives sitting nearby. The service includes spoken hymns, sermons and benedictions. They emphasized preparation for the "end time," more than focusing on the individuals who have died. The services lasted two hours, or more.

Then the handmade wooden coffin is moved to a convenient viewing place, and everyone filed past it. The mourners returned to their buggies, and followed horses, plodding slowly, carrying the dark hearse conveying the body to the cemetery. Services at the gravesite, in a family plot, were relatively brief. They bury the child, and filled in the graves by hand. The school, the homes of the dead girls, and the cemetery, are all within a short distance of each other. In a territory where the children spent almost all of their lives, and now, where a tight-knit community gathered to grieve, as the world watched.

Funeral services were announced on Wednesday. The first service, for Naomi Rose Ebersol, 7, a second-grader, was scheduled for Thursday morning at 8 a.m.

This was my angel. I was saddened to my core.

Services for 13-year-old Marian S. Fisher were scheduled for noon. At 1:00 p.m., services for Mary Liz Miller, 8, and her sister, Lena Z. Miller, 7, were to be held at the Miller's home. A funeral for Anna Mae Stoltzfus, 12, was scheduled for 9 a.m. Friday, at the Stoltzfus' home.

As preparations for funeral services were being made, the county churches were holding services and vigils. The world poured out its collective heart. Funds were established to cover the expenses of the victims. Their "English" neighbors reached out to embrace the victims' families.

The Amish are humble people, and they wanted to be certain that people understood that they were not promoting this, but they were willing to accept help. One Amish elder explained to me, "This is our 9-11, this is our Hurricane Katrina. It would be un-Christ like to not let these people help us, when they want to help."

The donations would assist the victims of the murders, by helping them pay for medical and other urgent care for the victims, as well as the ongoing needs of their families and the community. Transportation was needed for the families to travel to visit their injured children in hospitals. The outpouring was overwhelming. Donations were received from all over the world, and amounted to more than $4.3 million.

Friday's paper continued with a huge headline, "LAID TO REST." More details emerged, as the funerals continued. Marian's 11-year-old sister, Barbie, who was wounded in the attack, was now awake and talking.

Barbie told her family that Roberts had asked the girls in the classroom to pray for him. One of the girls asked him, "Why don't you pray for us?" He answered bluntly, "I don't believe in prayer."

When the girls realized he planned to kill them, Marian said, "Shoot me first." Barbie said, "Shoot me next." They were trying to offer themselves, so the younger girls could be saved. Their courageous effort failed. He shot them.

What followed, were the longest ten days of my life.

Thursday, October 12th, at 4:45 a.m., an excavator, equipped with a backhoe, began ripping down the one-room schoolhouse. A contractor arrived at 4:00 a.m. and removed the white picket fence surrounding the school, which had been built in 1976. Under bright spotlights that illuminated the entire schoolyard, excavators reduced the concrete and wooden structure to rubble, within a half hour. Dump trucks hauled the bloodstained debris to two Lancaster County landfills. By 8:15 a.m. there was little evidence the tiny school ever existed, as the workers graded the land, blending it with surrounding pastures.

Certainly the Amish would have been capable of tearing down the structure on their own, but I was glad to see they enlisted the aid of contractors, who swiftly demolished the school. The Amish community had their own other thoughts to bury. Though the tragedy at West Nickel Mines School will remain in our hearts forever, the greatest physical reminder of the killings no longer existed.

One evening I was waiting in line, at the Bart fire hall, for a snack, before a counseling session. There was a group of two or three Amish boys in front of me. They appeared to be about eight or nine years old. It was only a day or two after the school had been torn down. I overheard one little boy say to the other, "They can take away our school, but they can't take away what we remember." His statement pierced my heart, as I wondered what he remembered. I was filled with awe and sadness at the profound wisdom in his statement.

The boys had now returned to a makeshift school, in a nearby garage. Try to imagine their feelings, as they went into the room, and ten girls out of twenty-six students were missing. I can't imagine it.

Mail and gifts began arriving, and Bart Fire Company station was set up as the collection and distribution center. One letter from Australia was simply addressed, "Amish Families USA," and found its way to the Bart fire station.

Mail and letters began arriving to the coroner's office. One was from one of our county dispatchers. Parts of his letter included, "I just wanted to say that I have been thinking about you and your staff during the last couple of days. I saw your (Dr. Kirchner) crew in action, and have the utmost respect for the job that you folks had to do. It was gut wrenching watching from the command post. I cannot imagine the horrific sight inside. I tip my hat to you sir and want you to know that we are here for you and your staff, around the clock. I hope that Ballenger and Rottmund come out of this OKAY. Know that we are here for each other."

But possibly the greatest gift to emerge from this tragedy was the lesson of forgiveness. The Amish struggled to adjust to a changed world. They are like anyone else. The sorrow is both personal and communal. While forgiving is a central part of their beliefs, it is still difficult.

When Charles Carl Roberts IV murdered five young girls and maimed five others, he burst the bubble of rural security, and invited grief to enter Lancaster County's Old Order Amish community. But the man who so carefully planned his assault on the school, and his own suicide, also accomplished something

I'm certain he never anticipated. He guaranteed that the core Amish belief in extending forgiveness to everyone, even this man so consumed by hate that he murdered innocent children, would command world-wide attention.

The world learned what I already knew.

To the Amish, it's not about their way of living, it's not about their way of not driving a car, rather, it's about taking care of their community, wanting to keep the community as it is, and keeping life pure, as Christians.

I believe the Amish had inadvertently sent a message to the "outside world," by the way they handled this tragedy, with great compassion and amazing grace. Many people were not aware of the close interaction between the Amish and non-Amish here, where many Amish serve in volunteer fire departments.

It seemed the same question kept arising, "Why?"

We can't expect to be able to understand everything in this life. I believe there usually is no answer to, "why?" I believe we should never put a question mark where God has put a period.

Cards began arriving for me. I was shocked when I received the first handful. People across the country actually took time to write to me, and expressed their hopes and prayers for me to find strength. Those acts of kindness meant more to me than anyone will ever know.

Cards, counseling and faith in the belief that we are never given more than we can handle, are what kept me going. I had selfishly felt so alone in the first few weeks following that Monday. When cards began arriving, it was as if others were reaching out to help me through those first hazy, dark days and weeks. I replied to each one of them.

While most were on a personal note, there were those that were not. One was from a group, "S.A.V.E.", "Stop Antidepressant Violence from Escalating". They were inquiring as to whether Mr. Roberts had any traces of antidepressants in his bloodstream at the time that he committed the shootings.

One from Mary, in Pasadena, Texas, had a beautiful, dark stone inside the card, with the word "HOPE" engraved on the stone. A note was included. "Dear Janice, I felt compelled to write you this letter and let you know that you are not alone with the heartbreak you are feeling. The compassion you have shown for the families involved in this awful, awful crime is commendable. The tenderness in which I know you know you did your job when you encountered these innocent children showed so much respect and love for them, even in their deaths. Please do not despair. There is still so much hope in the world. Through all of this, the Amish have stood above all others in their steadfast compassion and forgiveness of others. I pray that God will give you peace and erase the terrible things that you had to see on that dreadful day. As long as there are people in the world who care, there is always hope!" I will cherish that simple, but powerful, stone forever. Mary and I continue, to this day, to write to each other.

It was my first night back with ambulance, following the day in Nickel Mines. I had agreed to do a football standby with Gene. After the standby, we returned to the station and there was a message for me to call Elva at her restaurant, which is directly across the street from our ambulance station. I called and she said a few people from Canada were there, and interested in the Amish story. Elva asked if I could come over and answer a few questions.

By now, my mind and soul had become immune to the questions. I begged Gene to go with me, and he agreed. We walked in the front door of the restaurant, which was now closed, and I saw cameras and lights, all set up, obviously for an interview. I did an interview with Lorna Dueck, a reporter for "Listen Up", which is a Canadian television station. Their reporters just happened to stop at Elva's restaurant for dinner, and mentioned to her the reason for them being in the area. Elva told them of my involvement, and hence the interview.

Lorna Dueck was another one of the nicest reporters I have ever met. She later sent me a beautiful card, along with a copy of the two-hour airing on the Amish tragedy. She wrote, "Your willingness to forgive and serve in such an involved profession as yours—wow. Thanks for making the heart in the show."

A lady from New Jersey wrote, "You do not know me, but I was moved to write this after seeing your interview on ABC's "Nightline." There is no way to make sense of such a tragedy. Even saying it was God's will seems wrong, as I perceive God as loving and not evil. You try to help people—both the victims, whose lives are lost, and their relatives who have to figure out how to piece together their shattered lives and go forward. Both your jobs can be very hectic and hard. It's common to lose sight of ourselves in such tests. Please remember to take care of yourself in dealing with this tragedy. Those 5 little lives may be gone physically, but they live on in the hearts and spirit of the community—your community. I'll pray for them and you."

I received a card of encouragement from my letter carrier. He had mailed it to me! Just offering a note to hang in there. But his small note meant so very much to me.

One from Wichita, Kansas, was simply addressed, "Deputy County Coroner. Janice Ballenger. Lancaster County. PA, USA," and it found its way to me. That card is one of my favorites. The front has a picture of mountains and clouds, and the words, "The beauty of the world has two edges . . . one of laughter . . . one of anguish . . ." while the inside simply said, "My thoughts are with you." As I looked at the saying on the front of the card, I realized how true this was. Inside the card Brenda wrote, " . . . your humanity, compassion and tears helped us all grieve. May each day bring you blessings."

Another lady wrote, "Saw your picture in the paper; my tears fell, knowing what hell you had witnessed. Unbelievable. I worked with Charles' mother at Armstrong. The devastation of the Amish and Charles' family is unreal. My heart goes out to you and all."

A female from Red Hill, Pa., wrote, "I felt compelled to write to you after I saw your interview on tv. Your words and your expression caused me to feel the depth of the tragedy. Instantly I knew the depth of the innocence, and the weight of a bizarre peak of psychiatric misfiring of an individual. I wanted to hug you like only a sister could at that moment. Consider yourself hugged. Someday I would like to meet you." I wrote back to her and said that I don't have a sister, although many times I wished I did, but I never heard from her again.

Many, many brochures and pamphlets containing various religious scripts and readings were sent to me. Bibles were mailed to me from many different religious groups. The Book of Mormon was sent by the Church of Jesus Christ of Latter-Day Saints.

Jehovah's Witness's sent a book titled, *What Does The Bible Really Teach?* A two page, handwritten, letter was enclosed with it. Parts from the letter included, "Can you imagine a world without wicked ones? Crime and hatred would be a thing of the past."

No, I can't imagine a world without crime and hatred. I wish I could.

While each and every card and gift was precious to me, I believe the most humbling gift I received was from The Episcopal Church of the Advent. It was sent from their Kennett Square pastoral care center. When the box arrived, it was about the size of four shoeboxes. I pondered, "What could be inside this large box?" I opened it to find a beautiful shawl. There was a letter with it. "We read *The Washington Post* article about the shooting at the Nickel Mines school. The picture of you at the church in Paradise said so much about what a heavy burden that is for you to carry. There is a Prayer Shawl Ministry here at Church of the Advent, and we are sending you a prayer shawl to wrap you in prayer. We hope it gives you comfort and helps you to heal. We will continue to keep you and the Amish community in our prayers. This shawl has been knit for Janice Ballenger for comfort and healing. On this date, October, 2006 and around our gathered circle, this shawl has passed through our praying hands and been blessed by our loving hearts."

I literally wrapped the shawl around my shoulders. I could feel the caring and prayers that went into making it. I had never heard of a prayer shawl before, but I was moved to tears, as I remained wrapped in it and re-read the letter. I laid down on my sofa, and for the first time in weeks, I experienced a peaceful sleep.

I decided to sleep with the shawl that evening, and again had a very peaceful sleep. But when I woke up in the morning, I found that during my sleep, I had pulled on some of the yarn. Small holes were starting to develop, so I decided to hang it on a special chair in my living room. The chair was my grandmother's parents' first piece of furniture, when they set up housekeeping, and it's a very special piece to me. The shawl continues to hang there, and when I'm in need of a quick comfort fix, I look at the shawl and I'm good to go.

Most letters and cards came within the immediate weeks following the shootings. I will never forget the day I brought in my mail, and all that was there were bills.

My first thought was, "Okay, I'm supposed to be back to normal now?" I didn't feel back to normal. How could everyone think that I was back to normal?

I knew I would never be the normal person that I used to be. But through counseling, I learned that the day I went to my mailbox, and found only bills, was the first day of my "new normal."

Other cards and letters continued to straggle in during the following year. One from Mobile, Alabama, was received in March of 2007. It read, "Dear Janice, I had watched your special on The Learning Channel about the tragedy and was deeply touched . . . I wanted to do something special so I decided to send a gift of money for you to pass onto the Amish. Whether they use it to buy some seeds for their crops, or whatever, I am sending my deepest condolences to all who were affected by this terrible event." A ten dollar bill was neatly folded and tucked into the letter. Once again, nearly a half a year later, I found myself crying. But these tears were different. These tears were tears of thanks to those who realized how all of us had suffered.

Another one arrived quite some time later. It was a blank card, with writing inside, "Time has passed since that awful tragedy in Nickel Mines, but I know that the day's events are still so present for you. Please know that the thoughts, prayers and tears of many of us surround you in empathy for what you had to witness and endure. I felt your pain when I saw one of the interviews you did and just want you to know that you are not alone . . . we all grieve the loss of innocence and are greatly affected in our daily lives. Thank you for your compassion in doing your job that day/week. God obviously gave you the strength to carry you through. God is carrying us when we can't find the strength to walk. . . ."

One card had a separate piece of paper inside it, "I sent this card immediately following watching everything on the news, but it came back so I finally got online and found this address to re-mail this card to you." My immediate reaction was one of awe. I thought, "In this day and age of email, how many people would spend the time researching the mailing address, and take time to re-mail the card. I was overwhelmed with gratitude.

The same words seemed to be echoed, over and over, "I saw you on the news and wanted to let you know I am praying for you. Your job last week was so difficult my heart aches for you and the Amish families and the Amish community. May you feel the peace and comfort that only God can give. You seem like such a compassionate person and I know this is something that will take time but I will continue to pray for you. God bless and comfort. I am a mother of three and I can't imagine the pain these families and you and the officers and all involved are feeling. I hurt, and I only watched it on television. It is so hard to understand why anyone would want to hurt children and the Amish, they are such a kind, caring group of people. Love & prayers & understanding will get you through this difficult time."

Most of the cards appeared to have been purchased in the sympathy isle of a store. Yet they seemed so appropriate in the wording, "Praying for You. Sometimes it's hard to understand why God allows us to go through certain situations . . . but please remember that, no matter what, God is there with you through it all and that others who care are keeping you in their prayers."

The handwritten notes overwhelmed me, "I am writing you today in view of the recent atrocity that you have personally had to cope with. Being an eyewitness to the tragedy must really be difficult and I am sending my deepest sympathy to you for having to deal with it. I'm sure you can never be prepared when it is violence against innocent children. It seems the most common question right now is 'Why?' Yet no matter what answer was given, it wasn't good enough. It really doesn't make a difference."

She was right. Immediately following the incident, nothing seemed to matter or make a difference to me. I had trouble fathoming that I could ever move on. But as time went on, I realized that if I'm going to move on, I have to accept this as God's will, and not question why.

Through the caring expressed by complete strangers, and my faith, I was able to move on. While some of my friends seemed to understand the trials I was experiencing, I remained amazed at relatives and friends who seemed clueless to my emotions. I was sharing this thought with a close friend, and he told me something I hadn't thought about before.

Some people cannot understand what it's like to go through a life-altering event until they experience one. I thought about that for a long time and I believe he's right. The people that never even mentioned it, or the one that suggested that I, "Put it all behind me, not remain immersed in it and move forward," are those that have never dealt with a horrific, unexpected death.

But how do you "put it behind you?" How do you get the images out of your mind? As hard as I tried to put it behind me and move on, there were always reminders. The sight of an Amish boy riding his scooter. Passing a horse and buggy on the road. Watching children enter their schools, many skipping merrily as they approached the entrance, as I watched and shook uncontrollably. I was filled with so much grief and sadness.

Then came my first coroner call after October 2nd, 2006. It was exactly two weeks later. It was another beautiful fall day.

The call was for a motor vehicle accident, involving one occupant. The car was traveling at a high rate of speed, lost control and was stopped by a large tree, after going down an eighty-yard embankment. As I was driving to the scene, I thought, "This is it! This will be my last call. Why am I subjecting myself to this? I pulled up and saw another horrific sight. The intrusion to the front of the car was so heavy that a vin number was not able to be found.

It took every ounce of courage I could muster to get out of my Jeep and walk to the car. I found a wrist, and pronounced time of death. I gathered my information for my reports. I remained professional. I prepared the toe tag and death certificate as the extrication continued. After the funeral home arrived and removed the body, I left the scene and returned home. It suddenly hit me. I can continue doing this job. I had just proven that to myself. I must be addicted.

On November 15th, 2006, our county honored the responders to the Nickel Mines tragedy. Their faces betrayed nothing. They sat silently, their shoulders back, their faces solemn, as our county commissioners extended gratitude to the men and women who handled the tragedy. A few statements were made by some, all reflecting the same thing. There were no heroes to be singled out. They were all part of a united team that day, even as each of them now seeks peace in their own way. One voice trembled with emotion as he asked that the county be granted healing and grace to move on. One echoed my feeling, "It's good to live in Lancaster County."

Law enforcement units that responded that day were: PA State Police; Lancaster County Sheriff's Office; Lancaster County District Attorney's Office; Christiana, Quarryville, Strasburg, East Lampeter, and Southern Regional police departments and Maryland State Police.

Medical groups honored were: Bart Township Quick Response Service; Christiana, Gordonville, White Horse and New Holland ambulances; LEMSA; Susquehanna Valley Emergency Medical Services; Manheim Township EMS; Ephrata Hospital Advanced Life Support; and Chester County's Oxford, Parkesburg and Pomeroy ambulances.

Air Medical Services: Sky Flight Care; Lifenet 6-1; Pennstar 2; Pennstar 4 and Medevac 6.

Fire companies: Bart Township, Christiana, Gap, Gordonville, Highville, Intercourse, Kinzer, Lafayette, Lancaster Township, Paradise-Leaman Place, Quarryville, Refton, Ronks, Strasburg, Upper Leacock, West Earl, Willow Street, Witmer, all of Lancaster County; and Chester County's Atglen, Avondale, Honey Brook and West Grove.

In Lancaster County, the following agencies responded to the event: County Wide Communications, Emergency Management, Public Safety Training Center, Critical Incident Stress Management Team, and the MH/MR Disaster Emergency Crises Outreach Team. Other agencies contributing on the day of the shooting were: South Central PA Task Force; state Emergency Management Agency; Salvation Army Canteen; Chester County Department of Emergency Services; Lancaster County Association of Constables (security); and the Lancaster County Coroner's Office.

By November 21st, three of the wounded girls had returned to school. One remained hospitalized at Children's Hospital in Philadelphia and everyone hoped that she would be home for Christmas. Six-year-old Rosanna was at home, in a semi-comatose state. She is not expected to recover much function, if any, and is considered a case of palliative care. All of the surviving girls had severe gunshot wounds to the head and, or upper torso, with long-term implications expected.

I wondered what long-term implications those, whose lives were changed forever, on Monday, October 2, 2006, would suffer.

Chapter 9

Ordinary
and Extraordinary

Many ordinary and extraordinary events have occurred in my life. Many of the significant ones followed October 2nd, 2006.

Most of them fell into my lap while I was still in a daze.

In late October, the pregnant woman, Lydia Mae Zook, who survived the shootings, gave birth to a daughter. She named her "Naomi," after Naomi Rose Ebersol. Lydia was a teacher at another nearby school, and had gone to the Nickel Mines School on October 2nd to visit. Lydia, her sister-in-law, Ruth Ann, and Sarah's 2-year-old and an infant, were trapped inside the school. Because Roberts released the women with young children, Lydia felt her unborn baby had saved her life.

Lydia recalled journeying from the school to the neighbors, and hearing pounding, which was Roberts nailing barricades to the doors and windows. Lydia's 6-pound, 4-ounce baby was delivered three weeks early at a birthing center in Georgetown. The staff at Georgetown had delivered four of the ten girls who were shot.

By the end of October, four of the five Amish girls who survived the shootings had returned to their homes. The fifth remained hospitalized, but was reported to be making progress. The girls talked about their experiences. They had all suffered horrendous injuries, and some will deal with lifelong disabilities. As I sat with the families, and mostly just listened, I wondered which had done more damage, the bullets or the horrific experience and injury to their souls.

December 22, 2006, might have appeared to be an ordinary day. But it was extraordinary in the fact that Sarah Ann Stoltzfus, who had been critically wounded, returned to her home and school. She caught up to her class by the time the term ended.

Emotionally, she recovered enough to talk about the tragedy. Physically, the only visible effects were scars, and her hair was short, from being shaved before her surgery. She doesn't have full vision to the left side, although it has greatly improved. Her brain surgeon said it's a miracle that she recovered as fully as she did, to which her family responded, "Which we thank God for. We also know that healing is not always as complete as we would wish for everyone, but we do know that God is with us in all things."

Everyone had been praying that she would return home by Christmas. Another miracle was answered. Amidst the ordinary days, there are always the extraordinary days. The days filled with miracles.

A school soccer game is usually an ordinary event. Five-year-old Bryce Roberts kicked a soccer ball down the field, while fans cheered on. The extraordinary part was that these fans were not relatives, they were strangers. They were varsity soccer players on the sidelines of Bryce's games. These fans had come out to show him that people care. They came out because they had seen a sad thing happen to Bryce's family. He had lost his father, Charles Roberts, on October 2nd. The varsity players knew that sports were still there for Bryce. It was a place he could turn to. They just wanted him to know that they cared about him.

WIOV, a country radio station based in Ephrata, was instrumental in the distribution of prints of Bruce Becker's painting, "Kindness and Compassion." One of the signings was held at Ephrata Ambulance. Bruce was to begin signing prints at 1:00 at our ambulance station. By mid-morning, hundreds of people were waiting in line. Kevin and I watched in awe as the line grew. A few hours later, a van pulled up in front of our station, and family members of the Amish girls stepped out from the van. They were taken inside our building, where Bruce signed prints for each of them.

Some were signed "In memory of . . ." while others were "In honor of . . ."

Several weeks later another signing was scheduled at Christiana Ambulance. Anita and I had become close friends, following our first counseling session, and Casey and Murph from WIOV continued to go above and beyond the call of duty to assist in these signings. We formed a tight bond. My life became blessed by having Anita, Casey and Murph as new friends.

Casey sent an email, that said it all, "To my new Best Friends . . . Where do I begin? The past few months have been such an emotional rollercoaster for all of us. From the tragedy, to the healing, we've been there for each other. A bond like that is special. Though we met under horrific circumstances . . . I feel richer because I've found some new people in my life that will forever be special in my heart. I love you all, and wish all you a wonderful holiday and a New Year of Peace."

Christmas Day was around the corner. I kept thinking of the words in one particular Christmas song, "Where are you Christmas? My life is changing; I'm re-arranging. I'm not the same one, see what the time's done, is that why you have left me go?" Another one seemed to be constantly playing, and rattled my soul. "We are reflections of God's love."

Another carol that tugged at my heart, was one that contains the words, "Let there be peace on earth, and let it begin with me."

Why can't there be peace on earth? Why has it become such a vicious world? There I go again, asking why, when I know there aren't always answers to the question "why?"

Sometimes I think it's not really much different today, than "in the good old days." My late grandfather's aunt told me that when she was young, they too, were always busy. But it was a different sort of busyness. She said that they made time at the end of each day to just sit and socialize with neighbors who would stop by, or they would walk to visit neighbors. Wouldn't it be nice if we made time to just sit and socialize? Or just sit. Or made time to listen to others?

Maybe some of those successful suicides would have been unsuccessful ones.

The news in Lancaster County in 2006 had a decidedly negative tint. Our county, noted for its peaceful nature, was rocked by three grisly murder cases in a 14-month span, with the most recent being the West Nickel Mines murders.

I realized that this Christmas would be unlike any other for our Amish community that remains mostly to themselves. I realized this Christmas would be unlike any other for those of us non-Amish that had been thrust into the event.

But in their grief, the Amish also demonstrated why they are unique among God's children. In the immediate aftermath of the killings, they forgave the killer and reached out to his family. Their act of forgiveness touched the world, as it was truly a gift from the heart, the greatest gift of all.

I'm a firm believer that you shouldn't feel compelled to purchase gifts for all of the people on your "list." Giving Christmas gifts should be something we want to do, not something we feel we have to do. To me, random acts of kindness throughout the year are more important than opening gifts on Christmas Day, except for children. There I make an exception to my self-imposed rule.

The ending of each year always brings the "Top stories of the year." For Lancaster County, the year 2006 was marred by unthinkable tragedies and tumultuous events. Someone asked a reporter to sum up the year in one word, and he replied, "Tragic."

I called it a year of fury. The killing spree in Bart Township, that shocked the world.

Earlier in the year, Jesse Dee Wise, Jr. killed six of his family members in their Leola home, stuffed their bodies in the basement, and then went shopping, and hung out with his friends. I must admit, that after the Leola murders, I thought the worst coroner call was now water under the bridge, and it wasn't my call, so I was safe from any horrific calls. Little did I know how wrong that thought was.

And who could forget Lancaster County's Floyd Landis? The Farmersville native won the Tour de France, after stunning the field, two days earlier, with a remarkable comeback in one of the toughest stages of the race. Commentators were calling it the best single-day ride in race history. But Landis tested positive for high levels of testosterone on that particular date, and our hearts were broken again. Lots of other things happened in Lancaster County in 2006—good, bad and bizarre—but those events captured the top stories.

On December 29, 2006, I received what I thought was an ordinary letter, along with a brochure. Parts of the letter included, "Dear Janice, I am sending a small book to you written by a friend, Cheri Lovre, Director of the Crisis Management Institute in Salem, Oregon. Cheri was called in by the Solanco School District to help school staff and community to deal with the aftermath of Nickel Mines. The book was intended to help the families learn if parents or children were experiencing nightmares, flashbacks or nervous discomforts, these are a result of trauma, not grief. They are not failures of faith, but indications of injury to the nervous system, to the brain.

"While the book was initially written for the Amish families, it quickly became apparent that there were more souls that would suffer deep wounds as a result of their work in the schoolhouse. After reading accounts in the newspaper, you came to my mind and that thought has not left me. I asked Cheri for a copy for you and she wanted very much for you to have one. While you have already likely availed yourself of professional counseling, I hope you will read the book. Cheri's work with trauma is internationally known and research based, but most importantly, comes from a place of deep understanding and compassion. With sincere appreciation for the heart-breaking service you rendered on our behalf, Warm Regards, Linda Shoemaker."

I opened the book and began reading. I read the book over and over. The words engulfed me and flowed through my body, like I can only imagine morphine bringing comfort to an aching body. The book is titled, *When the World Turns Upside Down*.

I felt like someone else finally understood what I had been feeling, and put everything into words. The dedication reads, "A book for understanding psychological trauma for the Amish following the tragedy at Nickel Mines School. Dedicated to all law enforcement and emergency responders who came so quickly to help. Written with love and great respect by Cheri Lovre."

I didn't know at that time, how my life would change, by Linda and Cheri entering it. Some of the paragraphs were extraordinary.

"Almost all of the time we live with life being 'normal' and we get used to what we think our days will be like. Once in a great long time, something happens that is so far outside our normal life that we can't get through it the same way we usually do, and we don't understand how we will overcome the challenge. The deaths and injuries of the girls at Nickel Mines School are an example of this kind of overwhelming event.

"Any time something occurs that makes our hearts beat fast and we feel that surge of fear and energy, it is because our bodies have released a whole complement of chemicals. These chemicals are helpful for us in the first moments, when we need lots of energy to run or lift heavy equipment or save a life. They're good when we have to react quickly. Our reactions are fast when it really matters. It is known as the 'fight or flight' response.

"But later, when we are safe from the event, our bodies don't know how to turn these chemicals off very quickly. These chemicals continue to make us feel on edge. Easily upset. Angry. Small things seem to provoke a big reaction.

"What is happening is while grief is a part of the heart and of the emotions, the other responses in our body, called trauma, is a matter of the brain and of our body chemistry. Trauma is like an injury to the brain. It changes the brain just like having a farming accident and losing an arm changes your body.

"Prayer won't make the arm grow back and we can't pray away the chemicals that injured our brains.

"Our bodies want to keep that chemistry pumping through our bodies all the time. So when a door slams, we jump because we react with alarm. When we sleep we have dreams that are frightening. And just when everything seems like it should be okay, we find ourselves on edge or irritable or unable to get through the day.

"The part of the brain that gets injured from trauma is the limbic system. We can't pray that better, just like we can't pray a new arm to grow. We need to use the advanced part of our brain to quiet down the limbic system. The fastest way to engage the advanced part of the brain is to talk. Talk about when things were normal. Then talk about what happened. Then talk about things you do now that are a part of normal life. Remember, when you speak out loud, you are engaging the advanced part of your brain. Sometimes even our best friends and closest family members don't know how to help us. We need to tell people what we need when they can't figure that out.

"In the middle of all the sadness, it feels like things will never be the same. For many, losing so many little girls at Nickel Mines school, life won't ever be the same. But that doesn't mean that it won't ever be okay again.

"This will always be the saddest chapter in the book of Lancaster's Amish community. But there are many stories yet to be written. Many babies yet to be born. Many weddings yet to celebrate. So we must do all we can to cope and to grow and to move forward. To find our new normal."

There it was again, the "new normal."

There is so much more to her book that enriched my life. I had never known the process, perhaps I did at one point in my life, but when I desperately needed to understand it, it wasn't there. Not until I read her book.

On Friday, January 5, the morning blog from Dr. Kirchner contained the following:

> *Good morning. Last evening after birthday dinner we returned home to watch the Ford funeral, which we had recorded. Regal but simple eulogies when the combined organ and orchestra did the Ralph Vaughn Williams "To All The Saints"; I lost it. Maybe a build up from Jim Beittel's death and maybe from the Amish murders just came out. Ann Curry asked me, "Did I cry yet?", and I said, "No, but eventually it would catch up with me." And it did. If you didn't weep over the Amish murders you are over-medicated.*

A simple watercolor painting. Sounds ordinary enough, but it evolved into an extraordinary painting. Lancaster artist Elsie Beiler's painting shows the West Nickel Mines schoolhouse, on a beautiful sunny day, with children playing in the schoolyard. The painting is deeply symbolic. There are 26 children playing outside—15 boys and 11 girls. It's the exact number of students who were at the school the day of the shooting. Flying over the school are five birds, signifying the five girls who lost their lives that day. The painting is called "Happier Days."

If only we could freeze time and go back to 10:15 that day. But we can't. Rather, those involved have to remember the happier days. Limited editions were produced, and Emma Zook presented prints to the ten officers who were the first to arrive on scene. Beiler then offered the remainder for sale. I was fortunate enough to have purchased one.

For a long time, whenever I happened to notice Bruce Becker's "Kindness and Compassion" print, or Elsie's print, on my wall, it sent me back to the scene. I considered removing them both from my walls. But now they bring me comfort.

I witnessed the spirit of forgiveness shown by the families of the Nickel Mines community. Here was my backyard community, demonstrating its willingness to forgive the man who murdered five of their young daughters. They showed the world that "an eye for an eye" is not the way. Healing, forgiveness and love are the alternative.

The Amish set an example for us all to reach out with love. So much of life is push and pull.

Why can't we all pause to look out from our individual spot, whether it be on top of a grain of dust, or a mountaintop, and bring their example into our heart and let it burst forward in deep appreciation for our many blessings, enabling us to share everyday joys.

Why can't we turn our hearts into golden vessels of understanding and forgiving?

Why can't we each do a random act of kindness every day?

Why can't we keep the spirit of Christmas in our hearts all year round?

Kindness is not a sign of weakness, but rather of strength.

I found myself continuing to question why this and why that, knowing there was no answer, and knowing I had tried to make a commitment to myself that I wouldn't question "why?" anymore, but it's difficult to remove that word from your vocabulary.

Remember the book I received from Cheri Lovre that was written originally for the Amish to learn to deal with the tragedy? Something very extraordinary came out of that new friendship.

In March of 2007, I was contacted by an acquaintance of Cheri. Debra Wolfe was coordinating a multidisciplinary conference on child welfare with the theme, "An Opportunity to Heal." It was to be held on May 30th through June 1st and was sponsored by the Children's Hospital of Philadelphia. The Field Center for Children's Policy, Practice & Research were presenting three days of conferences titled, "One Child, Many Hands."

A Plenary Panel was being held on May 31st with Charles Figley, Ph.D., Editor of Traumatology; Fulbright Fellow and Professor; Director, Florida State University Traumatology Institute, College of Social Work, Tallahassee, Florida, moderating. Would I consider being on the panel? At first I was hesitant, the tragedy was still too fresh, still too raw, for me to sit on a question and answer panel, in front of 300 people, without falling apart, again.

Cheri wrote a stirring letter. "In my work with catastrophic school events, I have had too many times when I was there to serve the needs of the survivors, and people from emergency services and others were coming to our interventions because their needs weren't being met. It is a tough issue, figuring out who needs what, so anything we can do to further the cause is so important."

Debby wrote me the convincing letter. "Working with children takes its toll on professionals. Those who strive to help and care for children often suffer trauma themselves. This important session will explore Secondary Trauma and offer an opportunity to heal the helpers."

That was all I needed to hear. Heal the helpers. I committed.

As May 30th was my birthday, I looked at this as a piece of toast with both sides buttered. I'd get to spend my birthday out of town, and I'd hear how to heal the helper. I was still concerned that I would not be able to control my emotions during the discussions, but I kept thinking of the good that would hopefully emerge from this event. I asked if I could take Angie along as my navigator. They graciously agreed.

I was presented in advance the list of the others on the panel: James M. Callahan, MD; Cheri Lovre, MS; Joseph McBride, MSW, LCSW, ACSW; and Holly Smith, MA. A room was reserved for us at the Inn at Penn for the evening of May 30th.

Angie and I left Lancaster County around noon that day, and checked into our room. Guest speaker Amy Berg was scheduled for that evening. We chose not to do anything but relax. I was too nervous about the next day and besides, it was my birthday.

Cheri and her friend, Linda Shoemaker, met us for dinner. We had so much fun. It was nice and relaxing. After dinner, Angie and I walked the streets, stopping in at local taverns. Our Pennsylvania Dutch accents were quickly detected. That didn't stop us from enjoying ourselves.

The next morning we met for the Conference Plenary. I was very moved by the entire experience, and the people who came from the audience to speak with us after the conference.

We had agreed to meet for lunch at a nearby restaurant. I sat next to Holly. During our conversation, I mentioned that I've been keeping journals and writing was very therapeutic to me. Holly told me she had written a book, and hers was actually published. She took my personal information, and promised to mail me one of her books. She urged me to keep writing and work towards getting it published.

True to her word, she mailed me one of her books, *Fire of the Five Hearts, A Memoir of Treating Incest*. Holly is the supervisor of the Boulder County Sexual Abuse Team in Colorado. Her book is punctuated with her emotions. She laid it all on the line. I read the entire book in one day. It became an inspiration to me.

If I could learn so much from reading her book, perhaps I could help someone through my writings.

Holly helped me realize that I am not alone in my gut-wrenching, but satisfying world. She made me realize that so many jobs take great tolls on the caregivers. An ordinary event of reading a book turned into an extraordinary event of realizing that I was not alone in my feelings.

On April 2nd, 2007, children went to school. An ordinary event. That particular day was not. It was exactly six months since the incident in Bart Township, and the children were attending their first day in their new school. The new school was appropriately named "New Hope Amish School."

It was bittersweet. The excitement of the children to gather in a new school coupled with the stark reminders of those who were missing. State troopers provided protection from the media for the students and parents, as they attended their new school.

No one pretends that the tragedy's emotional wounds can be erased. It's hard work. You just have to keep working at it. But there were signs on the first day at the New Hope School that it was living up to its name. Children played baseball during recess and at 3:30 they burst out the front door to greet their mothers, waiting at the edge of the schoolyard.

A patchwork quilt, not an ordinary quilt, but an extraordinary quilt, a hand-colored patchwork quilt made by children at St. Hilary Catholic School in Fairlawn, Ohio, had been given to a Catholic grammar school in New Jersey. The intent was to soothe and bring hope to students who had lost parents and neighbors on September 11, 2001.

In 2005 the quilt moved to a school in Madison, Mississippi, to heal the wounds of those who had lost homes from Hurricane Katrina.

Then it was taken to Nickel Mines, where the quilt hung in the fire hall of the Bart Township Fire Company. It was a beautiful piece of artwork, full of phrases, "We Are Blessed" and, "We

Are Thankful," in addition to drawings of hearts; the American flag, rainbows, typical things children would draw and color during happy times.

Then came April 16, 2007. The circumstances in Blacksburg, Virginia, were hauntingly familiar to the tragedy in Bart Township. A man, angry at the world, barricaded himself inside a school with guns and began shooting. Thirty-three dead, twenty-nine injured. The families of the Nickel Mines victims said it was time for the quilt to move again.

On a warm, misty morning, at 4:30 a.m., a bus left Lancaster County with 29 Amish from Nickel Mines, including seven schoolboys from New Hope Amish School, and headed to the Virginia Tech campus. Once on the campus, the Amish presented the quilt, in a plain wooden box made by the Nickel Mines community. They walked solemnly outside Norris Hall.

They saw people crying as they read memorial stones dedicated to the Virginia Tech victims. They were strangers meeting strangers, but they all had something in common. They shared pain, loss and needed healing. They forged an immediate bond. One of the Amish commented that it helped him feel somewhat normal. He felt that they weren't alone in their suffering. While he hopes the quilt remains in Virginia for a long time, he had hoped it would stay with them longer, as it's moving on represented another tragedy.

As October 2nd, 2007, approached, I began dreading what should be an ordinary day for me. It was the one-year anniversary of that painful day in Bart Township.

My phone began ringing non-stop. All of the media wanted an interview. I just wanted October 2nd, 2007, to be over.

One hand was dreading the day, but the other hand was looking forward to it, hoping it would be a milestone in helping us to move forward. All of the occasions will have passed; the first Christmas since that day; the birthdays. A year had gone by, and at times I still felt so susceptible to being pulled down by my thoughts from that day.

I knew I wanted to go back to Bart Township, but I wasn't certain what I would do. Then I learned that counselors would be at the Bart fire station all through the day and into the evening. I was also told there would be a group counseling session on the 2nd at 7:00 p.m. I decided that's what I would do, attend the group counseling session. I looked forward to seeing the others, and to learn how they were doing. As you hurt together, you grow together.

I arrived early and saw they had refreshments. As I waited in line for a hot dog, I noticed Kelly, sitting at a table. I felt an immediate sense of relief. I gathered my hot dog and soda and headed towards Kelly's table.

I saw many other people I recognized. People who had become a part of my life. People who had helped me make it through the past year. We hugged, but this time, we didn't cry.

As we prepared to begin the counseling session, we learned there was a special being aired on our local channel. It was a half hour long reading of "Letters" that had been received following that Monday. It was aired without interruption and everyone wanted to watch it. The Amish families, who don't have televisions, had arrived to watch it at the fire station. So we sat, and stood, in silence, and watched the emotional program. Again, no one shed a tear, but it was a very solemn atmosphere. When it was over, some people left and the rest of us remained for the counseling session.

I was overwhelmed to hear the same thing over and over. So many commented, "It still so often seems like it happened yesterday." So many were still trying to find their "new normal."

A lot of ordinary problems now seemed insignificant. Each family of a daughter killed had created a memory card. These are handmade on plain paper, with the name, dates of their birth and death, a bit of personal insight about the girl, and a poem.

On the anniversary of the death, the families exchanged five new cards.

One man said, "Our schedule is about back to the way it was, but life won't ever be back to the way it was. We're never going to get back to normal. We'll never get back to October 1st but there is a new normal and we're moving toward it."

Bart Township Fire Company presented those on scene with a letter and a pin. The pin is a purple ribbon, with "October 2, 2006" on the ribbon, and "West Nickel Mines School" along the bottom of the lapel pin. The letter read, "The tragic event that took place at the West Nickel Mines Amish School on Monday October 2nd, 2006, will never be forgotten. Nor will the services you provided our community in our time of need.

"The resources that were required during the emergency phases and in the weeks that followed were overwhelming. So too were the selfless sacrifices of time and talents given by many.

"In recognition of your role during this difficult time the Officers and Members of the Bart Township Fire company hereby present you with this lapel pin as a token of our sincere appreciation. Please realize these pins are only presented to those individuals who served our community during this time and are not available to others."

I will never wear my pin. It sits on the mirrored jewelry tray that was my grandmother's tray. She kept her favorite jewelry on the tray, as I now do. I see it every day as I prepare for work. I see it every evening when I take my jewelry off for the evening. It's not something I want to wear. I'm too afraid I'd lose it, and I don't feel it's meant to be worn.

While some suggested that the Amish have this extraordinary gift of forgiveness, I don't feel that way. I have witnessed them grieve the same as anyone else. They adhere to the scriptural commandment to "love your enemy." Poignant and powerful words to live by.

I have learned so much in my multiple roles. I've learned that it's critical to build and maintain a support system.

I have learned that you are as young as your self-confidence; as old as your fears; as young as your hopes and as old as your despair. Many times, in my despair, I have been driven to my knees by the overwhelming conviction that I have nowhere else to go.

Once I read, "Don't ever let yourself become too angry, lonely, hungry or tired."

That just doesn't seem to work, as any volunteer will attest to.

I believe that sleep, riches and health, to be truly appreciated, must be interrupted.

If you want to see the rainbow, then you've got to muddle through the rain.

Despite the gruesome things I continue to see, smell and touch; and the anguish I hear in others' voices, I continue to go back for more. More life and death situations. I'm addicted. Sometimes I think the drug of my choice is "trauma." But it's a good addiction. As long as my heart remains large enough to carry my body, I will continue trying to help others.